D0929690

MOTHERS AND DAUGHTERS

Mothers and Daughters
The Distortion of a Relationship

Vivien E. Nice

Consultant Editor
Jo Campling

St. Martin's Press   New York

First published in the United States of America in 1992

Printed in Hong Kong

ISBN 0–312–06764–X

Library of Congress Cataloging-in-Publication Data
Nice, Vivien E.
Mothers and daughters : the distortion of a relationship / Vivien
E. Nice.
p. cm.
Includes bibliographical references and index.
ISBN 0–312–06764–X
1. Mothers and daughters—United States.   I. Title.
HQ759.N568   1992
306.874'3—dc20   91–21509
                                            CIP

To the memory of my mother Minnie Watkins,
who taught me to love myself,
and for my daughter Jennifer,
who continues to help me to grow.

Contents

Acknowledgements

A better understanding of my relationship with my mother has been the driving force behind ten years of research and thought that have gone into this book. In those years much has happened to change my understanding of this important relationship.

My move from working-class childhood into middle-class academic study created a barrier between me and my mother that grew harder to shift the more I used my newly-acquired academic skills to analyse it. The death of my mother and the birth of my daughter just over a year later led me away from a theoretical understanding and towards an understanding based in my own experience. Having regained some of the feelings of the real relationship my mother and I had as I grew up – our shared love, comfort and companionship – I was able to read theoretical accounts more critically and to find accounts which spoke to my own experiences. In particular here I am indebted to Adrienne Rich and her wonderful work *Of Woman Born*. My intense grief and guilt following my mother's death has slowly turned to deep 'ordinary' sadness. This book is part of my communication with her: I know she was with me in its writing.

My thanks to Shulamit Ramon who started the whole thing in more ways than one. To Carol Ann Hooper for her incisive comments which helped me not only on a particular chapter but informed my understandings in the whole of the work. To Jo Campling for giving me the opportunity, for her confidence in me and her special skills, and to the 'unknown reader' for her wonderful generosity. To my friend Sheila Melzak and my friend and sister Glenys Chatterley for their love and support; and to Terry for his unstinting love, and bravery in the face of exploding eggs.

Grateful acknowledgement is made to the following for permission to quote from published material: *Rosalie Sorrels*: excerpt from 'Apple of My Eye' (copyright 1974 © by Rosalie Sorrels) used by permission; *Ellen Bass*: 'There Are Times In

*I will not be divided from her or myself
by myths of separation*

Adrienne Rich (1978)

*Before sisterhood, there was the knowledge – transitory, fragmented,
perhaps, but original and crucial – of mother-and-daughterhood.*

Adrienne Rich (1977)

Introduction: Mothers and Daughters in Patriarchy

Mother-daughter relationships can be found at the core of women's writing. Women exploring their own experiences and the experiences of other women through fiction (for example Marshall, 1959; Morrison, 1974; Barefoot, 1986; French, 1987; Tan, 1989); through poetry (for example Alta, 1971; Astra, 1986) and through psycho/mythology (Hall, 1980), will often write about this fundamental and important relationship. Susan Koppelman in her introduction to *Between Mothers and Daughters: Stories Across a Generation* says

> Women who write fiction write stories about mothers and daughters. Often, a woman writer's first published story is about the relationship between a mother and a daughter. Nor do women writers abandon this subject as they grow in their craft and their lives. They return to the literary contemplation and portrayal of mothers and daughters again and again throughout their careers. (Koppelman, 1985, p. xv)

As Park and Heaton (1987) point out 'the short story form, with its immediacy and condensed imagery, appears perfectly to captivate the complexity of this relationship'.

In autobiographies and in biographies of women written by women the mother-daughter relationship is often central (for example Beauvoir, 1958; Martineau, 1877). Some daughter-writers have felt compelled to write about the intertwining of their own and their mother's story (for example Colette, 1966; Chernin, 1985; Gornick, 1988; Hopkinson, 1988; Steedman, 1986) or in writing about their mothers have gained some understanding of their own heritage (for example Walker, 1984; West, 1982).

The desire to understand this relationship better and to reflect on its complexities has led to collections of letters between mothers and daughters (Payne, 1983); to tributes in the form of anthologies (Olsen, 1985); and to a number of books specifi-

1

cally about the mother-daughter relationship (Neisser, 1967; Hammer, 1976; Arcana, 1979; Fischer 1986; Herman, 1989; Caplan, 1989; Apter, 1990; Dodd, 1990). All these works attest to the centrality of the mother-daughter relationship in the lives of women.

The mother-daughter relationship is also seen as central in texts on the psychological development and identity of women (Eichenbaum and Orbach, 1985; Bernay and Cantor, 1986), and in issues pertaining to women's mental health (for example Dix, 1986, on post-natal depression; Chernin, 1986, on anorexia).

Where fictional forms, poetry and biographies are used it may be easier for the relationship in all its complexity of lived experience to remain intact. However where attempts are made to unravel *the* mother-daughter relationship in order to understand its importance and influence in female development, problems of interpretation creep in.

Susan Koppelman goes on to say

> Women of every race, ethnicity, religion, region, and historical period write stories about mothers and daughters, and the similarities among the stories are greater than the differences because what we share as women, at least in terms of this primary relationship, is more than whatever else divides us. Stories about mothers and daughters seem like different facets of one great universal story that includes not only all the stories we have, but all those still lost and all those yet to be written. (Koppelman, 1985, p. xv)

While the similarities may seem greater than the differences in fictional accounts of mother-daughter relationships, we should not assume that those works which seek to interpret this relationship also offer us a universal picture. In this book I wish to explore the way current interpretations of mother-daughter relationships tend to distort that relationship both in theory and in experience.

PATRIARCHAL DISTORTIONS

The prevalence of male-dominated, white supremacist, and class-related language, concepts and knowledge has had a distorting effect in all areas of Western thought. History, philosophy, psychology, and so on, have all been developed out of the experiences of the white, middle-class (publicly heterosexual) male. Within this, those who are not white, not middle-class, not heterosexual and not male have been given a peripheral role in terms of their service to the dominant culture. Their own contributions and experiences have been rendered invisible. This ground is now to some extent being reclaimed (especially in terms of gender: in history see Anderson and Zinsser, 1989; in philosophy see Grimshaw, 1986 and Spelman, 1990; in psychology see Miller, 1978 and Gilligan, 1982).

Patriarchal distortion itself has a long history. Riane Eisler (1990) has explored in some detail what she takes as evidence of a pre-patriarchal society based on a Goddess culture. A culture which was matrilineal (line of descent through mother) and matrilocal (members of family living close to mother). Not matriarchal in the accepted sense of women dominating men, but of women preeminent in a society based on a partnership, an equality and complementarity between women and men. Eisler believes this to have been a time of great peace.

The 'dominator' model which followed, and which is said to form the basis of our current patriarchal structure, went through a process of 'standing reality on its head' in the (almost successful) attempt to eradicate knowledge of this previous existence. Eisler gives as an early example of this distortion the Greek drama of the *Oresteia*, where a son is cleared of killing his own mother, which she says 'was designed to influence, and alter, people's view of reality'. The *Oresteia* sought to impose the notion that children are not related to their mothers, but rather mothers are merely carriers of male seed, and only fathers are related to their children, thus making patriarchy (descent through the father and 'rule of the father') appear 'natural'. Despite our increased knowledge of reproduction this is still a basic tenet of current patriarchy, for proof of which we need only look to the contemporary use of mothers as 'surrogates' (Chesler, 1990).

Patriarchy is now generally taken to mean male dominance, and here I subscribe to Humm's definition of patriarchy as 'a system of male authority which oppresses women through its social, political and economic institutions' (Humm, 1990, p. 159). But in its technical sense patriarchy means 'rule of the fathers', and here the *Oresteia* is instructive, for in it we see patriarchy as imposing a patrilineal line of descent which denies the relationship between mothers and their children. This distinction is important when one is talking about motherhood, since although all contemporary societies appear to be male-dominated, not all are patrilineal (Rothman, 1989). There are a few, like the Trobriand Islanders, where men still rule but not as fathers. 'Women in such a system' says Rothman 'are not a vulnerability, but a source of connection', producing and re-producing 'the body of society itself' (Rothman, 1989, p. 30). In patrilineal societies such as ours women's power as reproducers of society has to be subverted and as far as possible denied: men look to their sons to continue the line, daughters will carry the seed of another man's line.

We can see from Nina Herman's (1989, pp. 73–91) inter-pretation of the *Oresteia* how it can also be used to suggest the daughter's hatred of the mother. Herman describes the mother (Clytaemnestra) as a 'narcissistic mother' who was 'simply not good enough' and through her neglect of her children caused in her daughter Electra a hatred so deep that she 'lashes her wavering brother into the act of matricide'. According to Herman it was not the 'simpler hands of Olympian crime and punishment' which led a son to kill his mother but mother-daughter conflict, 'the fury and despair of early infantile frus-tration, compounded by subsequent deprivation of a thwarted little girl, that finally drove the sword into the maternal breast'.

Patriarchy retains dominance through the repetition of distorting myths about women, and particularly about women as mothers, which become embedded in the cultural un-conscious of society. In contemporary society these myths are perpetuated through psychoanalytic interpretations. The aim is to disconnect women and deny the continuity in the mother-daughter line. The distortions of patriarchy combine with those of a racist and classist society to offer a very narrow view of knowledge generally.

Distortions operate through the structure of patriarchal knowledge which is characterised by dualisms and hierarchy (Du Bois, 1983; Hartsock, 1981). Patriarchal language and thought insist on dichotomised, polarised categories – dominant and subordinate; mind and body; instrumental and expressive; active and passive; independent and dependent; rational and emotional; objective and subjective; public and private.

Value is given to those 'qualities' seen as masculine: for example, intellectual activity; assertiveness; independence; rationality; objectivity; activities in the public sphere and so on; whilst those seen as feminine are devalued and often held in contempt, for example, concern with body maintenance (as in feeding and clothing those one is carer to); submissiveness; passivity; dependency; emotion; subjectivity; domestic activities.

Little credence is given to women's (private) experience until it is lifted into the 'public' arena and interpreted by (male) 'experts' who can be scientifically objective and rational. Women too are dichotomised – good mother, bad mother (note the wicked stepmother/good fairy godmother split in fairy tales); madonna and whore – in a way which offers women totally unrealistic models of womanhood, setting them against each other and in conflict with themselves.

Those human characteristics which are regarded as typically masculine are most highly regarded in a male-dominated society, and so *all* human development is considered in terms of striving towards and attaining these characteristics. So-called 'feminine' characteristics are not highly regarded.

Mothers and Daughters in Theory

It is not surprising, then, to find distortions in interpretations of mother-daughter relationships. Contemporarily we find these distortions largely in psychological theories, theories renowned for their white, middle-class narrow-mindedness and their 'mother-bashing' tendencies (Walters, 1988, p. 39).

Carol Gilligan had shown how dominant psychological theories not only ignore women's experiences but see them as 'deviant' and 'other' to the male 'norm'. Women, she says, speak in a 'different voice' from men, but this voice goes unheard in the espousing of dominant ideas and is rendered deviant and lesser. In the particular area explored by Gilligan – that of moral development – she found that this difference presented itself in terms of male concern with individual justice and rights, whilst women were concerned with connection, relationships and responsibility to others. Gilligan says

> Women's place in man's life cycle has been that of nurturer, caretaker, and helpmate, the weaver of those networks of relationships on which she in turn relies. But while women have thus taken care of men, men have, in their theories of psychological development, as in their economic arrangements, tended to assume or devalue that care. When the focus on individuation and individual achievement extends into adulthood and maturity is equated with personal autonomy, concern with relationships appears as a weakness of women rather than a human strength. (Gilligan, 1982, p. 17)

Because of the insistence on the dependence/independence dichotomy it does not appear possible to be both an autonomous person and one who upholds and values connection with others. A continuing relationship between mother and daughter is not only devalued in this way, but where it leads to strength for these women through connection it is regarded as a threat to male supremacy.

The male interpretation of women's experience has been about men controlling women – women have been told how to experience their sexuality (Freud, 1977), how to give birth (see Oakley, 1980) and how to be a mother (see Oakley, 1981b). They have also been told how to relate to their mothers, for just as *descriptions* of motherhood are really *prescriptions*, so theories which tell us that continued connection to mother can seriously damage our mental health are prescribing a particular way of relating to our mothers which insists on 'separation'.

In the field of mental health mothers have been blamed for most, if not all, the ills that befall their children (Caplan and Hall-McCorquodale, 1985). This has been most evident in the past in the diagnosis and treatment of schizophrenia (Bateson, 1972; Laing and Esterson, 1964) and is most prominent currently in the dominant literature on the sexual abuse of children, where despite (or because of?) the adherence to systems theory, a mother is seen as culpable when the father has sexually abused their children (for further exploration see Hooper, 1987; MacLeod and Saraga, 1988; Gavey et al. 1990).

The misogynist psychoanalytic theory which underlies much mental health and child abuse work has also been central in interpretations of the mother-daughter relationship. A core belief that adult mental health has its origins in the earliest relationship between mother and child accounts for this centrality. Even where feminists have sought to interpret the theory, there has often remained a mother-blaming, mother-hating emphasis (Dinnerstein, 1976) which seems to suggests that mothers are to blame for perpetuating women's oppression and that the answer lies in an increase in father involvement in early child care (Choderow, 1978; see Bart's critique of Dinnerstein (Bart, 1977), and of Choderow, (Bart, 1981)).

Not all feminist psychoanalysts start from the same base, however. In a British television programme on women and psychoanalysis ('Voices', Channel 4, 1988) three eminent women psychoanalysts debated the psychological development of women. Their seating arrangement, American psychoanalyst Jean Baker Miller on one side of the (male) host and English psychoanalyst Juliet Mitchell and French psychoanalyst Janine Chasseguet-Smirgel on the other was suitably representative of their views on the subject of gender acquisition. The viewpoints of Miller on the one hand, and of Mitchell and Chasseguet-Smirgel on the other were not merely opposed: the two sides in effect spoke in 'different voices'.

Chasseguet-Smirgel and Mitchell had obviously developed their theories of female psychological development out of male-based theories: their talk was of 'penis envy' (JCS) and 'potency-envy' (JM) and of fulfilling unmet need. Baker Miller, however, began from a basis of female connection in an attempt to develop a truly female psychology and not one based on women's 'deficiencies' in relation to men. As with Gilligan, Jean Baker Miller emphasises the value of women's connection to others and their ability (however learnt) to care – qualities denigrated by patriarchal society, whose effects are distorted by it in an attempt to set daughters against mothers.

The danger with psychoanalytic interpretations lies in their use of some essential truths about our experience and its manipulation to fit the theory which we are then seduced into accepting. This may happen for women especially when such theories are reinterpreted by psychotherapists who are also feminist. For example many (all?) women will recognise and relate to the idea of the 'little girl' within, the needy child who wishes to be looked after (Eichenbaum and Orbach, 1984). It is then only a short step to believing that this 'little girl' exists because we were not loved enough by our mothers as infants – especially since we all have at some times wished for a more 'perfect', more 'all-loving' mother. If we can understand that our mothers were themselves reacting to the presence of a 'little girl' within them, projecting that presence onto their daughters, and rejecting both their own feelings and the daughter who brought them to the surface, we can see this situation as a cyclical one for which we cannot blame our mothers themselves. But we do blame them, for who else is to break the cycle? Yet can mothers really be held responsible for the vulnerability which as humans we must all feel at some time, or for the fact that rather than accepting such neediness as natural, dominant, patriarchal society in its search for 'strength' has determined such needs to be weakness.

Our understanding of mother-daughter relationships has been distorted via patriarchal myths which aim to retain a male-dominant society. One of the ways this is perpetuated is by white, middle-class psychological theories which have misogyny and mother-blaming at their root. Theories do not just remain 'theories' but have a profound influence on lived experience. This distortion is not only a theoretical concern but affects the reality of mother-daughter relationships.

Women's Experience and Paradoxical Reality

Because women's experience is ignored in these theories, and because they dominate our educational and socialisation structures, women will try to fit their own experience into these theories – leading to feelings of abnormality, or an alteration in the perception of their experience. Uta Enders-Dragaesser points out that

> recurring paradoxical situations with strong misogynistic implications keep women locked within a female "normality": a fictitious social construction of femininity which excludes and devalues lived female reality. (Enders-Dragaesser, 1988, p. 583)

Rather than looking to early female socialisation (and hence to the early mother-daughter relationship) to explain typical sex-role behaviour and women's frustrations within that, Enders-Dragaesser considers it more important to be aware of the continual pressure on girls and women of this 'paradoxical reality' where 'lived reality is hidden beneath definitions, values and words expressing ideas of "normality" ' (ibid, p. 585).

An example of paradoxical reality is the way in which women are told that they are weak and dependent on men and yet are expected to meet man's dependency needs and to forgo their own need for emotional support. Perhaps the 'little girl' within is the feelings girls and women continually have reinforced about the 'immaturity' and 'selfishness' of their own neediness. This neediness then has to be seen as unmeetable in the present and is therefore consigned to the past and to that primary relationship where all our needs should have been met in a way which would last us a lifetime. The conceptual leap is taken from mother as the primary gratifier of infants' needs, to mother as the primary source of all developmental problems. For womanhood the ultimate paradox must be the need to deny our mothers in order to affirm ourselves (Walters, 1988, p. 41).

The mother-daughter relationship has been interpreted via psychological theories of development which are steeped in male-defined concepts. Individuation, separation, independence – the language of the individualised, competitive, hierarchical male – are considered developmentally mature, whereas women's connectedness, mutuality, concern with relationships are seen as developmentally immature. Daughters are seen as dependent on mothers: if the daughter 'fails to separate' from her mother she will fail to develop as an adult, autonomy being equated with separation from the mother. Later in life mothers are seen as becoming dependent on their daughters. These interpretations leave no room for positive images of connectedness, interdependency and support between women and between mothers and daughters. The language, concepts and theories of patriarchy seek to erect barriers between women, and in that first female relationship between a mother and her daughter. As Adrienne Rich says

> Truly to liberate women, then, means to change thinking itself: to reintegrate what has been named the unconscious,

the subjective, the emotional with the structural, the rational,
the intellectual; to 'connect the prose and the passion' in
E. M. Forster's phrase; and finally to annihilate those
dichotomies. (Rich, 1977, p. 81)

Mothers and Daughters in Classist and Racist Society

It is not only through male-dominated theory that a distortion
in interpretations of mother-daughter relationships takes place.
The writings of feminists and the theories they have produced
have themselves been dominated by white, middle-class women.
The dualisms and hierarchies of Western knowledge and concepts do not only apply to the male/female divide but are also
relevant in considering dominance and subordination in terms
of race and class. Thinking of people 'in parts' relates not only
to personality characteristics but also to the way gender, race
and class identity have been considered as separable and hier-
archically ordered in feminist theory, with gender treated as
the first and most fundamental form of oppression.

Elizabeth Spelman (1990) has shown how white, academic
feminist works (for example those by Simone de Beauvoir and
Nancy Choderow) have taken white, middle-class women as the
'norm' against which to measure all women by implicitly
assuming that sexism can be split off from other forms of
oppression, and is best explored where these other oppressions
do not exist. The effects of the race and class of white, middle-
class women on their experiences goes unexplored, and by
being in a position to include or not include the experiences of
women from whom they differ, they are able to retain the
privileges of their race and class and their primary claim to
'womanness'. As Spelman points out 'Recent feminist theory
has not totally ignored white racism', but

> Much of feminist theory has reflected and contributed to
> what Adrienne Rich has called 'white solipsism'; the tendency
> 'to think, imagine, and speak as if whiteness described the
> world' [Rich, 1978]. While solipsism is 'not the consciously
> held belief that one race is inherently superior to all others,
> but a tunnel vision which simply does not see nonwhite
> experience or existence as precious or significant, unless in

spasmodic, impotent guilt-reflexes, which have little or no long-term, continuing momentum or political usefulness.' (Spelman, 1990, p. 116)

If we believe that the relationship between mothers and daughters is central to the development of gender identities, then we must be aware that gender identities cannot be split off from racial and class identities. The relationship between a mother and a daughter does not exist in a social vacuum. The context will to some extent determine the relationship, and only by attempting to explore all possible facets of social context can we hope to increase our understanding of what may be common factors in relationships between different mothers and daughters.

Ambivalence in Mother-Daughter Relationships: An Example of Distortion

Ambivalence is a central concept in writings on the mother-daughter relationship. The daughter is seen as having ambivalent feelings towards her mother, feelings of both love and hate which are interpreted as unhealthy and which are seen as causing the daughter problems in her relationship with her mother. To a lesser extent the mother is considered to hold ambivalent feelings towards the daughter in her desire to hold onto her daughter and also to push her away.

Ambivalence is an interesting concept. Whilst generally it is seen as a sign of stress and in an extreme form as a symptom of schizophrenia, in fictional characters it is seen as a sign of strength and as evidence of the subtlety of the creator (*The Fontana Dictionary of Modern Thought*, 1977). While swinging rapidly from the extremities of love to hate and back again probably is a sign of mental disturbance which would certainly cause some problems in a relationship, having profound feelings of both love and hate, the need to be close and to be apart, are surely the hallmarks of any close and emotionally binding relationship, whilst being aware of the complexity of one's own feelings towards another must be a sign of mental health and maturity.

Problems are caused when ambivalence is not considered normal in a close relationship and feelings have to be denied.

Whereas prescribed motherhood does not allow for the mother's ambivalent feelings – mothers must be wholly loving – it seems that the daughter's ambivalent feelings have to be turned to 'hate' in order for her to properly 'separate' from her mother (and in order to break any possible allegiance between two women). Even feminist psychotherapists have this to say

> The feminist approach accepts, indeed anticipates, that the mother-daughter relationship is bound to be *ambivalent and problematic* and that its legacy is that the daughter (and indeed the mother herself as a daughter) is unable to separate. (Eichenbaum and Orbach, 1987, p. 63) (my italics)

Nancy Friday's (1979) myopic view of her mother testifies to the bitterness and anger which can be directed at mothers when psychoanalytic theories are used to interpret (or reshape) female experience and to present an essentially male account of women's psychological development. Contrast this with the complexity of Adrienne Rich's account, which does not attempt to do away with the ambivalence of the mother-daughter relationship by splitting it and choosing hatred, but attempts rather to understand more fully this ambivalence which has to exist in a relationship between two people bound together by birth and by gender identity.

Ambivalence is used as a major trap of patriarchal thought for mothers and daughters. Caught within it, mothers and daughters seem unable to go any further in their relationship. It is a trap set by the different demands of patriarchy, which insists that the daughter identify with her mother but only by taking on her devalued status and her servicing role to men, whilst denying the mother her strengths and denouncing the mother and daughter's connection as women. It demands that the daughter reject her mother in favour of first the father and then the husband, and in doing so to denigrate her mother and herself. The connection between mother and daughter that is so dangerous to patriarchy is allowed only in so far as it serves male interest, that is in the passing on of the subordinate role from mother to daughter. The ambivalent feelings thus generated are then very difficult to separate from the ambivalence of profound physical, emotional and spiritual attachment.

STUDIES ON DAUGHTERS AND MOTHERS

The major works which have been produced on mother-daughter relationships vary in their degree of adherence to dominant male psychological theories. Neisser (1967) takes an 'anti-women's Lib' approach in her *Mothers and Daughters: A lifelong Relationship,* a book which seeks to instruct the mothers of daughters, and 'lets mothers know that they themselves practically write the script and coach their daughters – for tragedy': while the very title of psychotherapist Nina Herman's more contemporary anti-feminist work, *Too Long a Child: The Mother-Daughter Dyad,* suggests the developmental retardation she believes is caused to daughters through their relationship with their mothers. It is interesting to note that in Herman's index ambivalence is cross-referenced with 'hate/rage' but not with 'love', which is not referenced at all.

Judith Arcana in *Our Mother's Daughters* and Signe Hammer in *Mothers and Daughters: Daughters and Mothers* both use women's experiences to give a feminist perspective to mother-daughter relationships. Arcana is most successful in capturing the difficulties for women caused by patriarchal society and by allowing women their own voice she gets across some of the complexity of these relationships, although she fails to really give a voice to the mother. Hammer relies more heavily on her own interpretations.

Both works are still caught fast in patriarchal concepts. Hammer, for example, states that it is a concern of her book 'to explore some of the ways in which a weak sense of self has been passed on from mother to daughter' (Hammer, 1976, p. xiv). Both start from the basis of a problematic relationship between mother and daughter. Arcana, for example, prefaces her book with the comment 'For mothers and daughters to relate to each other in truth – even sporadically – is a terrible struggle for both women' (Arcana, 1979, p. xi). Arcana's work has been called 'mother-blaming', and somewhere between the daughter's experiences and the feminist interpretations there is some element of truth in this accusation: this is possibly due to Arcana's concentration on the daughter's view and her uncritical use of psychological concepts.

The more recent works of Fischer (1986), Apter (1990) and Dodd (1990) follow Arcana and Hammer in their use of interviews with mothers and daughters. Fischer and Apter concentrate on different stages in the life-cycle of the daughter, Fischer looking at the adult daughter's relationship to her mother and Apter concentrating on the teenage daughter's relationship. Celia Dodd's book is, as she puts it, 'a bit like a glorified problem page – although it doesn't only deal with the problematic side of the relationship' (Dodd, 1990, p. 4). These contemporary accounts of daughters' and mothers' own experiences shows our ongoing need to rethink mother-daughter relationships in the light of women's changing experiences and expectations.

All of the major texts on mother-daughter relationships, and indeed this one, have been written by white women, and by women who, if not *born* into the middle-classes, have been *educated* into the middle-classes. The interpretations that come out of such experience cannot be held to be universal for all women, or even for all women living in Western industrialised countries, even where, as in Signe Hammer's case the work is based on interviews with women 'from all classes and a variety of ethnic groups' (Hammer, 1976, p. xii).

Nina Herman's book manages not only to stay firmly entrapped in patriarchal theory, but also seems to completely ignore social context as having any effect whatsoever on relationships between mothers and daughters. She excuses herself from universality by the following statement in the introduction to her work

> I determined from the start that I was going to remain within my own, ancestral culture whose mainstream course through my veins. Within the Graeco-Judaean stream I might avoid such surplus errors as I would be bound to make should I attempt to cross the Nile or drift down the mighty Ganges. My sisters born along those banks are far better qualified to string their myths and phantasies into patterns of their own making. (Herman, 1989, p. xviii)

The lyricism of this may, like the rest of her work, lull us into a state of belief in her offerings.

ABOUT THIS BOOK

Through the use of male-dominated psychological theories, an adherence to patriarchal concepts and the experiences of white, middle-class women (or the imposition of their interpretation onto the experiences of all women), the literature on mother-daughter relationships has attempted to offer us what must be a distorted view of *the* mother-daughter relationship. The danger of this not only lies within theoretical realms but can, through internalisation, distort the lived experiences of mothers and daughters. This book is an attempt to explore those distortions as they appear in the literature on mother-daughter relationships. This is done largely by exploring those concepts – which have been used in a dichotomised way – in all their complexity as they relate to women affected by different social contexts.

While like all other works on the mother-daughter relationship, I generally take a life-cycle approach, unlike other works in this area I also attempt to include motherhood as a developmental process through the life-cycle. Nancy Mairs, in her essay 'On Being Raised by a Daughter' has noted the lack of attention in the literature to the power of the daughter to transform the life of the mother. She says

> The assumption seems to be that I'm the one in control, not just because I'm older than she is and, until recently, bigger and stronger, but because I have society's acknowledgement and support in the venture and she doesn't . . . Such lopsided accounts arise, I suppose from the premise – the consequence of a hierarchical view of human development – that adulthood signifies completion. But the fluidity, the pains and delights, the spurts of growth and sluggish spells of childhood never cease, although we may cease to acknowledge them in an effort to establish difference from, and hence authority over, our children. (Mairs, 1986, pp. 69–70; quoted in Kraus, 1990)

It is significant that the literature ignores the mother's view, for in taking it into account it would need to pay much more attention to the social construction of mothering and the conditions under which women mother. It would also need to be much more critical of 'mother-blaming' theories and concepts.

This book is an attempt to do this.

Despite what appears like much evidence to the contrary, I start with a firmly-held belief that the mother-daughter relationship is not inherently and does not have to be problematic, but has the potential to offer the basis of supportive, affiliative growth for women whether they are daughters or daughters and mothers.

Chapter One begins with the woman becoming a mother and the birth of the daughter. The value or rather lack of value given to daughters in patriarchy is examined for potential effect on the earliest stage of the mother-daughter relationship. The dependency of the child and of the mother, and the myth of women's dependency generally, are explored. The paradoxical nature of the mother's power is introduced as a theme throughout the book, and we see how motherhood itself has been distorted.

Chapter Two explores a central theme in the mother-daughter literature, the issue of 'separation'. The daughter is growing and the first separation of early childhood is explored. This is an important time in terms of the psychological theorists since 'failure' at this stage is believed to lead to women's 'immaturity'. This issue of separation is again explored in some depth in Chapter 4, at the time of the daughter's 'second individuation' in adolescence.

Chapter Three explores the so-called loss of the mother to the daughter. Here we see that in the literature the mother is blamed not only for not allowing her daughter to separate but for not merging with her in the first place, that is in failing to give the daughter enough early nurturance. The literature also accuses the mother of not offering the daughter an adequate role-model and of not encouraging a positive image of womanhood in her daughter. This is linked to the assumption that mothers are held solely responsible for the socialisation of daughters despite the obvious effects of all other interactions and influences, and the regulation of mothers to socialise daughters in specific, socially acceptable ways.

Chapter Four looks at the daughter's move from childhood to adulthood, the bid for self-identity and the mother's role in this. Competition between mother and daughter is considered along with evidence of connection and ego-supportive relationships. Adult life choices and their effects on the mother-daughter relationship are also explored.

Chapter Five is about the search for the 'ideal mother'. It looks at how mothers have been both idealised and denigrated in the patriarchal splitting of the Great Mother into the loving and terrible mother. Psychotherapy's offer of 'remothering' is critiqued and alternatives considered.

In Chapter Six the daughter becomes a mother – the time of 'reconciliation' in the mother-daughter literature. We see that in psychoanalytic theory mothers are blamed for most things that can go wrong in the daughter's pregnancy, labour and bonding with her child. But from women's own experiences we see the potential for support of the daughter by the mother at this time, a support which male-controlled child-birth has sought to denounce.

Chapter Seven concentrates on the positive possibilities of connection between mother and adult daughter, by looking at sisterhood, reclaiming the heritage of women in history and through reclaiming the heritage from our own mothers in what has been called matrilineage. The difficulties presented by living and being socialised into a society that aims to split women on their racial and class differences is explored, as is the possibilities of connection between mothers and daughters offered in the writings of multiply oppressed women.

Chapter Eight looks at the relationships between older mothers and their adult daughters, the myth of 'role-reversal', and the effect of the increased physical dependency of the mother on mother-daughter relationships and its interpretation in social policy literature. The death of the mother and the daughter's reactions to her death are also explored.

In the concluding chapter the mother's story is emphasised and future possibilities for connection and reciprocal adult relationships are considered.

Through the use of psychological, interactional and sociological literature, as well as novels and poetry, I hope to offer a critique of current thinking on mother-daughter relationships and set these relationships in their historical and social context.

By considering motherhood as well as daughterhood I hope to offer a more complete understanding of mother-daughter relationships; and through emphasising connection I hope to explore the transforming powers of these relationships, both for individuals and for society.

1 An Exclusive Relationship

POEM TO MY DAUGHTER

'I think I'm going to have it',
I said, joking between pains.
The midwife rolled competent
sleeves over corpulent milky arms.
'Dear, you never have it,
we deliver it.'
A judgement years proved true.
Certainly I've never had you

as you still have me, Caroline.
Why does a mother need a daughter?
Heart's needle – hostage to fortune –
freedom's end. Yet nothing more perfect
than that bleating, razor-shaped cry
that delivers a mother to her baby.
The bloodcord snaps that held
their sphere together. The child,
tiny and alone, creates the mother.

A woman's life is her own
until it is taken away
by a first particular cry.
Then she is not alone
but part of the premises
of everything there is.
A branch, a tide . . . a war.
When we belong to the world
we become what we are.

(Anne Stevenson, 1982)

This chapter is about the beginnings of a mother-daughter relationship. It is about the way our society constructs the mother-infant relationship out of a very particular, historically and socially specific, understanding of the needs of infants and the way in which those needs should be fulfilled. It is about the distorting effect of this construction on the mother and on the mother-infant relationship, particularly when the infant is female.

Psychoanalytic theory determines this as a crucial time in human development. The necessity for a primary attachment in which the infant can have needs met and frustrations contained is confused with the necessity for an exclusive relationship between mother and infant. Mental health problems in later life are always seen as having their root in this crucial period and are related to the mother's 'failure' to meet the infant's need or to reflect reality for it. Within this exclusive relationship the mother is seen as all-powerful in relation to the infant's dependency.

The infant's early relationship with its mother is marked by dependency – the infant's dependency on the mother, the mother's dependency within the mothering role and generally as a woman in our society. Dependency has been imposed on women in patriarchy, women have then been considered weak and mothers have been blamed for perpetuating their daughters' dependency.

Dependency is here explored both as the beginning stage of the life-cycle of the infant daughter and as an important concept in our understanding of motherhood and womanhood.

WANTING AND NOT WANTING A DAUGHTER

Jung tells us that 'Every mother contains her daughter in herself and every daughter her mother – every woman extends backwards into her mother and forwards into her daughter' (C. G. Jung, 1971, p. 162). The mother-daughter relationship does not begin with the birth of the daughter but with the thoughts, feelings and fantasies the mother has about being the mother to a daughter. This will relate to her own relationship with her mother, her expectations of herself as a mother and her expectations of the as yet unknown daughter.

When you ask a pregnant woman whether or not she wishes to have a girl or a boy the most accepted response, in white

Western society, is 'I don't mind as long as the baby is healthy'. This may be true for some women but it seems unlikely that all will share this lack of desire for a baby of one sex or the other.

Ann Oakley (1979) in a study of London women having their first babies in 1975–6 found that three-quarters of her sample stated a definite sex preference during pregnancy and many of those who said they had no particular preference and didn't mind stated after the birth that they had minded. Of the 76 per cent who stated a preference during pregnancy 54 per cent wanted boys and 22 per cent girls. Oakley also found that on the birth of the baby more women were pleased if they had had a son (93 per cent who had had a boy were pleased) and disappointed if they had had a girl (44 per cent of those who had a girl were disappointed). As Oakley (1981a, p. 95) points out 'Whatever treatment girls receive in childhood to point them in the direction of femininity, it is clear that they are more likely to start off as a disappointment to their parents' and to 'provoke less positive and more negative feelings in their mothers than sons'. Dana Breen (1975) also found more cases of post-natal depression occurring in mothers of daughters than in mothers of sons.

But what is the mother's preference for a son about? It seems likely that this 'preference' is socially induced in societies where men are valued more than women. Adah, the Nigerian-born Ibo child of Buchi Emecheta's novel *Second Class Citizen* felt early the experience of not being valued because she was born a girl.

> She was a girl who arrived when everyone was expecting and predicting a boy. So, since she was such a disappointment to her parents, to her immediate family, to her tribe, nobody thought of recording her birth. She was so insignificant. (Emecheta, 1977, p. 7)

When Adah herself became the mother of a first-born daughter she recalls the reaction of those around her

> After a long and painful ordeal she had come home to Francis bearing a girl. Everybody looked at her with an 'is that all?' look. She had had the audacity to keep everybody waiting nine months and four sleepless nights, only to tell them she had nothing but a girl. It was nine good months wasted. She paid for it, though, by having Vicky [a son] soon afterwards. (Emecheta, 1977, p. 122)

It is generally understood in patriarchal society that men prefer to have sons and it may be to please men, to continue the male line, and to be seen as having 'got it right' (by producing a male) that a son is preferable as a first child to women also.

Judith Arcana's study of mother-daughter relationships may better reflect the personal preferences of women, since she found that 'many more women prefer to have female children, or children of both sexes, than desire male children though most understand that making males will garner more praise and status' (Arcana, 1981, p. 193).

Of interest also are the reasons women give for wanting or not wanting a daughter. In Arcana's study we have a number of examples. When a woman says 'I want a daughter. I want to be the mother I never had. To the daughter I never was. That's what I want. I want a sister', we see both the desire to relive the mother-daughter relationship (but to do it differently) and the strong desire for a female bond (a sister). Another woman talks of the continuation of that bond and of being able to identify with a daughter: 'I wanted girls for that connection; the connection with my mother is that we are women, and my connection with a daughter would be the same thing.' For others there is a feeling of valuing women and oneself: 'I want a girl. I like girls. I'm a girl . . . ' and 'I wanted a girl. Why? To grow a woman, you know'.

Having recognised difficulties in the relationship with her mother, a woman may decide that she wants to go through that relationship again as a mother, in control and able to do it differently: 'I would want it so badly to be different with me than it was with my mother – so I think about it in terms of a daughter'. Or she may decide she would not wish to risk a repetition or may fear rivalry with a daughter: 'I didn't want the competition – the kind my mother and I had' (Arcana, 1981, pp. 195–7).

For those women who actively wanted a son, some related this to status: 'something special about having a male child', some to their own low self-esteem 'At that point in time I didn't like myself. I related more to men', and some because they believed it would be easier to raise sons, they wouldn't be so 'messed up', saying something about the difficulties felt to be inherent in raising daughters in our society (Arcana, 1981, pp. 202–3).

Adrienne Rich's desire to have a son was related to her wish to 'give birth to my unborn self . . . someone independent, actively willing, original . . . If I wanted to give birth to myself as a male, it was because males seemed to inherit those qualities by right of gender' (Rich, 1977, p. 193). It may seem easier, then, to raise boys to be active and independent as this is what is expected of them: a mother who wishes to raise her daughter in this way may well find this much more difficult.

Marianne Grabrucker (1988), on finding out following an amniocentesis, that the baby she is carrying is a girl, feels that she already knows the child 'for my imagination has created her: a beautiful, strong, self-confident, lively and intelligent creature. All the qualities she will, in my opinion, need and must have in order to be happy and successful in this masculine society'. Talking to other pregnant women who already know the sex of their child, she finds that those expecting girls see the child as a repetition of themselves, already feel a strong sense of attachment to their daughters, and can envisage their futures; whilst those carrying boys will 'wait and see how things turn out and then adapt to the "character" of the child' (Grabrucker, 1988, pp. 15–16). There is already a connection between mothers and daughters which is not there between mothers and sons, carrying with it some expectation of who the daughter will be.

DEPENDENT INFANT

The newborn infant is dependent for its survival on the adults taking care of it. Probably in all societies the person with primary responsibility for this care is the mother. In white, Western society, the ideology of the exclusive mother-infant bond sets the context for childcare and for the physical and psychological interaction between mother and infant. Although early psychoanalysts like Freud and Klein did speak of a gendered infant, they did so in a way which set the male infant's development as the norm and the female as the 'other': from the earliest developmental interaction, then, female has been 'deviant'.

The later and popularised versions of psychoanalytic thought (via Winnicott and Bowlby, Mahler and Kaplan) refer for the most part to a 'genderless' infant – although again it can be seen they are taking a male 'norm'. More recent works by feminist psychotherapists have put gender centre stage with particular reference to the interactions between the mother and infant daughter, but they also have done so in order to highlight problems in female development.

Does gender matter in this early mother-infant interaction? Research into the actual physical interactions between mothers and their infants suggests that it does.

Physical Interaction

The child care manuals produced by white, middle-class 'experts' talk of the handling and taking care of a genderless infant (although they refer to the baby usually as 'he') and it seems strange to us to believe that at this early stage there may be some differences in the way we relate to infant girls and boys, but close observation suggests that there are indeed differences.

Certainly in Britain today parents are more likely to want to ensure that the sex of their small child is known to all immediately by dressing them from day one in pink or blue, in 'boy's' clothes and 'girl's' clothes: even some disposable nappies are now differentiated by sex.

How infants are dressed seems to be important in terms of the responses they get from people generally. Our perception of an infant differs on whether we believe them to be a girl or a boy. Statham draws our attention to research studies highlighting the differences:

> parents asked to describe their new-born baby when the child was less than a day old were more likely to describe daughters as 'little', 'pretty' and 'cute', while their sons were firmer, better co-ordinated, stronger and bigger. The researchers concluded that these differences were 'in the eye of the beholder', since the girl and boy babies did not differ overall in size, weight or reflex responses. (Statham, 1986, p. 31)

We can see then that expectations may be set from the moment of birth depending purely upon the sex of the child.

The way we talk to and handle infants also differs on the basis of what we believe their sex to be. Moss (1973) observed mothers with their first-born infant in the first three months of life and found that boy babies tended to be handled, looked at and stimulated more, mothers tended to hover over male babies more in an attempt to anticipate needs, while girl babies were talked to more often, encouraged to smile more and more often 'quieted and restored themselves to a state of equilibrium' rather than needing mother's attention.

These studies are limited. They were probably carried out with white mothers and infants, and what they mean in terms of differences in male and female babies, and the reasons for differences in treatment by mothers is really open to conjecture. But it does seem likely that mothers and others relate differently to an infant depending upon the sex of that infant from the earliest moments.

What observation of mother-infant interactions does more clearly tell us is that the infant is not a passive recipient of the mother's actions: rather the infant initiates as well as responds to interactions between them. Stern (1985) points out that this tells us that the infant is born with a sense of herself as separate from the mother – a fact which it is important to remember when we look at psychoanalytic interpretations of this stage.

Psychoanalytic Interpretations
In the work seeking to develop our understanding of the psychodynamic interaction between mother and infant, the sex of the infant (and indeed the effects of the sex of the mother) is largely ignored.

The Object-Relations School of psychoanalysis (Fairbairn, 1952) has explored in some depth the very earliest stage of development and the importance of the mother-infant bond. This work has been popularised in Britain by paediatrician and psychoanalyst Donald Winnicott and through him has reached beyond the professional community and become part of the dominant understanding of early childcare. The major work of American psychoanalyst Margaret Mahler (1968; 1975) and her colleagues on the psychological 'birth' of the infant and its translation into more 'lay' terms by American psychologist Louise

Kaplan (1978) is also noted as being very similar in spirit to that of Winnicott.

This work tells us a lot more about the way mothering is constructed in our society than about the reality of that experience for either infant or mother. The interaction between the mother and infant is seen to lay the foundation for the future mental health of the child and the adult. The earliest stage of life is for the infant a time of 'absolute dependence' followed by a more aware dependency on the physical and emotional environment. Mahler calls these stages 'autistic' followed by 'symbiosis'. In all these accounts this 'environment' is taken to be the mother who is the infant's 'primary attachment' figure (Bowlby, 1969).

'Symbiosis' is a continuation after birth of the fusion between mother and infant. For Winnicott (1960) the identification of the mother with her infant begins in pregnancy and increases throughout pregnancy as 'a willingness as well as an ability on the part of the mother to drain interest from her own self on to the baby' in what he refers to as 'primary maternal preoccupation'. It is this state of 'primary maternal preoccupation' (which no-one but the mother has) which gives the mother 'her special ability to do the right thing' because 'she knows what the baby could be feeling like'. The mother interprets the world for the baby, giving the baby 'the illusion of being at one with her' such that 'An abundance of these near-perfect interpretations holds the baby together and begins to anchor him to the world of reality' (Kaplan, 1978, p. 93).

In these early months, then, the mother and infant are bonded together in 'oneness' described by Kaplan as a physical and emotional bonding.

> The baby curves his body and expands it, especially in the chest and stomach regions, until its contours fit perfectly with the contours of the body of his mother . . . The fit, as far as the infant is concerned, is so perfect that all boundaries melt away. It is as though he and his mother are merged – the being of one dissolved into the being of the other. (Kaplan, 1978, p. 100)

Similarly Bowlby's (1988, p. 9) 'ordinary sensitive mother' is naturally able to understand her infant's needs and to give the right sort of care. This can of course go wrong – if the mother is unable to give herself over to this preoccupation with the infant, having other interests which are 'too compulsive to be abandoned' (that is she is too selfish) – or at the other extreme where the mother tends to become over-preoccupied with any-thing she does and the infant now becomes 'her pathological preoccupation' (Winnicott, 1960).

If, for some reason, say depression, the mother is unable to enter a symbiotic relationship with the infant, he is likely to suffer from what Bowlby (1969) has termed 'insecure attach-ment': this will show itself later in 'separation anxiety' and the infant will find it difficult in Mahler's third stage of separation-individuation to actually separate from his mother.

In order to become independent, then, we must first have experienced dependency. This notion of 'insecure attachment' and the consequent inability to separate is central to some of the writings on the mother-daughter relationships as we will see in Chapters 2 and 3.

The idea that it is the mother and no one else who can best offer this intensity of care to the infant, and who should do so, is not questioned. None of this is considered too great an expectation of mothers because the mother's ability and willingness to abandon herself to the needs of her infant are seen as the natural behaviour of a 'healthy' woman. (Choderow's (1978) work uses object relations theory to show how this capacity to mother is reproduced in female but not male infants in their primary relationship with the mother.)

A mother who is not 'good enough' can however have disastrous consequences for the infant's development, for

> it is the infant whose ego is strong *because of the mother's ego support* that early becomes himself or herself, really and truly. Where the mother's ego support is absent, or weak, or patchy, the infant cannot develop along personal lines, and the development is then related . . . more to a succession of reactions to the environmental failure than to the internal urges and genetic factors. (Winnicott, 1960, p. 17) (italics in original)

The 'environmental failure' is then the mother's failure.

The consequences of the mother's 'failure' to be emotionally present for the infant shows itself in the 'splits' in the baby's consciousness, resulting in the development of a 'true self' which is suppressed, and a 'false self' which is presented to the world. As Sayer points out, Winnicott

> treats the child's internal world as a reflection of an essentially uncontradictory external world, as whole and integrated if its mother is good enough and consistent in her care of the child, and as split, divided and pathological if its mother's care is pathological and not good enough. He thereby overlooks the contradictions in external reality (involved, for example, in the baby's contrary experiences of gratification and frustration) that Klein and Freud recognised to cause consciousness to be split and divided however good or bad the mothering the child receives . . . splits that are, in fact, inevitable given the ambivalences and contradictions intrinsic to social interaction. (Sayers, 1986, p. 67)

Klein (1937) believed in the infant's ambivalence towards its mother from birth, based on an instinctual endowment of love and hate and the experience of gratification and frustration in the interaction with the mother. The mother (or more accurately for Klein the mother's breast as being the first part of the mother related to in feeding) is experienced by the infant as both 'good' and 'bad' 'even under the best possible conditions' (Klein 1959). The 'good' mother, that is the one who satisfies the infant's needs, is split off from the 'bad' mother who fails to do so.

No mother can constantly respond to her infant's needs in just the right way at just the right time, but this is regarded as acceptable because by helping the infant to master the frustrations caused by the 'bad' mother, the mother allows the infant to experience that anger against the 'bad' mother will not destroy the 'good' mother. Eventually 'good' and 'bad' will be seen as contained in the same person, and what Klein called the 'depressive position' will have been reached and the mother will be seen as a separate person. (We can see here how the theory begins to link up in terms of the mother-daughter relationship, where the daughter does not integrate the 'good' and 'bad', but remains ambivalent and unseparated.)

However, where the mother is not able to hold the infant through this process, the infant will repress the negative experiences in order to preserve the 'good' mother in a way which may later result in an idealised internal mother-image, and the projection of the 'bad' image into other relationships, or onto oneself.

While for Klein this constitutes a pathological state, this 'splitting' and the inability to see the mother as a separate person recurs as a major theme in the literature on mother-daughter relationships, until we almost can believe that ALL mother-daughter relationships are pathological, and that daughters are constantly striving throughout the life-cycle to get beyond this earliest stage of development to see themselves and their mothers as separate people.

Feminist Psychoanalytical Interpretations

The social context of gender construction traditionally ignored by psychoanalysts in this early state of development is seen as crucial by feminist psychoanalytic writers. Gender is important in two major aspects, which often merge and which reappear throughout the various stages of the mother-daughter relationship: these are the mother's experience of being mothered; and her identification with her daughter because they are both female.

In terms of identification, for example, a mother may unconsciously act on a belief that because she is 'like' her daughter then she is more likely to 'know' what her daughter's needs are, whereas she will need to be more attentive to her son in order to discern those needs (the hovering we saw earlier?).

A mother may also see herself and/or her own mother reflected in a female infant in a way she would not do so if the infant were male. The reactions to this 'recognition' may then depend on the mother's feelings about herself and about her own mother. Alternatively the mother may see a potentially different mother for herself in her baby daughter and may unrealistically look for a 'mother' in her infant.

Sheila Ernst has used both the writings of Winnicott and of feminist psychoanalysts to show the importance of gender – both in terms of the mother's gender and that of the infant – at this early stage of development. For example she points out that

> Winnicott's account of primary maternal preoccupation is illuminating but also limited. Some feminist writers have

argued that mothering a girl infant and being 'at one' with her is different and unconsciously more threatening and powerful than merging with a boy infant. (Ernst, 1987, p. 83)

This could be because of the mother's fear of reawakening the distress felt at her own unmet needs (that is those unmet by her own mother), or her fear of merging too much with her daughter and losing a sense of her own boundaries.

Ernst also looks at what Winnicott (1971) has described as 'mirroring'. This is seen as a crucial aspect of the infant's development. The baby when it looks into the mother's face should see itself reflected, that is, should see the mother looking at and concentrating on the baby. If the mother does not reflect back in this way because she is reflecting 'her own mood or, worse still, the rigidity of her own defences' and this happens frequently then the baby sees the mother rather than herself and has to 'learn to predict its mother's moods instead of focusing on itself and its own image'.

Ernst believes that daughters are unlikely to receive adequate reflection back from their mothers, but indeed may have to in some way provide a corrective experience for mothers 'who are emotionally deprived and lacking in the social mirroring of their reality' (Ernst, 1987, p. 85). Mothers, it seems, cannot help but 'fail' in their early mothering of daughters. They cannot offer daughters the adequate mirroring which leads to the secure attachment necessary for the infant daughter to see her mother as a separate person, and so, the theory goes, daughters are unable to separate psychologically from their mothers.

Although Ernst offers us an understanding of the early psychological development which seeks to take account of gender, she (and psychotherapists generally) are still in danger of ignoring to a large extent the way society impinges on and effects the mother-infant relationship. While Ernst points out that social expectations can tend to reinforce certain psychological 'difficulties' for girls and women, she and others still concentrate on the individual 'failure', as it is seen, to work through particular phases in the process of psychological development, whilst ignoring the patriarchal imposition of such a process and the effects of this on women. Chapter 2 offers the most relevant example of this, where we see women's 'failure' to work successfully through the process of separation from mother linked to weak ego development and psychological problems in adult life. But we can see it too at the earlier stage of dependency and particularly in the notion of the 'facilitating environment'.

The Facilitating Environment

The 'facilitating environment' which Winnicott decided is absolutely necessary for the infant's healthy development IS the mother. So where is the rest of society in this? The father gets a mention – just – as the protector and provider to the nursing couple, but he does appear rather peripheral to it all (and his increased involvement at this stage is offered as a solution to the 'reproduction of mothering' by Choderow, 1978). Other relatives are hardly mentioned, either as helpers or as recipients of mother's care.

Winnicott gives fathers the role of providing mothers with the care and protection they need in order to devote themselves to their infant. Bowlby suggests that mothers need help 'not in looking after her baby, which is her job, but in all the household chores' (Bowlby, 1988, p. 13). This help, it is said, will very often come from the father, but it is also recognised that quite often this help comes from grandmothers.

What we have then is a hierarchy of dependency – infant dependent on mother, mother dependent on father. But what of the mother who has no partner? Or the disinterested father? Or the father who insists his needs come before those of the infant? Very often mothers have to balance the needs of baby with those of other children and of the father himself. Men in our society largely expect to have their physical and emotional needs catered for by women, as I will go on later to explore in relation to the paradoxical nature of women's dependency. The effect of this on mother and child is clear.

> My disappointments at times worked themselves out on her. There were days with guilt feelings when I became the doormat for both of them. He who sat in his study and wanted to own me alone. And she who could barely walk, and cried for me from the other end of the house. I rushed from one to the other, always with a bad conscience. Never able

to completely give what I yearned to receive. (Ullman, 1977, p. 124)

A mother without a male partner may actually then be better off in some ways, as she does not have to continually balance the needs of children and partner, and she may feel freer to seek the support and companionship of female friends or relatives without being accused of disloyalty. However, she will also most likely be trying to survive on state benefits or low wages since economic structures are determined to ensure the continuation of patriarchy (Glendinning and Miller, 1987).

The further we venture out into the real environment surrounding the mother-infant couple the less consideration we find given to it in the psychoanalytic literature. Social constraints barely get a mention, it is as if poverty, poor housing, social isolation, ill-health and so on, make no impact on the kind of care an infant receives. Psychoanalytic accounts ignore the *actual* environment into which the infant is born, including the relationships surrounding the child, and also ignore the mother's own history and experiences (except insofar as these are pathologised in terms of her not being able to be a 'good enough mother').

Dependent Mothers

The exclusivity of the mother-infant tie already tells us something about how mothering is constructed in our society. A mother is expected to be wholly available for her children: all-giving, all-understanding and totally selfless, she should immerse herself in motherhood to the exclusion of all else (except being a wife — after all fathers have needs too). Women's attempts to fulfil this ideal often leads to depression and guilt.

The 'good enough' mother (and mothers are allowed to fail sometimes, as this is good for the child's development – but not deliberately or too often) is seen as a natural phenomenon, no effort is expected, mothers will do this instinctively. Underlying this is the idea that the needs of the mothers and children are complementary, belying the effort that goes into the work of being a mother and the effort, via child care texts and so on, that has also gone into telling mothers how to be good enough, while it is accepted that mothering involves (and should involve) sacrifice and selflessness.

Ann Oakley in a review of child-care advice literature concludes that 'normal motherhood is an exercise in the denial of self'. She finds that children's and father's needs are paramount; that mothers are expected to get all their own needs met within the roles of wife and mother; and that mothers should accede to the overriding authority of medical 'experts' (Oakley, 1981b). In fact the 'ordinary sensitive mother' is a figment of the middle-class, white, male 'experts' ' imagination, and has more to do with the idealised image of motherhood than its reality. The fact that many women believe in the ideal themselves and also believe that it should come naturally leads to a lot of striving, heart-ache and guilt, only adding to the burdens of being a mother. How then to give the infant the feeling of harmony and sereneness which is the madonna's role?

The work and effort involved in mothering in our society is rendered invisible by the ideology of the 'ordinary sensitive mother'. Hilary Graham (1982) in a study of 200 mothers concluded that motherhood is 'a state of perpetual coping' noticed only in failure and involving both responsibility and culpability. Any failure in the child's development is seen as mother's failure.

The mother and infant are living in a world which, in white, Western society at least, is most certainly not geared up to their needs, and it is the mother who must daily negotiate this often hostile environment (McConville, 1987). Neither will this be the same for all mothers. The extent to which a mother can successfully negotiate the rigours of everyday life with baby will not necessarily (as she is led to believe) depend on her abilities as a mother but on her position in society's class and racial structure. It will also depend on her access to economic and social resources – whether or not she has a car to carry home both shopping and baby; whether she lives in a house with enough space and a garden, or in a block of flats with a faulty lift; whether she has relatives and friends around or is isolated; whether or not she can get the services she needs, like decent child care; whether she has to fight a daily struggle against racism, and so on. These are all resources mothers do not directly control and which they cannot change by being 'taught' how to be 'good' mothers, but which largely depend on one's class and race and on the way oppressions operate structurally in our society.

Take the situation of Beatrice Henry, grandmother to Tyra, who was expected by social services to act as Tyra's surrogate parent and first line protector. She was

> a woman, recently widowed, previously traumatised by the death of a young son and recently traumatised by the maiming and the loss of a baby grandson, living on social security with five children in a grossly overcrowded flat and precious little financial or other help. (London Borough of Lambeth, 1987)

And yet it was not until Tyra's death at the hands of her father that it seemed pertinent to ask 'could she be expected to cope'. Here the racial stereotype of 'strong, black matriarch' inter-twined with the expectation that 'mothers will cope' to lay a massive burden of responsibility at this woman's door. As Parton and Parton point out:

> That Black mothers do demonstrate great strength and skills in coping with the pressures of a racist society *is* evident (Bristol Child Health and Development Study, 1986). Yet the stereo-type of the Afro-Caribbean mother figure as all-pro-viding matriarch prevents them being treated as an individual with individual needs. (Parton and Parton, 1989, p. 44)

Even in the best of social circumstances, the exclusivity of the mother-infant relationship can bring isolation, exhaustion and a heavy burden of responsibility in the daily grind of catering for an infant's needs (see Kitzinger, 1978, p. 33). This leads to a reality of motherhood which contrasts sharply with the romantic image of fulfilled togetherness. It doesn't have to be like this as Jessie Bernard points out

> The way we institutionalise motherhood in our society – assigning sole responsibility for child care to the mother, cutting her off from the easy help of others in isolated households, requiring round-the-clock tender, loving care, and making such care her exclusive activity – is not only new and unique, but not even a good way for either women or –

if we accept as a criterion the amount of maternal warmth
shown – for children. It may, in fact, be the worst. It is as
though we had selected the worst features of all the ways
motherhood is constructed around the world and combined
them to produce our current design. (Bernard, 1974, p. 9)

Effects of Motherhood on Mothers' Mental Health

Becoming a mother involves massive changes in life-style and a
shift in identity, all of which takes its toll on the woman's
emotional well-being. It may therefore come as little surprise
that childbirth is the highest risk point for depression in the
female life-cycle (Formanek and Gurian, 1987). Nor can this be
reduced to a purely hormonal change (as it has been in the
labelling of 'post-natal depression') since although depressive
illness has been shown to be most prevalent amongst mothers
of young children, within this group those most at risk are
working-class women with fewer material and social resources
(Brown and Harris, 1978).

Gavron's (1966) study of mothers of young children showed
that working-class mothers have fewer social contacts than
middle-class mothers and are more likely to be isolated within
their own homes. Tivers (1987) notes the mobility restrictions on mothers with young children which are considerably
worse if the mother cannot afford to pay for any form of substitute child care or have the use of a car. Particularly for new
mothers, who have not as yet established social links in their
close neighbourhood, the early stages of motherhood can be
extremely lonely.

Yet this can also be a time of the development of supportive
relationships between women, and as we will see in Chapter
Six, a time of increased involvement between the new mother
and her own mother. Both these factors are often hidden,
denied or discouraged by male child care 'experts' who prefer
to see such support as interference. This is in keeping with the
dominant (that is white, middle-class, patriarchal) ideology of
exclusive motherhood, exclusive marriage and the self-contained
nuclear family which seeks to obliterate the close relations
between women (except perhaps in Black and white working-
class families where sociologists have tended to dismiss close
female relationships as 'abnormal').

The social and economic constraints on the mother have an effect which is generally ignored when the psychology of the mother-infant interaction is being considered. The psychological accounts are concerned that a depressed mother cannot adequately 'reflect back' or 'mirror' her infant's emotional life, thus leading to psychological problems for the infant. What is not considered is the construction of mothering in our society which is abusive to women (Ong, 1986) and can actually lead to varying degrees of depression in the mother.

Depression has been largely seen as linked to loss. The new mother suffers a great deal of loss – of employment, of money, of independence, of status, of mobility, of social contacts, and of sleep, much of which is exacerbated by the emphasis on the exclusive mother-infant tie, and the lack of consideration of the mother and child's needs in our society. Yet despite all these reasons for depression in mothers, psychoanalysts manage to ignore these in favour of the influence of past relationships.

The psychoanalyst Malan considers maternal deprivation to be 'the most important single root cause of depression' (Malan, 1979, p. 144). As an illustration of this Malan describes a twenty-nine-year-old mother of four (the youngest of whom was eighteen months old) who is suffering from depression. She was feeling 'that everything was getting on top of her and she couldn't cope; at its worse she felt she couldn't look after the household . . . she reproached herself for not being a good enough wife and mother.' Malan ignoring totally the reality of the situation for a mother of four children in our society, considers this mother's difficulties as originating in her own childhood with her own mother who did not give her enough 'genuine care and affection', this 'inadequate mothering leads to resentment; resentment leads to guilt; the guilt is held at bay by compulsive giving' (this mother had previously been a nurse caught in what Malan refers to as the 'helping profession syndrome') 'the giving leads to a deficit in the emotional balance of payments, which leads to more resentment and a vicious circle'. The guilt the mother feels is taken as 'the main surface manifestation of her depressive illness' and as a way of 'hiding the negative feeling of resentment'.

The notion that women are brought up to give to others and are made to feel guilty when they 'can't cope' is never considered. Indeed, Malan considers the mothers 'depressive self-reproaches – that she is not a good enough wife and mother' as having some justification as well as being true about the woman's own mother (Malan, 1979, p. 147). In all of this Malan never once sees this woman as anyone other than a wife and mother. The resentment the woman feels is not considered to be the resentment of a woman forced to deny her own needs in order to be this 'good wife and mother'.

Vivienne Welburn in her book on postnatal depression does consider such needs as valid. She begins her book with an example of the drastic lengths some women have to go to meet both their own needs and fulfil the mothering role

I am haunted by the image of Sylvia Plath in the months before her death, rising at four a.m. to write her poetry before her children woke and she embarked on a day's hard mothering. What sort of society do we live in that requires a woman to drive herself to breaking point if she is to care adequately for her children *and* fulfil her own needs! We can only react as the people we are, not the eternal martyrs we are expected to be. (Welburn, 1980, p. 13)

It isn't only the expectations of others that drive women to immerse themselves in motherhood, but also their own expectations of themselves. The image of the all-embracing, perfect mother haunts us all: the desire to have and to be that mother is strong. Jane Lazarre describes her feelings shortly after the birth of her second child

In those early days, all the mythical aspects of motherhood hung in the air around us. And once again I tried to piece all of our expectations into the image of a beautiful woman whose being I would then don like a golden gown . . .
Mother, goddess of love, to whom we all can go for protection and unconditional love, perfect human being we have all been taught to believe in, whom poets have compared to the earth itself, who kneels down, arms outstretched, to enclose us and fend off the rains, whom none of us has ever met but who continues to haunt us mercilessly; Mother, I can't find you, let alone be you. (Lazarre, 1987, p. 9) (italics in original)

The notion that we can actually be the all-giving mother leads to guilt, depression, a 'loss of self', as Welburn says:

> By being caught up in the unconscious projections connected to the archetype of the Great Mother, human mothers easily lose all sense of their own individuality and worth. They are stretched to fit impossible expectations and forced to cut off their own needs. Women who have a strong sense of individuality and worth escape the rack but the most vulnerable easily start to disintegrate. The most terrible loss is the loss of self. (Welburn, 1980, p. 162)

This is bound to have an effect on the mother's interaction with her baby. A mother may hear her baby's cries as an accusation of being a 'bad mother' as did Jane (quoted in Ernst 1987, p. 71), although the feeling can occur with both male and female infants the fact that Jane's baby was a girl and that Jane herself had 'a particularly unsupportive relationship with her own mother' is taken as significant by Sheila Ernst, since the 'shared gender intensifies the mother's identification with her daughter' and presumably also with her own less than perfect mother, and is 'too encumbered by her daughter's re-evocation of her own early infancy' and thus unable to 'mirror' the baby's feelings. But what of the fact that society does not 'mirror' the mother's feelings, but presents her with a distorted image of how she should be'?

Some mothers enter motherhood with a strong expectation of having their own needs for care met within their relationship with their baby. When this fails it can have dire consequences as with Kathy:

> 'I have never felt really loved all my life. When the baby was born, I thought he would love me: but when he cried all the time, it meant he didn't love me, so I hit him.' Kenny, aged three weeks, was hospitalised with bilateral subdural hematomas. (Steele and Pollock, 1978, p. 119)

The 'cause' of this baby's injuries is likely to be seen as his mother's own 'maternal deprivation' as a child, thus relieving us of the responsibility of considering how this woman's need currently go unmet, and how she has been led to believe, through the myth of romantic motherhood, that they will be met by her baby.

POWER AND HOSTILITY

Women are said to have power through nature, that is, power because they are able to give birth, but as Bernard (1974) points out the hand that rocks the cradle does not rule the world, precisely because it is too busy rocking the cradle. Here we see the difference between the private, fragmented, interpersonal power that women are said to hold within the family, and the public, political power held by men in the wider world.

To the infant in the exclusivity of the mother-infant relationship the mother must be experienced as having awesome power. Dinnerstein (1976) emphasises the 'absolute power' of the 'mother's life-and-death control over helpless infancy'. The mother is also considered to have considerable power over the socialisation and therefore the behaviour of her children. For most mothers this 'power' is felt more as responsibility towards the infant and towards society, indeed the infant may be felt as having the power to keep its mother near, serving its every need. The mother is also conscious of her lack of power in the world outside her relationship with her infant, both as a woman in a patriarchal society, and as a mother in a society that ignores her needs.

Power, like dependency, is a paradoxical concept for mothers. Power in decision-making in relation to one's child is rigidly circumscribed by societal expectations (New and David, 1985, p. 54); and having power over the infant invariably means servicing the infant's needs.

The psychological needs of the infant have been made to parallel the physical needs in terms of importance – if its physical needs are not met the infant will die, if the psychological needs are not met it will suffer severe psychological damage or 'soul murder' (Shengold, 1978).

While the psychological literature looks at the anger of the infant feels towards the mother because its needs are not totally met, much of this literature and that on child-rearing ignores the hostile and angry feelings of the mother (Graham, 1980). This anger is sometimes repressed (as women are generally taught to repress anger and aggression) until it seeps out in depression or bursts out in physical assaults. This is rarely, if ever, discussed in child-care literature because a mother who abuses her child is considered an aberration. She is 'mad' or 'bad', or she is under an unusual level of stress; she is not an 'ordinary sensitive mother' under 'normal' (in our society) conditions of motherhood, experiencing justified anger at her situation which then gets misdirected onto the only person she has power over – her child.

A mother who abuses her child is difficult to accept, after all mothers are expected to protect their children – and for the large part they do. This protection does not only involve protecting the child from starvation, the extremities of the weather, ill-health, accidents, attacks by strangers and so on, but also from her own hostile moods and anger and those of her male partner.

But mothers do not really have this omnipotent power to protect. Their power is limited – especially when it comes to the violence of men – where women may have difficulties protecting themselves. Mothers do neglect and abuse their children, and children are (often) angry with their mothers for this (although for a daughter this anger may take longer to get to, or may seem more threatening to the self). But mothers, because of their protective function, are also blamed when the abuse comes from elsewhere (often the father, or the mother's male partner). Physical abusers of children are found in about equal numbers amongst mothers and fathers: but when one takes into account the disproportionate amount of time mothers spend with children, it becomes clear that a simple count of numbers does not reveal the truth of the situation.

Looking at other forms of abuse, neglect is, by the definition of motherhood in our society, a form of abuse perpetrated by mothers, since it is mothers who are expected to care for their children; while sexual abuse is almost wholly perpetrated by men.

In the dominant 'dysfunctional family' model of child sexual abuse where in theory blame is ascribed to the family system, and not to an individual, it is in fact clear both from the theory and the 'treatment' that mothers are really regarded as 'at fault'. We can see this in influential works from both sides of the Atlantic, for example the British-based 'experts' Mrazek and Bentovim suggest that

To a family with a mother who claims she knew nothing about the incest and is a passive victim in it all, an unexpected intervention would be: 'This is a powerful woman here – to have accomplished all this and avoid sex herself. She's rather like an orchestra conductor, creating lots of sound without playing an instrument herself'. (Mrazek and Bentovim, 1981, p. 172)

Meanwhile in America Giaretto's Child Sexual Abuse Treatment Program appears to need a mother to admit responsibility for her part in the incest as evidence of the programme's success, for Giaretto states 'by termination, 50% of the evaluator's sample [of mothers] admit that they were "very responsible" as opposed to none who admitted this at intake' (Giaretto, 1981, p. 195).

It seems we have not moved as far away from Freud's denial of sexual abuse by fathers (Herman and Hirschman, 1977; Masson, (1985) as we think we have, for now rather than blame the 'fantasy' of the child (and this also still happens) the mother is blamed. The mother is expected to protect her child and where the abuser is her partner she has been blamed for being 'absent' (dead, or in hospital, or emotionally absent). The mother is very often considered to have 'colluded' with or even encouraged the abuse (Forward and Buck, 1981). Mothers have been blamed for not allowing husbands 'conjugal rights' (CIBA report, 1984); for wanting too much sex; for being sick; having a baby; going out to work; filing for divorce; being passive but scheming and so on, all of which are seen as precipitating the male partner's sexual abuse of children. Even the perpetrator's mother and grandmother may stand accused of dominating him as a child (see Driver and Droisen, 1989, p. 36).

In those much rarer instances where mothers do sexually abuse their children they are not excused in this way, nor are fathers held to blame at all. Deborah Valentine (in a review of Evert's (1987) personal account of survival of physical and sexual abuse by her mother), comments that

one cannot help but wonder if Evert ever felt betrayed by her father who did not protect her from her mother's abuse or feel rage at the male relative who also sexually abused her. A common theme among girls who are victimised by fathers or other males is that their mothers did not protect them from harm. Yet Evert does not express these feelings of anger and betrayal towards her father. Why not? Do only mothers protect? (Valentine, 1989, p. 101)

The danger in writing about the stresses and powerlessness of motherhood that can lead to the abuse of the even less powerful child is that it may be read as an apology for mothers who abuse and an ignoring of the very real pain that abuse inflicts on the child (see Kathy Kea's letter to Bie Nio Ong, 1987). It is as if one has to take sides and see either the child's pain or the mother's but not both. It is perhaps wrong to expect the child (as an adult survivor) to see her mother's pain and forgive her – she needs her anger to be validated, it is the responsibility of others to see and alter the construction of motherhood and devaluation of women which may lead to abusive situations.

While a woman may be able to empathise closely with the abused daughter, it is more dangerous and more difficult to relate to the abusing mother, and easier to consider her 'not like me'. This is even easier to do if we consign abusing mothers to a different class from our own (just as so-called 'dysfunctional families' are consigned; Parton, 1985) as we see in the attitudes of middle-class social workers to working-class mothers; or to a different culture (how do we feel about the mother who aids in the female circumcision of her six-year-old daughter?: Nawal el Sa'adawi, 1980).

The responsibility and powerlessness of mothers is related to their so-called dependency as women, and it is this we will go on to explore.

WOMEN AND DEPENDENCY

Dependency is an important concept in women's lives generally. Erikson (1971) would have us believe that women's identity is grounded in dependency, in that identity is achieved for women when they commit themselves to the future father of their children and transfer their dependency from their parents (presumably their father) to their husband.

Dependency and autonomy are crucial concepts in an understanding of women's psychology and women's experience. The separation from mother that is thought to lead to independence and autonomy is worthy of detailed exploration in its own right, Chapter 2 will therefore look at separation as a concept and a life stage/process.

If we concentrate here on dependency, we can see that it has a number of meanings and can be experienced in different ways, and that on the whole for women their dependency is paradoxical in that it means looking after others and having them dependent on you for physical and emotional care and also often for economic security.

The stereotypes of masculinity and femininity would lead us to believe that men are essentially independent while women are dependent (Bardwick and Douvan, 1971). But who are women dependent on and for what? If women (generally) are considered dependent and men (generally) independent we may then assume that women are dependent on men, and this is usually taken to mean that women are economically and emotionally dependent on men (although what it really means is that males dominate females).

The ideology of white, middle-class family life confirms this dependency. The man works and earns the family income, the woman stays at home in order to provide for their physical comfort and is financially dependent on the man. Their relationship is exclusive in that they are as a couple expected to wholly meet each other's needs. This involves the woman in emotional dependency on her man without whom she is not a 'complete' woman. We can see how this operates if we consider how the combining of economic self-reliance and motherhood which has characterised the lives of many Afro-Caribbean and African-American women has been stereotyped into the 'black matriarch'

> as a powerful symbol for both Black and white women of what can go wrong if white patriarchal power is challenged. Aggressive and assertive women are penalised – they are abandoned by their men, end up impoverished, and are stigmatised as being unfeminine. (Collins, 1990, p. 75)

Dependency involves a number of strands – economic, physical and emotional. Let us first consider economic dependency.

The dominant ideology of husband as breadwinner and wife as housewife ignores the 65 per cent of married/cohabiting women and the 56 per cent of women with dependant children who are economically active in Britain (Martin and Roberts, 1984). That many of these economically active mothers work part-time reflects the fact that they are having to balance their paid work with the unpaid work of caring for the family. Women's paid work is seen as secondary to her role as wife and mother (or daughter where she is caring for elderly relatives) and her wage is certainly seen as secondary to that provided by her husband. Yet for many families the income of the woman is crucial, and whether the woman earns money or not, it is often her responsibility to keep the family healthy without getting into debt (Graham, 1987).

Women are generally less well paid than men and their access to better-paid work is restricted. Psychological texts (e.g. Horner, 1972) have considered women's general lack of involvement in high income positions as women's own fault related to their 'fear of success'. This 'fear' is related to jeopardising one's 'femininity', and certainly adolescent girls may devalue and deny their own academic abilities at a time when it is thought important to appear attractive to boys (Oakley, 1981a, p. 124).

But the sexist structures of the paid workforce cannot be so easily dealt with. It is in effect made very difficult for women to secure financial independence from men, especially as a mother. This dependency is not attributable to women's 'weakness' but to those structures which force her into financial dependency and keep her there, from the earliest socialisation into 'marriage in preference to career' and 'suitable (underpaid) work for women', through sexist assumptions and treatment in the education system (Spender and Sarah, 1980), to the evident lack of equal opportunities in a workforce which does not take women's abilities or requirements seriously.

In terms of physical and emotional care it is largely women who are depended upon. Men's dependency on women is well hidden. The expectation that women will take care of men's physical and emotional needs begins with the mother and extends to sisters, girlfriends, wife and secretary. This is so well grounded in our socialisation and our belief systems that men do not have to articulate their needs as they will be met as a matter of course by the women in their lives. If the woman does not fulfil this role the consequences can be dire – economic hardship, violence, even death (Edwards, 1987). Women's physical care of men is more overt and quantifiable than their emotional care. Women on the whole still do the bulk of the household chores (Hoschschild, 1989) and thereby service men.

Emotional care is less easy to define. Women are said to be emotionally dependant on men – to need a man to love them. But if we look at emotional care and what it actually involves, we see again women taking care of men in terms of supportive listening, ego-stroking and ego-building, approval and support, and see girls being taught to do this from an early age (Cline and Spender, 1987).

Men's dependency on the physical and emotional care of women has been seen as a consequence of male domination (Miller, 1976) and as a cause of women's devaluation (Westkott, 1986). A weakness (that men cannot take care of themselves) has been socially transformed into a strength (they can command service from women). That women take care of men both physically and emotionally is a fact every woman knows, and it is said to fulfil one of women's needs – that to be needed and approved of.

Men and women win social approval in different ways, men by being stereotypically masculine – independent and strong, women by being stereotypically feminine – attractive and caring. It may be said that both are constrained by such stereotypes, but we note that 'femininity' is very much formed in relation to approval from men. Jean Baker Miller (1976) explains this in terms of dominant and subordinate groups. Men as dominants have certain expectations of women as subordinates which women have to fulfil in order to survive. She says

> Subordinates, then, know much more about the dominants than vice versa. They have to. . . . They become highly attuned to the dominants, able to predict their reactions of pleasure and displeasure. Here, I think, is where the long story of 'feminine intuition' and 'feminine wiles' begins. It seems clear that these 'mysterious' gifts are in fact skills, developed through long practice, in reading many small signals, both verbal and non-verbal. (Miller, 1978, p. 11)

That women are often dependent on male approval and permission whether inside or outside the home, can be seen as a consequence of male domination, but it has also been seen as a need within the woman herself. This is not surprising, as women are taught from an early age that in order to be loved they must be 'good' girls – unselfish and caring for others, and also that they must be attractive (in order to get a man to look after).

Psychoanalyst Karen Horney (1950, pp. 17–39) believed that the sexualisation and devaluation of girls in childhood leads to a 'dependant character structure that is dominated by the idealised self'. This 'idealised self' is the person who the dependant individual believes she should be. It is the 'internalisation of culturally prescribed femininity' as demanded by the devaluing oppressor. 'The female idealised self is an inner critic that demands ideal appearance, perfect understanding, and selfless caretaking' (Westkott, 1986, p. 146).

In trying to live up to this 'idealised self' women are constantly judging themselves and looking to see how others are judging them to see whether or not they are worthy of attention and care. A woman is taught that if she is a 'good' daughter, wife and mother then she will receive care in return. So she suppresses her own needs for care and looks after her father, brother, younger sisters, and mother, all the time endeavouring to look and behave as they would want her to, looking for approval and acceptance of her own need to be cared for (Westkott, 1986, pp. 145–6). This may be particularly so with mother, for if only the daughter can be the 'ideal' daughter she thinks her mother wants, she may get the 'ideal' mother she hopes for.

If women find they do not get the care and attention they need in their family of origin, they may expect to get it within marriage. The myth of romantic marriage in white, Western society is that it will meet all the couple's needs and it comes as quite a shock to many women when they find their husbands cannot understand their needs, let alone fulfil them, whilst they are still expected to meet all their husband's needs and to bow to his superiority. (This may be less hidden in arranged marriages and women may enter these with a lower expectation of getting their own needs met.)

On discovering this some women take flight (women are more often the instigators of divorce) whilst some enter an exaggerated state of dependency in the form of phobias (agoraphobia may be seen as the fear of flight preventing flight; Symonds, 1971; Fodor, 1974). A woman may look to motherhood to meet her needs – certainly she will find approval for she is fulfilling her feminine destiny, as well as finding a new source of love in her relationship with her children – but being a 'good' mother is expected, and wins no medals; and now she has another person wholly dependent on her.

As we see women's dependency is by no means as straight-forward as patriarchal knowledge would have us believe – where women are deemed to need men because they are, after all, only weak women. Perhaps women's 'dependency' on men can best be understood by looking at the term we often use as its opposite – autonomy. Autonomy means self-government and self-determination, it suggests that we not only have independent thoughts and feelings, but that we can act upon them. It is the constraints imposed on women when they seek to act upon their own wishes, desires and decisions which makes them appear dependent on men, and the strength of this denial of action which leads many women to lose touch with, or rather to suppress, their own independence of thought.

In exploring dependency as a concept related to mothers and women, I may seem to have strayed somewhat from the mother-daughter relationship. This has seemed necessary for unless we try to understand those concepts on which mother-daughter literature depends we cannot begin to see how interpretations of mother-daughter relationships have been distorted in the literature.

The relevance of women's 'dependency' to the mother-daughter relationship is clear in that mothers are seen to 'teach' their daughters, through socialisation and identification, to meet men's needs and suppress their own. Girls are taught to be attractive and caring, not to outshine men intellectually, to offer support (including to mother herself) and look for approval. The paradox of women's dependency is clear, and is felt from an early age, as Eichenbaum and Orbach point out

> A girl may develop tentative and clingy behaviour. She *appears* dependent, incompetent and somewhat fragile. She learns

to look outside herself for guidance and leadership. But behind this outward facade is someone who, whatever her inner state, will have to deal with the emotional problems met in family relationships, a person who knows that others will expect to rely and lean on her, a person who fears that she will never really be able to depend on others or never feels content about her dependency. (Eichenbaum and Orbach, 1984, p. 21)

A daughter may blame her mother for this, she may feel that her mother chose not to give her the care she needed and needs, or the confidence to face the world 'independently'. Learning to look after others, while not feeling worthy of being cared for oneself, may be felt to be the mother's legacy to her daughter.

While complete dependency is only justifiable in infancy, we do not as we grow become completely independent. Dependency, as Eichenbaum and Orbach point out is 'a basic human need', with the achievement of 'autonomy and independence resting on the gratification of dependency needs' (1984, p. 16). The need to be cared for by others does not disappear in adulthood and it is not a weakness. Yet because men get this need met through women without having to articulate it they are seen as not having such a strong need for emotional care as women, while women – who have first to realise their needs (which have been suppressed in childhood), then to articulate them and then to look for someone to meet them – are seen, by others and themselves, as having an overwhelming need for emotional care. So overwhelming that many women suppress these needs further and blame themselves for being 'unloveable', since loving oneself can only come from a basis of being loved and feeling loveable.

The resultant devaluation can lead to low self-esteem and depression. If women do express their own needs they may be judged selfish, aggressive, unreasonable. If they seek to have their own needs met by caring for others (which is what after all they have been taught to do) then they are seen to be making undue and exaggerated claims for the affection of others, and may be labelled 'dependant altruists' giving 'to others the care that she craves but cannot give to herself' (Westkott, 1986, p. 161). Perhaps some forms of care can only come from others (and in the here-and-now) and in asking women to give that care to themselves (having first acknowledged their mothers' early failure in this area) we are asking the impossible, as well as continuing to blame women for their own neediness.

If a woman makes her needs overt but also states that she does not expect them to be met she will be denigrated as a 'martyr' because she has usually made the recipient of her care feel uncomfortable. But women learn that asking for what they need doesn't work – 'We learn helplessness not in the sense that we learn to ask for help but in the sense that we abandon all thoughts of help' (Apter, 1985, p. 79).

It may be seen why dependency is an ongoing theme in the mother-daughter relationship. It is not only the first stage of the relationship with the daughter wholly dependant on the mother, but is an important and paradoxical element in the daughter's psychological development and in her experience of being a woman. It will show itself again as mother's dependency on her daughter and as a daughter feeling responsible for the care of her mother. We will also meet it again in the altered form of mature and mutual dependency/interdependency.

Within that first relationship with her mother is said to lie the basis for the daughter's feelings of self-esteem. Children are said to need unconditional love and acceptance – how realistic are these needs and how possible to meet? As daughters we may feel that if only our mothers had loved us enough then we might love ourselves more. If they had fulfilled our dependency needs then we could go on to achieve autonomy and independence – those sought-after, male characteristics. But is this so?

We are using here concepts loaded with value judgements – dependency is bad (and female), independence is good (and male). And what of interdependency – it isn't mentioned. Patriarchal knowledge has split and polarised our understanding of this concept. Women are dependant because they have not achieved psychological independence; they have not achieved this because they have been unable to separate from their mothers in infancy; mothers are responsible for this because they do not fully meet their daughters' needs in infancy and so provide a secure attachment from which the daughter can separate – the distortion begins.

2 Growing Apart?

The Greek myth of Demeter and Persephone has been used in the feminist literature on the mother-daughter relationship (Hall, 1980; Davidson and Broner, 1980; Rich, 1977) in an attempt to regain historically the 'essential female tragedy' (Rich, 1977, p. 237) of the loss of the daughter to the mother.

Demeter, the Mother Goddess, vents her anger upon the earth when her beloved daughter Persephone is abducted and raped by Hades, lord of the underworld, having been led to him by her own father, Zeus. Demeter forbids anything on earth to grow until her daughter is restored to her, Zeus intervenes and the daughter returns to her mother. But because Persephone has eaten some pomegranate seeds given to her by Hades, she must return to the underworld for 'a third part of the circling year'. On Persephone's return to her mother, Demeter restores fruitfulness to the earth but only for the nine months in the year that her daughter is with her.

While feminist writers understand this myth to illustrate the way patriarchy separates mother and daughter, it is interpreted quite differently by Nina Herman in her psychoanalytic text on the mother-daughter relationship *Too Long a Child*. Herman considers the abduction by Hades as desired by Persephone, who 'was drawn into the "paternal circuit", from the maternal one, not nearly as unwillingly as a more conventional and superficial reading would have us believe' (Herman, 1989, p. 56). Herman considers the wandering of Persephone away from 'the watchful mother' to indicate her wish to dissolve the mother-daughter symbiotic bonds while Demeter is the 'Terrible Mother', the 'witch' possessively holding on to her daughter. This latter interpretation of the myth is in keeping with the psychoanalytic understanding of the desperate attempts of the daughter to separate from the powerful and possessive mother without which separation the daughter remains retarded in her psychological growth and 'too long a child'.

Eichenbaum and Orbach write of the daughter

> the daughter's sense of self is fused with her sense of mother, so that in her attempts to separate from mother she may not

know who she herself is. Trying to be her own person, she is nevertheless confused about where she begins and mother ends. In her early development she has taken mother into her, and now, because she does not have a strong sense of her own separate self, the sense of mother inside her may outweigh her own independent identity. Unlike her brother, she cannot use gender difference to differentiate herself. Psychologically and socially she is a miniversion of mother, someone who will have a life like mother's . . . Inevitably, then, the daughter's attempts at separation are somewhat ambiguous and dovetail with mother's ambivalence. (Eichenbaum and Orbach, 1985, p. 54)

In this chapter I shall examine the issue of separation with a critical eye towards this concept which has been so freely used in discussions of the mother-daughter relationship and in the psychological development of women.

SEPARATION-INDIVIDUATION

We return, then, to the early psychological development of the child and the process which is said to follow on from the symbiotic mother-infant tie, the period of separation of mother and infant and of individual psychological growth for the infant. This process if successfully completed leads to the child's psychological separation from the mother and the beginnings of the autonomous self. The move, then, is from symbiosis to separation, from dependency to autonomy, from identifying with the mother to the establishment of the ego and the beginnings of a separate identity.

For Mahler the 'separation-individuation process' follows 'a developmentally normal symbiotic period' and 'involves the child's achievement of separate functioning in the presence of, and with the emotional availability of the mother'. The separation-individuation process begins in about the fourth or fifth month and lasts until around the thirtieth to thirty-sixth month (Mahler et al., 1975). 'Separation means establishing a firm sense of differentiation from the mother, of possessing one's own physical and mental boundaries. Individuation means the development of a range of characteristics, skills and personality traits which are uniquely one's own' (Flax, 1978, p. 172).

This process, so the argument goes, can only go ahead at the right time and in the right way if the mother has been able to offer the infant an emotionally 'holding' environment in the symbiotic stage and if she has not been over-eager in this 'holding', that is, too possessive and unable to let go, for then Kaplan says the baby will want to 'move into separateness as quickly as possible' and may be seen to prefer strangers to 'the entrapment of oneness' with the mother (Kaplan, 1978, pp. 122–3).

Having experienced 'oneness' with the mother the infant begins to explore the world beyond the mother with the confidence that she will not abandon him. The mother must also encourage the baby's exploration of the world, putting him down on the floor with toys near enough to reach for, and as he begins to crawl and walk, ensuring enough freedom of movement in safety. The mother will sometimes be away from her baby, but this should not be too unreliable or for so long that the baby imagines he has lost her forever.

Where is the father in all this? Essentially he is around as a reminder of the separateness that is to come. For Kaplan it is important that the father is 'a father' and not 'a mother', offering the baby a 'different dialogue' to the one he has with his mother, the possibility of other things in life than the mother-baby oneness. While mothers offer 'rootedness and anchoring', fathers, says Kaplan, 'embody a delicious mixture of familiarity and novelty. They are novel without being strange or frightening'. Fathers offer babies the chance to 'experiment with danger' by 'ignoring the well-plotted routines that mother set up to ensure the baby's safety and wholeness'. They also keep 'a mother and baby in touch with the fact of their separateness' (Kaplan, 1978, p. 138).

Again we see that the infant is viewed as 'male', the argument always being that if you are going to write of the mother – always she – it is easier to clarify the written word if the infant is referred to as 'he', yet it is not felt necessary to change the pronoun to 'she' when referring to father-infant interaction. This is no literary device, the infant in the developmental literature is very definitely a boy, and his development is presented as 'normal' development. Any differences that occur when the infant is a girl are considered deviations from this 'norm'.

So what might these difference be? We have already seen in the period of symbiosis that the mother, because of her close identification with her daughter and fear for her loss of self, may have some difficulties in merging with her infant daughter – here we have the basis for the argument that because a daughter never experiences 'oneness' with the mother she cannot successfully separate, but is continually returning to the mother to get her earliest dependency needs met.

Alternatively this identification of the mother with her daughter may lead to her merging with the child to such an extent that she is unable to encourage the daughter's separation. The sense of oneness and continuity that the mother experiences with the infant is

> stronger and lasts longer vis-a-vis daughters. Primary identi-fication and symbiosis with daughters tend to be stronger and cathexis of daughters is more likely to retain and emphasise narcissistic elements, that is, to be based on experiencing a daughter as an extension or double of a mother herself. (Choderow, 1978, p. 109)

Choderow suggests that it is this identification which makes separation and individuation a 'particularly female develop-mental issue' and which leads to 'a tendency in women towards boundary confusion and a lack of sense of separateness from the world'.

The daughter's extended preoedipal stage (as the symbiotic and separation-individuation stages are classed) has an effect on the whole of her development, making her 'more open to and preoccupied with those very relational issues that go into mothering', and leading to mother and daughter maintaining 'elements of their primary relationship which means they will feel alike in fundamental ways' (Choderow, 1978, p. 110).

During the later stages of the separation-individuation process, called by Mahler 'rapprochement', the child realises the import of being separate from the mother, that symbiosis cannot be fully returned to and that neither of them (the child or the mother) is omnipotent. Mahler did note some differences here dependant on the gender of the child. Boys willingly disengaged from mother, while girls seemed more ambivalent about this and tended to demand greater closeness to their mother when in her presence. Mahler, echoing Freud, put this down to a girl feeling her mother had failed to give her some-thing (a penis) and clinging to her in order to try and get this, whilst also fearing she would be loved less because of this lack.

Flax, along with other feminist psychoanalysts (for example Juliet Mitchell, 1974), prefers to interpret 'penis envy' symbo-lically as the girl's realisation of the power held by males and not held by herself or her mother. The realisation that mother is not all-powerful is a blow to the self-esteem of the child, but especially, says Flax, to the girl, who is 'less likely to have com-pleted the earlier phases' and will not have 'the resources from the symbiotic period to develop an autonomous ego or to absorb blows to her self-esteem'. The daughter then is seen to blame her mother and because she has to identify with her mother she will blame herself for her own inadequacies. Unlike the little boy, the girl cannot 'through identification utilise the authority of the father to build her own sense of power and to protect herself from her mother and from regression to the helplessness of infancy' (Flax, 1978, p. 178).

In this Flax appears to hold the same opinion as Eichenbaum and Orbach, that the daughter's 'failure' in psychological development and her low self-esteem are due to an early lack of nurturance by her mother. One wonders how this differs from the Bowlby/Winnicott notions of 'insecure attachment' due to mothering that was not 'good enough'?

Eichenbaum and Orbach (1984) explain how the mother's identification with her daughter causes separation difficulties by way of a 'push-pull' dynamic. They consider that the mother 'transmits both a positive and a negative sense of self' to her daughter and that the 'mother's complex feelings about her own, and in turn her daughter's emotional dependency needs create the push-pull between mother and daughter'. The daughter, then, wishes to stay close to her mother to have her dependency needs met but the mother is unable to fully meet these because of her own ambivalent feelings: the daughter therefore experiences the mother pushing her away. The 'second push' comes when the father 'enters' the scene in the oedipal stage of development.

The major role of the father is to enable the infant to move out of the oneness with mother into the outside world – or as Herman tells us, to aid the move from the 'maternal' to the 'paternal' circuit. The major oedipal task, the move from mother to father, is for Freud the preparation for heterosexual adult relationships.

In order for the oedipal outcome to be heterosexual orientation in both girls and boys, the theory is set up to ensure that for boys the oedipus complex is destroyed by the castration complex (fear of castration by his father), so that boys end up identifying with their father and repressing their sexual feelings towards their mother, ready to transfer these to another woman in adult life, thus successfully completing the oedipal stage of development. For the girl, however, the process begins with the castration complex, that is penis envy, which leads a girl to turn to her father – who can give her a penis (symbolically changed into a baby), and to turn away in hostility from her mother who denied her a penis and who is now the rival for her father's affections. However, the girl must identify with her mother because they are both female. The daughter's denigration of her mother becomes the denigration of herself. The gender of the infant in relation to the gender of the parent, then, has such an effect that boys grow 'normally' and 'healthily' while girls do not.

For Freud the formation of the superego requires the successful resolution of the oedipus complex. As, according to his theoretical representation, women are by nature deprived of the impetus (the castration complex) for such a resolution, women do not develop strong superegos but remain concerned with preoedipal issues of relationship and are therefore developmentally delayed. That this tautological argument is offered as proof of the moral superiority of boys over girls, men over women, highlights the misogyny of Freud.

Although the oedipal stage of development is about the entrance of the father into the child-mother dyad for the daughter it seems that the relationship with the mother remains the most important influence at this time. Choderow points out that the 'continuity of preoedipal issues in women's lives suggests that girls do not give up this preoedipal relationship completely' and that explanations regarding the daughter's turning away from her mother to her father 'testify to the strength of a girl's ongoing relationship with her mother as much as to the importance of her relationship to her father'.

So, for example, we see that Chasseguet-Smirgel (1964) regards penis envy as the daughter's wish 'to detach themselves from the mother and become complete, autonomous women', and that oedipal daughters 'hate and fear' their mothers. On the other hand Alice Balint, Lampl-de Groot and others suggest that it is love for the mother that leads her into penis envy.

> What a girl comes to realise is that her common genital arrangement with her mother does not work to her advantage in forming a bond with her mother, does not make her mother love her more. Instead, she finds out her mother *prefers* people like her father (and brother) who have penises. She comes to want a penis, then, in order to win her mother's love. (Choderow, 1978, p. 125)

The oedipal daughter is seeking her mother's love and approval or is turning from her mother in bitterness and hatred – or rather ambivalently, she is doing both. Eichenbaum and Orbach say this stage is experienced by the daughter as the 'second push' away from mother towards father, and, as with the first 'push', experienced as rejection by the mother. We have here the basis for the hostility between mothers and daughters, which is said to characterise this relationship in patriarchy (Arcana, 1981), in the form of sexual rivalry for the father, and the daughter's feelings of rejection by the mother.

> Every step of the way, as the analysts describe it, a girl develops her relationship to her father while looking back at her mother – to see if her mother is envious, to make sure she is in fact separate, to see if she can in this way win her mother, to see if she is really independent. Her turn to her father is both an attack on her mother and an expression of love for her. (Choderow, 1978, p. 126)

That daughters are continually 'looking back' to their mothers for whatever reason seems to be used as evidence of their lack of separateness from their mothers. It is as if the very act of looking back invalidates any separateness the daughter may feel she has achieved. Ernst, for example, tells us that

> A daughter who is apparently autonomous in directing her own life, having a clear sense of identity, may unconsciously be living her life according to her fantasies of how her mother would perceive her and cannot therefore be seen as psychologically separate. (Ernst, 1987, p. 69)

Even a woman making every effort to be different from her mother is said to be still caught up in this mother-daughter symbiosis because it is her mother she uses as a model – albeit a negative one.

What role do fathers have in this? Only a positive one, it seems, of aiding the child to separate from her mother – any failure in this being mother's responsibility. Because fathers are not expected to offer the same nurturing to their children that mothers do, but indeed are expected in psychoanalytic literature to offer something quite different, then their influence on the daughter's development comes in for much less notice or criticism than the mothers.

Herman refers to the 'positive' way in which Zeus played his part in 'aiding' Persephone's move away from her mother's hold by growing the narcissus which drew her away from safety and into the clutches of Hades, 'as a fragrant phallic symbol which proved irresistible to his maiden daughter'; she also describes how Florence Nightingale's father stepped in to give her an allowance 'her basic economic freedom that she might remove herself, in the very nick of time before succumbing to madness, from the maternal roof quaking at its every seam'; and approves the way that 'Mr Garrett stood staunchly at Elizabeth's side in furthering her education'. Herman gives no thought to the fact that education and money are largely male gifts to bestow (Herman, 1989, p. 334).

The effect of the father's absence – physical or emotional – or indeed of his presence, is generally ignored. The effect of his expectations on the daughter are rarely, if ever, addressed, despite the fact that research does show fathers to have quite a socialising influence on their children, and also that some fathers already impose expectations of traditional femininity and sexuality on their three-year-old daughters, referring to them as 'flirtatious' and 'coy' and wishing them to be dressed in a feminine way (Johnson, 1982).

The daughter's 'difficulties' in passing healthily through the early stages of psychological development is then mother's fault. Flax tells us that

> it is not that women totally lack the experience of being nurtured; but it is rather that their experience takes place within a context in which the mother's conflicts render the experience less than optimal and, in some cases, profoundly inadequately. (Flax, 1978, p. 175)

What we have so far, then, is the daughter getting 'stuck' in this preoedipal stage between symbiosis and separation-individuation, where the mother's failure to allow complete merging with her infant daughter, and her holding onto her daughter because of her own needs to maintain the symbiotic relationship, leads to the daughter being unable to move on from this stage. We have the mother failing to give the daughter a penis and the daughter retaining her closeness to her mother in the hope of having this put right. We have the daughter's realisation of her lack of penis (power) being an added blow to her self-esteem which she cannot easily sustain because of her fragile sense of self, and therefore we see a regression back to the helplessness of infancy. We have the daughter seeing her mother's lack of penis (power) and turning away from her in anger and hatred.

Nina Herman sums up for us the psychoanalytic view of the withholding, envious and possessive mother denying her daughter any hope of selfhood in a 'partial' list of reasons why 'separation poses a specific impasse to the mother-daughter dyad'. This includes the mother withholding sufficient milk from the daughter; keeping father possessively to herself and not facilitating a closer father-daughter bond; withholding a penis that is power and authenticity in the world; withholding sexual satisfaction and a baby; the mother being envious of her daughter's growth; the mother wanting to keep the daughter at home to aid her in the care of other children (depriving her of a childhood) and her own care in old age (presumably depriving her of an independent adult life); mother 'projecting her neediness and feminine dissatisfactions into her' daughter; these 'unresolved grievances' says Herman 'provide a most potent glue' between the 'two protagonists of the mother-daughter dyad', only to be unstuck, it seems, by the role of the father and 'growing prospects for women in the wider world' (Herman, 1989, p. 332).

By her withholding and holding onto her daughter the mother both keeps her close and forces her out into the world. The mother is both too close and not close enough, pushes the daughter away and tries to hold her back.

Observed Behaviour

Do mothers keep daughters close, while daughters strive to move away? Or do they push their daughters away whilst the daughter attempts to remain close? Unfortunately observation of the mother-infant interaction gives us few answers. Observable differences in the way mothers interact with daughters and sons are open to different interpretations. It has been noted, for example, that girls receive attention by staying close to their mothers whilst boys are attended to whilst they are off exploring (Lewis, 1972); and that boys are left alone more often than girls (interpreted as boys having more freedom), and that girls' requests for help are responded to more positively than boys (interpreted as keeping girls dependant) (Fagot, 1978). It would seem likely that with increased mobility boys are encouraged to explore more whilst girls are kept close and interact more with their mothers. Whether this is also due to the girl infant's desire to remain close to her mother is not known.

Walkerdine and Lucey found that the four-year-old daughters of their study frequently offered resistance to the notion of growing up, and preferred at times the 'helpless' and dependant position of infancy vis-a-vis the mother, for example wanting to be spoon-fed or carried. Walkerdine and Lucey interpret this as a wielding of power by the girls and suggest the possibility of 'the girl not wanting to separate from her mother, not because her needs are not being met, but because the forfeiting of such a powerful position is frightening' (Walkerdine and Lucey, 1989, p. 154).

The daughter, then, may take up a position of helplessness which offers them a fiction of power and control and wards off fears of losing the mother (Unwin, 1984). How the mother herself relates to this has been discussed by Eichenbaum and

Orbach (1987a) and more recently by Walkerdine and Lacey (1989).

Eichenbaum and Orbach suggest that daughters feel both an injunction to stay close to mother but with the unconscious message not to expect too much from that closeness. For Eichenbaum and Orbach the problem for women does not lie in the inability to separate from mother in these early stages but in the 'difficulties that have occurred in the original merger'

> Separation, we contend, is such a very difficult area for women because it rests on the dilemma of the person who has not yet had sufficient emotional supplies to consolidate a psychological self which can allow for a genuine separation. (Eichenbaum and Orbach, 1987a, p. 63)

This suggests that daughters never have, or lose early on, the nurturance they need from their mothers.

Walkerdine and Lacey, however, have emphasised some important class-related differences which suggest a more complex situation than that of Eichenbaum and Orbach's idea of the 'never joined and therefore never separated mother and daughter'. Their study was largely concerned with the class differences in their sample of fifteen white working-class and fifteen white middle-class mother and daughter pairs (their analysis of four-year-old interactions is based on data gathered for an earlier study by Tizard and Hughes, 1984). They found a class difference in the types of dependency the mothers sanctioned in the daughters.

Middle-class mothers tended to sanction physical dependency but push their daughters hard to be intellectually independent, while working-class mothers tended to expect their daughters to be more physically self-reliant but were much more willing to tolerate their daughters not knowing about intellectual matters. So, for example, a middle-class mother tolerates her daughter not wiping her bottom after going to the toilet, but does push her to improve her reading skills even though these skills are already much higher than could be expected for her age. Working-class mothers stress physical independence from the mother:

> Big girls are girls who keep out of Mum's way when she is busy, they can play by themselves, go to the toilet by them-

selves, wash their own hands, they can 'look after themselves' in the home, and learn how to survive in the dangerous world outside. There are also strong elements of nurturance, for big girls look after not only themselves, but others too. This comes up most often in relation to helping Mum and in the care of younger siblings. (Walkerdine and Lucey, 1989, p. 165)

While both working-class and middle-class girls often displayed dependency and helplessness, working-class mothers resisted this more than middle-class mothers. It seems that middle-class girls 'can occupy a position of physical helplessness because *intellectual* self-reliance is stressed by mothers'.

Both sets of mothers are teaching their daughters to master the world as they see it. Working-class mothers may be more constrained by household chores and so encourage their daughters to be more independent of them so they can get on with these, but they also are preparing their daughters for the physical self-reliance they view as necessary to cope with the outside world and future paid and unpaid work. Middle-class mothers, meanwhile, consider intellectualisation as the path to 'getting-on' in the world.

Essentially all the mothers are relating to their daughters in the context of how they experience the world. A girl who sees her mother constrained by material circumstance 'always working, always rushing, never having enough money and so on may make the girls want to remain babies, not want to grow up to be like them, but to be protected from the world of growing up' (Walkerdine and Lucey, 1989, p. 162). Indeed any daughter seeing her mother constrained by motherhood as it is constructed in our society may feel the same.

If Walkerdine and Lucey's analysis of class differences is correct then working-class girls learn even earlier than middle-class girls that they must relinquish their physically dependant status and the pseudo-power which goes with it. But need this physical independence mean a loss of closeness?

If we start from the basis of separation as developmentally healthy, based on the positive regard of individualism and heterosexism, then any closeness in the mother-daughter relationship will be interpreted as unhealthy and denigrated.

The assumption is always that the mother's identification with the daughter leads the daughter to be unsuccessful in her bid to move through these early stages of psychological development. The daughter is said to experience a longer (compared to the son) preoedipal stage, and the issues of this stage are said to remain with her throughout her life. If the only way to healthy psychological growth and maturity is via completion of these early developmental stages, then the girl fails miserably. The argument is that daughters do not separate from their mothers in the healthy, normal way that sons do, they remain emotionally retarded, dependant, with weak ego boundaries and lacking a strong sense of self.

Sense of Self

What is a 'strong sense of self'? If we look at some of the literature on ego strength we find that it is linked to an awareness of one's own needs, a capacity to plan realistically for them and a clarity of goals (Gump, 1972), a capacity for delay, future orientation, firm ego boundaries and objectivity (Carlson, 1971). We can see that ego strength is about fulfilling individual needs and self-assertion, not qualities which women are encouraged to adopt, and certainly not wives and mothers who are expected, as we saw in Chapter One, to have their own needs met through caring for others.

Carlson, in a study of sex differences in ego functioning, found that while men represent experiences of the self in individualistic, objective and distant ways, females do so in interpersonal, subjective and immediate ways. If we adhere to the traditional criteria for ego strength we may then conclude that women have weak egos. Carlson, however, suggests that this serves as an indicator of different kinds of ego strength. Again we find that describing characteristics which are stereotypically masculine (independence, assertiveness, task orientation) as being also the basis for ego strength devalues those characteristics which are expected to be more developed in females (interpersonal orientation, nurturance, supportiveness, subjectivity) in a way that determines that to be female is to be developmentally retarded (Bardwick and Douvan, 1971).

The bias of males towards 'agency' and females towards 'communion' (Bakan, 1966) is well highlighted in research into people's expectations of typically masculine and feminine styles (Rosenkrantz et al., 1968) and of how men and women view themselves (Carlson 1970). Although women may value their interpersonal skills these generally are not seen as identity enhancing, but rather have been used to suggest that women take much longer than men to develop individual identities (Sanguiliano, 1978), or even that a woman requires a man to 'give' her her identity (Erikson, 1971). As we have seen this 'lack of identity' in women is said to have its source 'in the particular nature of the unconscious process of psychological separation of daughter from mother in early childhood' (Ernst, 1987, p. 68).

AUTONOMY OR AFFILIATION?

Does the development of interpersonal and nurturing skills, the caring for others that women do, really mean an inability to separate and have one's own identity? Paula Caplan thinks not, rather she sees this as a misinterpretation of women's nurturing behaviour. She points out that 'The failure to regard oneself as separate from others is an extremely serious psychological disturbance that is very rare' (Caplan, 1981, p. 34). Caplan refers to Signe Hammer (1976) who says of daughters that 'to some extent they never achieve a clear sense of a separate (from mother) self at all' and of mothers that the 'tendency to live in and through other people – to behave as though there were no difference between self and other – is an essential part of being a good mother'. Caplan wonders if what Hammer meant to refer to 'was the frequency with which mothers suppress their own feelings and wishes in order to meet the needs of others'.

Meeting others' needs, as Caplan and others (Jordon and Surrey, 1986; Grimshaw, 1986) have pointed out, actually requires a degree of separation from them, in order to see their needs and not impose one's own needs on them. As Grimshaw says, 'a capacity for an imaginative understanding of other people, or for holding their welfare very close to one's own heart, does not at all entail that one cannot differentiate one's own needs from theirs, or that one defines one's life goals as the same as theirs' (Grimshaw, 1986, p. 181). Rather, as Caplan points out, 'successful nurturing involves a substantial degree of psychological separation of self from others.'

Grimshaw believes the mistake is made in equating 'women's greater capacity for care for or empathy with others' with a supposed 'lack of separation' in women. This comes about because theoreticians have related the daughter's 'lack of separation' from her mother (her remaining in the preoedipal stage of development longer) with the daughter's increased capacity for nurturance (for example, Choderow, 1978). A 'problem' in the girl's development is therefore seen as the basis of her interpersonal and caring skills, thus devaluing them.

If we remain with a developmental model that has separation and individuation as its only aims, then any development that is about connection to others and relational aspects of identity is by definition seen as retardation. What we should rather be considering is that such a model of development misses out on the positive developmental aspects of concern with others (Franz and White, 1985). The development of a strong sense of self can, and it can be argued, for women does, include a concern for connection to and care of others.

The difficulty lies in the fact that these two aspects of identity are split by theory: one is rendered female (and negative) and the other male (and positive). In our society women are not encouraged towards individualism (concern with oneself) but towards developing interpersonal and nurturing skills (concern for others) – skills which are greatly devalued. As Jean Baker Miller points out, 'women have been led to feel that they can integrate and use all their attributes if they use them for others, but not for themselves' (Miller, 1977, p. 64).

This is well illustrated in a paper on autonomy in women by Natalie Shainess, who also points the way to an integration of autonomy and relational issues for women. Shainess uses the story of Antigone, daughter of Oedipus, as an example of autonomy in a woman. What is interesting in this is that Antigone uses her 'strong, healthy superego and ego', not to further some selfish end for herself but in a relational capacity. Defying the powerful Creon's orders, and risking her own life, she sets out to bring back her brother's body from the battlefield so that he can be properly buried. In doing so she shows 'qualities of independent ethics, caretaking and autonomy' (Shainess, 1986, p. 109). Antigone is a woman 'willing to take risks to live authentically', she is held up by Shainess as an example to all women of who we can be – a person of autonomy and high principle. Electra (used by Freud as an example of women's development), on the other hand, is 'incapable of autonomy', she is a 'passive, father-worshipping woman'.

Shainess here rather ignores the power men have as 'dominants', which is well understood by Jean Baker Miller as determining women's actions to a degree, and the competing demand this can make on a woman (in duty to her dead brother or in response to a live male authority). When our mothers 'teach' us to be less of a woman than Antigone, are they doing us a grave injustice or trying to protect us from the powerful forces they have experienced and we have yet to understand?

This issue of 'care for self' and 'care for others' shows itself again if we consider Freud's concept of superego. This is the outcome of the smashing of the oedipal complex for boys, and so because girls never quite manage this they do not develop strong superegos. This means that women are impaired, in Freud's view, when it comes to judgements concerning morality and justice. However, Gilligan has pointed out that rather than an impairment in moral development, women show a *different* understanding in this area than men. Once again we find that while men are concerned with individual rights and justice, women are concerned with relational issues, responsibility to others and the 'ethic of care' (Gilligan, 1982).

As George Klein has pointed out, '"We" identities are also part of the self' (Klein, 1976, p. 178). Concentration on the development of the self as an autonomous unit has led Freudian and Object-Relations theorists to view relational issues in regressive terms. So mothers and daughters 'fail' to separate, remain 'merged' and 'undifferentiated', suggesting always a failure in development, a standing-still or a return to more primitive forms of functioning.

Talking to women, as did Arcana and Hammer, it is very easy to conclude that separation from the mother – or lack of it – is indeed a major issue for daughters. Hammer puts it thus:

Most of the daughters in this book have received enough support from their mothers to emerge from the stage of complete symbiosis in early infancy. But for the vast majority of mothers and daughters, this emergence remains only partial. At some level mothers and daughters tend to remain emotionally bound up with each other in what might be called a semi-symbiotic relationship in which neither ever quite sees herself or the other as a separate person. (Hammer, 1976)

However, these works are based on the same theoretical model of development, steeped in male concepts of individualism and autonomy.

If we view relational issues in development as positive, then 'lack of separation' between mother and daughter can be reframed and called connection. It can take on a positive rather than a negative stance. Indeed, studies of development based on connection and individuation have found that supportive behaviour from the mother has a very positive effect on the ego-development of the daughter (Grotevant and Cooper, 1983).

Relational Theory

Jordon and Surrey, using Kohut's (1971) theory of self-psychology and George Klein's (1976) critique of existing theories about the self, formulate a relational model of development looking at the positive aspects of these early stages of the mother-daughter relationship.

Reframing the 'frequent mirroring, mutual identification and accurate empathy' that the sharing of the same gender can produce in the mother-daughter relationship, they point out that the use of concepts like '"semi-symbiotic" merely reflect the paucity of our language and theory in describing relational development' (Jordon and Surrey, 1986, p. 88).

Jordon and Surrey consider that the mother's identification with the daughter leads to her feeling more connected to her daughter at an affective level and more able to encourage 'emotional sharing' with her daughter, which forms in the daughter 'the origin of the capacity for empathy and the process of relational development'. This is not considered as retardation in the daughter but as a 'positive developmental pathway' and posits a new developmental model of 'growth through relation-ships'. Remaining in a close, connected relationship with mother can enhance the daughter's ability to relate to others and lead to the development of accurate empathy. Jordon and Surrey place great emphasis on empathy as 'central to an understand-ing of the aspect of the self that involves "we-ness" '. 'It is this process' they say

> through which one's experienced sense of basic connection and similarity to other humans is established . . . Without empathy, there is no intimacy, no real attainment of an appreciation of the paradox of separateness within connec-tion. (Jordon and Surrey, 1986, p. 85)

In similar vein to Caplan, and Grimshaw, Jordon and Surrey point out that with empathy one sees the 'differentiated image of the other' which is quite the opposite to the regressive form of merging which has generally been seen as the outcome of the mother-daughter connection. Jordon and Surrey see women's potential for intimacy and connection as deriving from that early empathic relationship with mother, which is very different to Eichenbaum and Orbach view that this is the source of women's problems in this area (Eichenbaum and Orbach, 1987b).

Choderow also sees the mother-daughter identification as leading to the development of empathy in girls, but rather than seeing this as a capacity to understand to some degree the needs and feelings of others, she sees this as experiencing another's needs and feelings as one's own, and experiencing oneself as continuous with others.

But empathy actually suffers if one cannot differentiate self from others. Mothering involves being aware of the difference between the child's needs and one's own and trying to meet both (Jacobson 1965, p. 57). Where this often goes wrong in our society is in the ideology of mothering as seen in Chapter One where a mother is not supposed to have needs of her own, or is expected to suppress her own needs in a selfless manner for the sake of her children and husband.

Instead of 'separation-individuation', Jordon and Surrey use the concept 'relationship-differentiation'. In this model growth does not involve greater degrees of autonomy and the breaking of early emotional ties, but is about maintaining connection whilst fostering, allowing or adapting to the growth of the other and of oneself. The mother-daughter relationship is then interactional and allows for the growth of each through the relationship, leading to mutual self-esteem and mutual empowerment. Because the mother is more open with her daughter and more willing to share emotionally, Jordon and Surrey believe that this will 'probably leave the girl feeling more emotionally connected, understood, and recognised than would a boy'. They go on to describe the 'mutual empowerment' and 'mutual self-esteem' this leads to between mother and growing daughter in rather rosy terms, 'both mother and daughter becoming highly responsive to the feeling states of the other over the life cycle' and a 'good relationship' developing and being 'highly valued by both mother and daughter', becoming 'a fundamental component of women's self-worth' (Jordon and Surrey, 1986, p. 91).

Although Jordon and Surrey point out that 'Such a relationship is very difficult to maintain, especially in a culture that stresses separation as an ideal', in their eagerness to value the connection between mother and daughter and the empathic skills of women in relationships which has been so devalued in our society, they are in danger of romanticising the mother-daughter connection and not giving enough credence to the strength of the cultural aspects which can and do distort this relationship in reality.

Within patriarchal societies it is still possible for women to offer each other emotional support and to find their strength in relation to other women. Yasmin Alibhai tells us that she grew up 'in the midst of a powerful practical display of the independence and power of women' but that younger Asian women settled in the West may be losing out on that 'particular sisterhood' with its 'organic closeness'. This she puts down to the different context.

> The dominant philosophy in the West is divisive, splitting people into egocentric little atoms, people so split think primarily of themselves, and they are at a loss to know how to give up a little of that self and form genuine rooted human links. . . . People are afraid that if they extend themselves, the "me" in them will be diminished, or lose shape . . . This

concept remains totally alien to me. Our inner world tells us that the more you give the more you grow. (Alibhai, 1989, p. 35)

Christine Renee Robinson (1985) also gives us a different picture of the mother-daughter legacy for Black women. She tells us that 'self-reliance, independence, assertiveness, and strength are inherent characteristics of Black women which are passed on to Black girls at a very early age'. African women have carried with them a legacy of autonomy from their traditional societies which has enabled them to survive the 'gruelling and dehumanising years of slavery'. But these traits have not been developed in a Western, individualistic mode, but in an etiology of a 'collective-consciousness', a community strength and support which Robinson tells us still exists today 'in practice and in ideology'.

Again we must be careful. By considering strength and assertiveness as inherent characteristics of Black women, we play down and devalue the development of these positive characteristics in the face of colonialism, racism and sexism. Black daughters may themselves 'inherit' strengths from their mothers via a feeling of connection and an understanding of and pride in their mothers' accomplishments in the face of massive oppression. Our Western theories of psychological development offer us a very poor starting-point in understanding the psychological development of women from other cultures, or the legacy they bring to their daughters growing up in white dominated society. Chapter Seven examines this further.

A danger also lies in trying to transpose the idea of a female community and the daughters' growth within this into a society dominated by an ideology of familism and possessive individualism (Dalley, 1988), where women are the carers and men hold the power, where community and caring skills are devalued. If we are not growing up in a community of women – where we can clearly see women's strengths for what they are – but in a nuclear family where mother carries the work and responsibility of caring without the power, we may wonder why our mothers are such martyrs to the needs of others, and feel angry with her that she does not offer us a better model of independence and assertiveness.

Anger and Love

In our society, the denigration of female values of caring and empathy, and of women themselves, the limited opportunities for women and the expectation of women's submission to men will all have an effect on that first relationship between women. We want our mothers to show us the way to be strong, to be ourselves. We also want their nurturance, love and approval. We feel the lack of this 'perfect' mother and our anger shows.

It shows in the studies of the mother-daughter relationship (Arcana, 1981; Hammer, 1976), it shows in the feminist therapists' consulting room (Eichenbaum and Orbach, 1985; Robbins, 1985; Herman and Lewis, 1986). Although feminists may have gone some way in understanding where that anger really belongs, it seems almost impossible not to direct it at mother. Adrienne Rich tells us

> When I think of the conditions under which my mother became a mother, the impossible expectations, my father's distaste for pregnant women, his hatred of all that he could not control, my anger at her dissolves into grief and anger *for* her, and then dissolves back again into anger at her: the ancient, unpurged anger of the child. (Rich, 1977, p. 224)

Mothers too feel angry at times with their children, some quite a lot of the time, and some especially with their daughters who may reflect back at them their own feelings of inadequacy and low self-worth.

In contrast I am struck by that other side – when a mother offers her daughter the nurturance she needs and feels the warmth of that sharing with the daughter. A poem by Ellen Bass and a narrative from Mary Gordon highlight this in very similar ways at different stages of the daughter's life cycle.

> There are times in life when one does the right thing.
> The thing one will not regret,
> when the child wakes crying 'mama' late
> as you are about to close your book and sleep
> and she will not be comforted back to her crib
> [. . .]
> an articulate person now, able to converse, yet still
> her cry is for you, her comfort in you,

it is your breast she lays her head upon.
you are lovers, asking nothing but this bodily
presence.
[. . .]
. . . and it is this sense of rightness,
that something has been healed, something
you will never know, will never have to know.

(Ellen Bass, 1984)

Charlotte watched her daughter cry. She had come home at
six forty-five and had spent the rest of the evening crying in
her room.
. . . "I was thinking maybe you'd better sleep in the bed with
me. I've turned the heat off in your room and it's chilly".
Felicitas sobbed.
"Come on bean", said Charlotte.
they got into the old hard bed with the metal headboard and
the horsehair mattress that had been Charlotte's mother's.
Charlotte lay down, said goodnight, kissed her daughter and
turned her back to her. Felicitas slipped behind her mother
like a spoon. Exhausted from a day of crying, she fell in-
stantly asleep. Charlotte lay awake and thought of mothers
who killed the men who hurt their daughters. Only she did
not know who to kill or why she had to kill him. And her
child was not a child. (Mary Gordon, 1982)

Where here is the 'possessive' witch mother, the mother who
cannot see her child's needs as separate from her own, or
'allow' her daughter her freedom and privacy whilst also offering her much-needed nurturance?

There is very little written by mothers themselves about the
process of separation from their daughters. What is written
tends to be of the type of 'what can I/have I offered my child?'
Partly this is because there is much less written by mothers than
by daughters on the mother-daughter relationship, but also it
may be because this separation is such a different process from
the viewpoint of the mother, and one in which mothers have
been made to feel that they have no right to certain feelings.

Western psychology concentrates on the rights of the (usually male) child and, as we have seen, blames the mother for

not offering the right environment for healthy development. No wonder then that mothers are loathe to write (or even to talk about except perhaps quietly to a close friend who is also a mother) their own feelings as their children grow and their relationship with them changes. Mothers are told to love their children enough to give them a 'self' and then to let them go (Friday, 1979), to have their own life and interest (but not before their children can cope with it) so that they have no expectations of having their needs fulfilled by their children. Mothers are expected to weep for the 'loss' of their growing child, but to hide these feelings from the child and not to hold onto the child for comfort.

But how do mothers really feel as their daughters grow and assert their individuality? It is difficult to know. Our literature has concentrated on the daughter's feelings, our theoretical base distorts what mothers might have to say. For example the mother, 'Barbara', in British psychoanalyst Dana Breen's book *Talking with Mothers* (1989) talks of the closeness and posses-siveness she feels for her five-month-old daughter, her wish to have 'some peace and quiet to enjoy her', and the fact that she would at times prefer not to have anything to do with her husband or her son. Breen allows no time or thought for the mother's feelings of connection with her daughter but delves straight into the interpretation that Barbara has 'problems with the "third" person', the father who comes in and disrupts the mother-daughter dyad. The message is that the mother's 'pos-sessiveness' will impede the daughter's development.

The issue of mother-daughter separation is a difficult one to grapple with. Western individualism, middle-class ideology and male domination all combine to offer us a distorted theo-retical standpoint from which to judge the mother-daughter relationship.

This chapter has been about the psychological process of separation between mother and daughter but we should not forget that the major concern of women from oppressed groups is more often enforced physical separation. In the past and still today daughters have been forcibly separated from their mothers, to be sold as slaves; to go into 'service'; to be wet-nursed; to be given to 'better' mothers when their own mothers were deemed 'unfit'. They have been separated by immigration, by racist immigration laws, and by the force of circumstances which leads to Black children being looked after by relatives or privately fostered with strangers whilst their parents seek to build a better life for them. They have been separated by adoption where a mother cannot afford to keep her child; by surrogacy agreements (Chesler, 1990) and by court orders where a father claims and wins custody by virtue only of his prior claim as father in a patriarchal society (Chesler, 1987). What effects do such enforced separations and subsequent maternal deprivation and child deprivation have on the daughter and on the mother?

This has been a difficult chapter to write, largely I think because of the elusive nature of the concept of separation – just what does it mean? The relationship between mother and child takes place on different levels – on the practical level of their reality of everyday life, which will be affected by their social context, and at the level of unconscious life, different for both mother and child and cutting across their interaction together. The intensity of the ambivalences surrounding the mother-daughter relationship are highlighted when considering separation and are difficult to deny. The desire for closeness and connection to others, and the opposing wish to be oneself is a struggle for everyone, but I think it is particularly pertinent to women in our society who are expected to provide that closeness for others.

Reading earlier works on the mother-daughter relationship, and listening to what (mainly daughters) have to say on this both in the books and in women's groups, it is hard to value the positive connection between mothers and daughters. Instead we hear 'mother didn't love me enough', 'mother didn't protect me', 'why didn't she behave differently so that I could value both her and myself?'.

Eichenbaum and Orbach's contention that women lack that very early merger with mother that would form the basis for self-esteem and a strong sense of identity is likely to be better understood by many daughters of Western patriarchy than is the connection and mutual empathy and empowerment posited by Jordon and Surrey. Both are based on a fantasy of the 'perfect mother'. Payne says that 'Separation is the psycho-logical term for the process of growing up and coming to terms with the fact that one's mother is a separate and imperfect individual who is not always available and who cannot and will not satisfy all one's needs and expectations' (Payne, 1983, p. 333). Women as daughters can think about and wish for a perfect mother, the same woman who as a mother would tell you it is a fantasy which denigrates what she has to give as a real mother. It is interesting that for many women the 'mother' in them does not tell the 'daughter' what she knows.

3 The 'Motherless' Daughter

The 'motherless' daughter is a recurring theme in women's writing and women's biography. We read that Virginia Woolf 'always thought of herself as a "motherless daughter" ' (Marcus, 1981, p. 13); Emily Dickinson stated 'I never had a mother' (Johnson, 1958) and Harriet Martineau 'conceived of herself as unmothered' (Davidson and Broner, 1980, p. 57), while Jane Austin's and George Eliot's novels portray 'a number of motherless heroines' (Davidson and Broner, 1980, p. 57). For Martineau, Woolf and Dickinson this 'motherlessness' meant different things.

For Harriet Martineau this 'motherlessness' began at her birth in 1802 in Norwich. She was almost a victim to the then relatively common practice of putting a baby out to a wet nurse which is so vividly described by Badinter (1980). When, as Martineau herself put it, she 'all but starved to death in the first weeks of my life, – the wet nurse being very poor. . . . The discovery was made when I was three months old, and when I was fast sinking under diarrhoea . . . ' (Martineau, 1877, 1, p. 10). Her 'unmothering' continued through a fearful and isolated childhood in the midst of a large family. She later observed 'a little more of that cheerful tenderness which was in those days thought bad for children, would have saved me from my worst faults, and from a world of suffering' (p. 11).

Mitzi Myers tells us that Harriet was the sixth of eight children of an 'unaggressive father' and a 'dominant' mother who 'governed' her household with 'high standards' and on an 'uncertain income'. Mrs Martineau was ambitious for her children and sought to prepare both her sons and her daughters for independence and to be self-supporting. In also expecting her daughters to show 'feminine propriety' and 'good manners' and to be 'proficient in all aspects of domestic management' she fulfilled the task of typical middle-class mothering. Harriet's mother, in both her own behaviour and her expectations, offered Harriet a 'complex female role model'.

Harriet continually sought the love and approval from her mother that she was missing. She 'elaborately mothered James and Ellen [her brother and sister], pouring out on them the love she felt herself deprived of'. She also continually tried to be the 'good' daughter, returning home at her mother's insistence and against her own wishes, at the age of twenty-seven; and later had her widowed mother come to stay with her in London against her own better judgement. Eventually she found physical release from her mother through her own long illness, and release from that illness and 'alienation' from her mother through hypnosis. Finally she created a home for herself with devoted nieces and servants as a surrogate family. Myers points out that

> Martineau never really succeeded in coming to terms with her mother, but she did succeed in coming to terms with herself. In a sense, she ultimately made herself into the mother she had always wanted to have – sympathetic, confident, just, and serene. Her complex experience richly illustrates both the strengths and weaknesses of Victorian mother-and-daughter relationships. (Myers, 1980, p. 79)

Martineau's experience of being unmothered began with early physical deprivation and developed with demands and expectations from her mother, some of them related to the social-isation of the 'good' daughter, which were not tempered with kindness and warmth.

Reading about Martineau one does feel that she was an unnurtured child who learnt to nurture others, and who was eventually able to provide nurturance for herself. We have little on which to base an understanding of her mother's life and feelings, a life in all probability dominated by trying to fulfil the rigid expectations of middle-class wife and motherhood, with a large family, on an 'uncertain' income.

From Virginia Woolf's biography we get much more a picture of a mother too wrapped up in the care of others, especially of her husband and her youngest son, to give her daughter the nurturance she needed. Virginia recognised the exhausting demands made on her mother, who not only concerned herself with the lives and problems of the people of the locality but also ran a home with eight children and a 'moody, dependant' husband, when she says

> I see now that a woman who had to keep all this in being and under control must have been a general presence rather than a particular person to a child of seven or eight. Can I remember ever being alone with her for more than a few minutes? Someone was always interrupting. (Woolf, 1976, p. 83)

Virginia grew up in a male-dominated family where her father 'godlike, yet childlike' occupied an 'extraordinarily privileged position' to which her chronically overworked mother (Julia Stephen) acquiesced (De Salvo, 1989, p. 125). Virginia could see that her mother gave her attention to her husband and sons and not to her daughters. Through her portrayal of mother-daughter relationships in her writings, we see how Virginia sought to understand her mother.

In *To The Lighthouse* Virginia portrayed her mother as the central character, Mrs Ramsey, and explored the potential mother-daughter relationship through the eyes of artist Lily Briscoe. Mrs Ramsey is a complex character ('"Fifty pairs of eyes were not enough to get around that one woman with" thought Lily') she is attentive to the needs of others (mainly men's) but unavailable to Lily who longs for intimacy and unity with her.

In her art, says Adrienne Rich, Virginia shows us 'the passion of the daughter for the mother, her need above all to understand this woman, so adored and so unavailable to her; to understand, in all her complexity, the differences that separated her mother from herself' (Rich, 1977, p. 228). On Mrs\Ramsey's death it is to Lily that Mr Ramsey turns to have his own needs met

> That man took. She, on the other hand, would be forced to give. Mrs Ramsey had given. Giving, giving, giving, she had died – and left all this. Really, she was angry with Mrs Ramsey. With the brush slightly trembling in her fingers she looked at the hedge, the step, the wall. It was all Mrs Ramsey's doing. She was dead. (Woolf, 1955/1927, p. 223)

Here we get some idea of how Virginia might have felt when her mother abandoned her completely by dying when Virginia was thirteen.

Rich interprets Emily Dickinson's statement that she 'never had a mother' to mean that she saw herself as very different from her mother, 'deviant, set apart, from the kind of life her mother lived; that what most concerned her, her mother could not understand' (Rich, 1977, p. 229). Certainly Emily Dickinson removed all traces of her mother's influence and presence in her life from her work. We are told that 'Following conventional nineteenth-century standards, Dickinson's mother is a "perfect" wife; but Emily Dickinson sees the world's contempt for this dutiful woman', a woman 'neglected by her husband and ridiculed by her children' (Mossberg, 1980, p. 133). Dickinson then attempts to disassociate herself from her mother and from the role her mother fulfils.

Even before her mother's death Dickinson was perhaps mourning a mother who could not give her the guidance and support she needed to be her own sort of woman: she was 'an ambitious woman without a role model or a mother adequate to her needs'. This is probably the case for many women struggling to have a life different to that of their mother, or even trying to be a different sort of wife and mother – this subject is explored further in Chapter Four.

Although the 'motherlessness' of Martineau, Woolf and Dickinson can be seen as experienced quite differently by them, they all have in common the social context of that experience and its effect on how they were mothered. Mothers' responsibilities as conveyors and upholders of societal values within the family, male dominance and female subservience, all served to shape the experiences of these mothers and daughters. Given the 'power' of these mothers to control their daughters and withhold nurturing, one might understand why women novel writers of the time made many of their heroines 'motherless', especially since it was also considered that nurturing mothers held back their daughters' growth.

In order for their heroines to be assertive and independent Jane Austin, the Brontës and George Eliot made many of them motherless (Broner and Davidson, 1980, Part 2). In this way the 'good, supportive mother' did not hold back the daughter's growth but could remain an 'ideal' for the daughter to emulate on maturation (MacDonald, 1980, p. 58). Nor are the heroines portrayed as mothers themselves 'because society provides no realistic model for healthy motherhood' (Zimmerman, 1980, p. 83). If mothers are portrayed then they must

> be flawed in some way, so that instead of preventing a daughter's trials, she contributes to them. The nurturing that we usually associate with motherhood, then seems to have to be withdrawn or denied in order to goad the daughter into self-assertion and maturation. (MacDonald, 1980, p. 59)

The implication is that with the presence of a 'good' and nurturing mother the daughter will remain developmentally delayed, that in order to grow daughters may be better off without a mother, since mothers cannot offer the kind of growth inducing nurturance that their daughters require. As with the psychological arguments in the previous chapter we see that mothers were held wholly responsible for the socialisation and development of the daughters.

The reasons daughters feel 'unmothered' will vary. These daughter/writers of the nineteenth and early twentieth century experienced a mothering set in the context of their particular social time and place – that is middle and upper middle-class, families ruled by men, where women's first duty was to the service of their men and where children's needs, especially those of daughters, were very low priority. Daughters' feelings of being 'motherless' can be seen in relation to the way the family was constructed and maintained within such values.

But daughters today can still be heard to say that they have felt 'unmothered' or 'motherless'. 'I'm angry at my mother for not mothering me' says Griffin (1977); 'I'm angry with my mother for what she never gave me' and 'Mom tolerated everything, she never got angry or said a harsh word, she was never physical with me. She didn't hug or kiss me, or play with me like dad did' (Robbins, 1985, p. 45). Eichenbaum and Orbach tell us 'When women talk of there being "something missing", they are trying to explain their mother's missing nurturance that makes them feel less than whole' (Eichenbaum and Orbach 1984, p. 49). Far from being an inherent part of the mother-daughter relationship, this can still be seen to be related to social context and the process of socialisation for girls and women.

LOSS OF NURTURANCE

As we saw in the last chapter, there is a strong belief amongst certain feminist psychotherapists that women generally lack that early nurturance from their mothers which would allow them to grow in self-identity and self-esteem (Eichenbaum and Orbach, 1984; Flax, 1978; Ernst, 1987). The belief has grown out of the repetition in therapy of women's neediness, lack of self-worth and anger (often needing to be 'uncovered' in the therapy) with their mothers. The interpretation of these feelings is based on psychoanalytic theory, grounded as it is in a belief in the overriding importance of early mother-infant interaction for adult mental health, with the added feminist stance that the devaluation of women in our society renders the mother's identification with her infant daughter negative rather than positive in its outcome. That this identification also forms the basis of women's nurturing abilities is seen as both positive and negative.

Eichenbaum and Orbach (1984; 1985) point out how the fact that women are raised to be nurturers whilst men are not affects the mother-daughter relationship in four particular ways. Firstly mothers have to prepare their daughters to be nurturers, 'a woman's self esteem suffers if she doesn't feel herself to be a "good giver"'. Secondly, because the mother does not receive the nurturance she needs from the father, the daughter notices and identifies with her mothers 'emotional dissatisfaction'. Thirdly, because of her own neediness and in teaching her daughter to look after others, the mother may offer herself as the first 'candidate' for the daughter's nurturing skills; and fourthly relating to her daughter may revive the mother's own feelings of loss of early nurturance from her mother (the mother is a 'motherless daughter' too), she may therefore look to her daughter to make up for this.

So, in all, the daughter is taught to care for others by her mother and it is her mother who she cares for first of all because of her mother's excessive neediness due to a lack of current and past nurturance. The mother then becomes the daughter's 'first child' and in so doing teaches the daughter not to expect to have her dependency needs met. A mother 'must wean her [daughter] very early from relying, at an emotional level, upon having her dependency desires met. For mother to continue to meet them would go deeply against the grain of socialisation to the feminine role'.

The needy part of the little girl, then, is experienced as unacceptable. The daughter finds that to get the love and approval she seeks she must act in a particular way – that is tending to the needs of others (including mother) – and hide that part of herself that is needy. Eichenbaum and Orbach refer to this as 'the little girl inside', the part of the psyche that 'still yearns for nurturance' and 'tends to carry feelings of isolation and depression, even despair'. This lives on in the growing daughter and into womanhood:

> from girlhood to womanhood women live with the experience of having lost these aspects of maternal nurturance. This nurturance is never replaced . . . This loss, which causes tremendous pain, confusion, disappointment, rage, and guilt for the daughter, is buried and denied in the culture at large as well as in the unconscious of the little girl. (Eichenbaum and Orbach, 1985, p. 52)

This loss is the loss of the mother. As we have already seen in Chapter Two, for Eichenbaum and Orbach the daughter's loss of mother's nurturance dates back to that earliest state of merger, which is seen as problematic (Eichenbaum and Orbach, 1987, p. 63).

Caplan does not believe that the early merger between mother and daughter is deficient, but rather that that merger has to be broken too early in order to prepare the daughter for the nurturant role, and because of a fear of homosexuality. She says

> A sudden failure in the meeting of a previously met need can cause one to experience that need as more intense than before (Freud, 1905). If, during the period of earliest infancy, a daughter has an intensely loving relationship with her mother and then is subjected to strict limitations on the expression of that loving intensity, she could well begin to experience herself as a person whose need for love is never met. Such a period of deprivation, begun early in life and following after a period of feeling well loved, can leave females with a sense of loss that can never be overcome (Caplan, 1981, p. 71).

The sudden cutting-off of physical affection between mother and daughter is vividly illustrated by one of Arcana's interviewees when she says

> Until I was about five there was a lot of it. But when I was about that age, we went to a movie and I put my head in her lap. She pushed me away, and said, "you're too big for that". After that there wasn't any physical attention from her. (Arcana, 1981, p. 74)

Arcana found that for most of the women she interviewed touching decreased through the first few years remembered, and then stopped around the age of nine or ten.

Caplan, believing the loss of physical nurturance to be linked to homophobia, considers that the age at which this happens will vary depending on how far the mother relates sensuality to sexuality, or when she has this 'link' pointed out to her as with Jane Allen's mother:

> I do remember when I was fourteen, my mother said we should stop holding hands when we walked down the street because a friend of hers had teased her and said we looked strange. She didn't explain exactly what the concern was, but I understood that adult women weren't supposed to be publicly affectionate or something bad would happen. (Rafkin, 1987, p. 52)

The mother may also, says Caplan, be forced to stop showing daughter physical affection because of her husband's jealousy. Preparing a daughter to be a nurturer and to be heterosexual are societal imperatives (coming from without and within) which the mother mostly feels compelled to obey.

We can see how particular beliefs about childbearing (which change with the current fashions) may affect the mother-infant interaction from the beginning. Tillie Olsen (1956) in her story 'I Stand Here Ironing' tells of a mother who, following the 'expert' advice of the times, nursed her first child on a rigid schedule, rather than according to the needs of the baby. Rigid feeding schedules may be old hat today but 'spoiling' is still frowned upon. When my own daughter was one day old I was told by a nurse that I would have 'a very spoilt little girl' because I was holding her just for the sheer pleasure of it (she was neither feeding nor crying at the time). Spoilt for what? In that she would go on to expect affection and not learn early enough that it is the giving and not the receiving of care that is the woman's lot?

While the ideas of 'spoiling' a child in this way is a social injunction which on the surface appears genderless, I wonder if this is in fact so. Friends tell me their infant boys are much more affectionate and willing to be cuddled than their daughters – is this the child's bias or theirs?

Some mothers ignore the social imperatives against showing their daughters 'too much' physical affection. Another of Arcana's interviewees tells us 'I was never down. I was always in her arms . . . We hugged and kissed a lot, and I still kiss her' and 'we used to cuddle together, and when I was scared at night I used to go into her bed with her and sleep' (Arcana, 1981, p. 79).

'GOOD GIRLS' AND 'GOOD MOTHERS'

In learning to nurture others, girls are said to lose out on their own early nurturance. They are expected to bury their own needs and look only to the needs of others, in this way they will gain (or so they are told) love and approval in return. It is our mothers as primary socialisers who teach us this and who bear the brunt if we don't learn to be 'good' girls.

Through example and through their attentions to us our mothers show us how to grow up female. The characteristics of the 'good' girl will vary between generations, cultures and classes but on the whole, in patriarchal society, it is about being a caring person, helpful and selfless, always looking to others' needs – especially those of men – about being heterosexual and attractive to men (although this attractiveness may sometimes have to be hidden from men other than father, brothers and husband); about being obedient and reliable, and only using one's skills and abilities in the service of others. 'Good' mothers produce 'good' daughters

> those who obey, follow and accept their inferior status . . . It is constant suppression, repression, and deprivation. Never a hair or a nasty feeling out of place. The daughter is the

mother's product. The mother is judged, her basic humanity evaluated, on the basis of her daughter's neatness, sweetness, and docility. (Gilbert and Webster, 1982, p. 30)

How the mother will bring this about is also clearly prescribed, for she 'should rarely have to resort to overt censure and punishment', indeed because such characteristics are viewed as 'natural' to the little girl, any waywardness on her part can be stopped by a look from her mother – a mere reminder of how she should 'naturally' be. In fact these 'looks' contain much more than this, they are the reminder to the daughter that in not behaving as she should she is causing her mother undue suffering, breaking her mother's heart – taught to care for others above her own needs, the daughter complies rather than risk losing her mother's love and approval.

But the risks both daughter and mother run if the daughter is not 'good' is often more than the mother's disappointment. As Gilbert and Webster point out, 'Each mother has to transit the rules of femininity to her daughter to help them survive in the world as she knows it'. In many cases, in a society where men hold the power, this 'survival' is really that. Not being a 'good' girl can result in poverty, social ostracism or even death for a woman.

We see this in Bouthaina Shaaban's book about the lives of Arab women, for whom to become pregnant outside of marriage can lead to death at the hands of a male relative (as it did for Yemen, see Shaaban, 1989, p. 3). Choosing one's own husband against family wishes can mean to ostracism from one's family (as it did for Bouthaina Shaaban herself) and lead to death threats and the locking up of one's mother (if she dares to want to see you) as it did for her friend Ghada, who says

My only regret is that I can't see my elderly mother, whom I adore. I'm not allowed to. She's been put under virtual house arrest by my brother, who would kill me this very moment if he found out where I was. My mother secretly manages to send me messages of love, a lock of her hair or a piece cut from her dress which I keep here in my bra to feel with every heartbeat. She knows nothing about the reality of my life. (Shaaban, 1988, p. 22)

No less threatening is the abuse that Western women suffer

at the hands of men within the family if they do not perform their proper duties as daughters, wives and mothers in accordance to the men's wishes. In 'Provoking her own demise', Susan Edwards shows how the civil and criminal justice system in Britain responds to violence against women on the basis of what is judged to be the women's 'contribution' to the assault (how she came to 'ask for it'). Some of the key factors she notes which influence whether or not action is taken by the police and how the court deals with a case once it gets there read very much like 'good' girl prescriptions and are to do with 'the degree to which women conform to or deviate from appropriate female roles of wife, mother, homemaker'. A woman is 'contributing' to her own assault or even death, if her behaviour has been

> sexually inappropriate, that is having friendships or relationships with men outside marriage, being bisexual or lesbian . . . inappropriate in terms of gender, that is, bad mothers, bad cooks, bad housewives . . . challenging either the gender assumptions of their expected roles or challenging male domination (Edwards, 1987, p. 158).

Our mothers have learnt the rules by which they are bound, they have seen the cost of failure to comply, it then seems little wonder that they will teach their daughters to protect themselves by being 'good' girls.

Not that our mothers may necessarily have made this connection. Some will try very hard to protect us from the difficulties in life. 'She really was much too kind. Her gentleness made it very difficult for me when I became older, to put up with the knocks you get' (Arcana, 1981, p. 45). Some will have internalised the 'good girl' bit so well themselves that they will see nothing but the joys of a 'good' marriage (often the one they didn't manage to get because they were not 'good enough') on the horizon for their daughters if they themselves manage to 'good' mother her into the right sort of girl – 'My relationship with her has a lot to do with satisfying her projected needs, like my having a "good" marriage' (Arcana, 1981, p. 9). Mothers are also sometimes heard to tell their daughters to look after their man properly because he is a 'good' man (a provider) and that if he 'strays' it is her fault for not meeting his needs.

Not all mothers rely on the 'good' girl model of protecting their daughters. Some do try to teach their daughters how to protect themselves by being assertive and confident of their own rights. This is most notable in the literature on Black mother-daughter relationships where we see mothers teaching daughters to have self-respect and to be self-reliant (Collins, 1990, p. 126; Sage, 1984). Julia, a Black American woman quoted in Stack (1974) has learnt from her mother that 'a woman has to have her own pride. She can't let a man rule her'. Likewise, Ladner's (1972) study of young Black women in America shows daughters being taught to be 'strong' and 'resourceful' to enable them to play a central role in their households.

Nancy Tanner points out that in matrifocal societies (that is where the mother's role is culturally and structurally central)

> there is little difference between women and men with regard to initiative, assertiveness, autonomy, decisiveness. In none of these societies are women socialised to find their identity in intimate dependence on men. Instead, they are socialised to become relatively independent, active women and mothers. (Tanner, 1974, p. 155)

We must not forget, however, that in imperialistic patriarchy 'good' white girls are also learning to be strong and resourceful in the service of their families, whilst maintaining an appearance of feminine dependency and weakness to earn their white male protection, while racism has decreed a different model for Black women who are not offered such protection at all.

TAKING CARE OF MEN

In Choderow's (1978) analysis of how daughters learn to care for others the father is 'absent'. Indeed it is the father not being present which leads to the reproduction of caring skills in daughters but not in sons, and Choderow offers an increase in father's role at this early stage as a way of making caring more than women's work. However in this Choderow ignores the very strong influence of the father, whether or not he is physically absent or present. For in learning to care for others it is men's need of care which is paramount.

In the biographies discussed above the fathers are largely notable by their absence – not in a physical sense of not having been there at all but in their daughters' interpretations of their importance. So we see that 'there is little mention of Martineau's father in her Autobiography, and that little shows him a gentle, supportive parent' (Myers, 1980, p. 72). Both Woolf's and Dickinson's fathers are present largely in their effects upon the mothers, Woolf's as an exacting, dependant and tyrannical man who took away mother's attention, Dickinson's as a man who ridiculed and neglected his wife.

Despite the emphasis in the socialisation and child development literature on the mother's role, fathers do have an effect upon their daughters' growth and socialisation by the very fact that in learning to be nurturers it is men, as dominants, who daughters are learning to nurture. It is mothers who are expected to teach daughters to be 'good' girls, and in so doing show the world that they are 'good' mothers. It is mothers who pay the price of 'failure' in that socialisation. It is fathers who reap the rewards – daughters, wives and mothers who will look after their every need and support their sense of superiority.

The expectation that women will look primarily to men's needs is highlighted in both middle-class and working-class studies of family life at the beginning of this century. Dyhouse, for example points out that 'one of the first and most important lessons learned by the young girl in the middle-class home was that the organisation of the household revolved around the needs of the male breadwinner', and that 'daughters learned from observing their mothers in their interaction with servants, or in their own activities, about the social expectation that a wife should be solicitous for her husband's needs'. Interestingly, in Jamieson's working-class study it was the deferential service girls were expected to give to their brothers which caused more comment (Dyhouse, 1986; Jamieson, 1986).

The more contemporary picture presented by Cline and Spender (1987) in their book *Reflecting Men at Twice their Natural Size* is not so different. They found a majority of the women they spoke to had experienced having to defer to brothers or fathers, usually at the request of their mothers, in order to keep the men in a good mood.

Angela McRobbie (1978) in her study of adolescent working-class girls in Birmingham found that it was quite normal for these girls 'to spend between twelve to fourteen hours per week engaged in some form of domestic labour (several babysat for neighbours and relatives as well as for their own mothers). Not surprisingly the girls were not joined in this work by their brothers'. Jill, a fifteen-year-old, says 'me brother doesn't do a thing in the house. He makes a mess and I clear it up after him. He doesn't even make his own bed, waits for me mum to do it when she gets in from work' (McRobbie, 1978, p. 100).

The way in which it is mothers who mediate between the power of the father and the behaviour of the daughter is well illustrated by Adrienne Rich's childhood. When her mother locked her in a closet for childish misbehaviour it was 'my father's orders but my mother carried them out', or kept her too long at piano practice 'at his insistence, but it was she who gave the lessons'; she was a child who 'felt my mother had chosen my father over me, had sacrificed me to his needs and theories', had a mother who 'was made to feel responsible for all our imperfections' (Rich, 1977, p. 222–4). Before judging and condemning Rich's mother, women who are mothers themselves may like to consider how often they have agreed to carry out a male partner's instructions against their own judgement in order to keep the peace or because they have been made to doubt their own judgement. Those who advise mothers may also like to consider how often they have condemned mothers for allowing children to play one parent off against the other by disagreeing with father's instructions.

Nancy Friday says that 'in mother's earliest and usually unconscious efforts to handle feelings of competition with her daughter, she teaches the little girl not to expect too much physical attention from daddy. "Come away. Daddy has important papers to go over." Mother is teaching us that men don't have "our" need for love' (Friday, 1979, p. 65). Or is the mother here saving the child from a more damaging 'request' from daddy to keep clear and let him get on with what is important (to him)? Many daughters feel that mother came between her and her father, preventing them from having a closer relationship.

Daughters learn their subordinate role from their mothers, they learn to put aside their own ambitions and needs as did their mothers before them. Adrienne Rich's mother gave up the possibility of a concert career; Sylvia Plath's mother Aurelia 'yielded' to her husband's wishes that she become 'a full time housekeeper' (Plath, 1976). That Aurelia went to terrible pains to avoid her husband's displeasure is typically interpreted in psychoanalytic fashion as the wife's pathology, seen by Herman as proof of her 'precarious personality' kept going 'with the crutch of primitive defences like omnipotence and denial' (Herman, 1989, p. 248).

Even where a mother expresses a desire to see her daughter succeed in paid work this may be tempered with the wish for a 'good marriage' for her. As one mother speaking to Cline and Spender put it: 'I know my daughter's bright and I'll do all I can to help her with her education – but I don't want her to be a career woman . . . A well paid job, that's what she needs. But not one that puts a man off. A good job and a good husband' (p. 34–5).

When the mother is not available to service her husband's needs then the expectation is that the daughter will take over her role. That mothers are blamed for their daughters' sexual abuse at the hands of fathers and step-fathers because they have withheld 'conjugal rights' affirms the entitlement of men to use women to service their every need. That daughters are often sexually abused concurrent with mothers' physical and sexual abuse by the same man illustrates the degree of men's power to enforce their 'entitlement' (Hooper, 1987).

MORE THAN MOTHER'S RESPONSIBILITY

So far we have concentrated on the mother's role in the socialisation of daughters largely because this is seen as mother's responsibility both by society, by the mother herself and especially by the daughter. But as we have already seen, this socialisation by the mother is really in the father's favour and on his behalf. This is the myth the mother-daughter relationship has been trapped within.

In the literature, in biographies, in women talking about their family relationships, the father is most often seen in a positive light or not seen at all. Even where it is father who has abused a daughter, it is the relationship with mother, and mother herself who is held responsible. (For example, see Justice and Justice, 1979; Kempe and Kempe, 1978.)

But fathers do have a more direct role regarding the socialisation of their daughters, both in how they treat their daughter and how they expect her to behave, and in how the daughter sees the father and herself in relation to him. We know that infants of both sexes form early attachments to their fathers as well as their mothers (Pederson, 1980; Lamb 1981). However, the way boys and girls experience their parents does differ – with mothers being seen by both boys and girls as 'doing things for you' whereas fathers 'do things with you' (Meltzer, 1943, p. 314). Also fathers do differ in their treatment of boys and girls, fathers prefer sons (Hoffman, 1977), they talk to and look at baby boys more than baby girls and spend more time with boys than girls (Lewis and Weintraub, 1972).

In reviews of the research on fathers' influence on daughters' development, both Biller (1976) and Johnson (1982) conclude that fathers are influential in their daughters' sex-role development, although they interpret this differently. Biller stresses the father's influence in terms of personal and social adjustment and his lack of involvement as leading to problems in personality development (mainly having problems relating to men and being disliked by boys!): Biller notes however that 'overly rigid sex typing and negative definition of feminine behaviour' (p. 126) can be detrimental to girls development.

> The well-adjusted female's identification with her father seems to involve understanding and empathising with the father rather than rejecting her basic femininity and wishing she were male. A positive father identification may also include the sharing of many paternal values and attitudes as long as there is no interference with the girl's development of a feminine self-concept and an expressive mode of social interaction. (Biller, 1976, p. 132)

Biller also finds that fathers 'influence their children's sex-role development more than mothers do' generally by being more interested than mothers in sex differences and encouraging femininity in girls – this involved not only viewing daughters as 'more delicate and sensitive than their sons' but also in the tasks they expected them to perform, 'for example, they expected girls to iron and wash clothes and baby-sit for siblings, while boys were expected to be responsible for taking out the garbage and helping their fathers in activities involving mechanical and physical competence'. Fathers also encourage their daughters to develop skills in social interaction.

Miriam Johnson (1982) interprets the findings of the research differently. Johnson breaks down the concept of 'femininity' into its maternal and heterosexual aspects and points out that 'while the maternal aspects of women's "femininity" seem more related to basic gender identity and to the mother daughter relationship . . . the heterosexual aspects of femininity more directly involve the father'. She stresses the negative impact of fathers' influence, noting that they 'seem to reinforce what is generally considered "traditional" femininity including passivity and attractiveness'. For example, a study by Sears (1970) reported that the degree of femininity in girls was positively correlated with the father's (but not with mother's) 'warmth'. Sears also stressed that 'femininity' was correlated with poor self-concept in girls as well as boys.

In terms of caring, a large study of adolescents by Leuptow (1980) carried out in 1964 and 1975, found that 'women *most* influenced by the father have higher expressive orientations than those influenced by the mother'. It would appear, then, that fathers do have quite an influence in the development of 'feminine' characteristics in girls, although in terms of 'caring' it is likely to be mother's behaviour that girls imitate with feminine women adopting 'expressive role behaviour by imitating their mothers' interactions with their fathers'.

Another interesting factor to emerge from these studies is that while fathers generally show a preference for boys (Gilbert et al., 1982; Fagot, 1978) and, in many important respects, a withdrawal from girls (Margolin and Patterson, 1975), 'mothers do not withdraw from boys nor step up their interaction with daughters in a complementary fashion'.

It is now being suggested that fathers should encourage 'autonomy' and 'achievement' in daughters (Biller, 1981; Lamb et al., 1979). However, it is not only father's direct influence on his daughter's development which needs to be considered, but also the way the relationship between the mother and father influences the daughter's perceptions of how men and women are. As pointed out by Johnson, 'to the extent that marriages remain male dominated, the influence of the father on the daughter may work against her psychological autonomy even though he may verbally encourage autonomy'. It is what the child sees and experiences rather than what she is told which has a lasting impact on her understanding of the world. A child may be told that mother and father consider themselves equal partners in their relationship but if that child observes mother tending to father's needs and deferring to him (Bell and Newby, 1976), then the child may learn a rather distorted definition of equality.

Social learning theory (Bandura, 1977; Mischel, 1966) and cognitive-development theory (Kohlberg, 1966) suggest that children are socialised into sexually specific roles by their observation and interaction with their parents. This has been explored in traditional psychological literature mainly as fathers' influence on boys' sex-role development (Hargreaves and McColley 1986) while the mother-daughter influence is largely assumed.

So it is expected girls will identify with their mothers and will be encouraged to do so. They will look to their mothers to see what sort of adult they will be, what they will be expected to do and how to do it, and they will rehearse for their future caring roles by helping mother in her household work (what Hartley (1966) has termed 'activity exposure'). As Jamieson (1986) found in her study of working-class mothers and daughters at the beginning of this century:

> in accordance with conventional gender divisions, mothers made girls do more housework that boys; young women were expected to continue helping with housework, young men were not. This gave daughters some experience of 'women's role', and some opportunity to identify this role as an aspect of the subordinate position of women in the gender hierarchy. My evidence suggests however that mothers rarely set about deliberately and consciously socialising their daughters into the role of future housewives. (Jamieson, 1989, p. 54)

Although more mothers today may consciously be attempting *not* to socialise their daughters into this role it should be remembered that insofar as mother herself carries out the caring work for the family, the daughter may learn via observation.

The cognitive-development model of Kohlberg (1966) argues that a child quickly learns that people are categorised into two genders that remain constant over time. They also learn that they belong to one of these categories and their identification with that category guides their understanding of later events.

Recognition of one's gender identity as unchangeable, says Kohlberg, is acquired by the age of six or seven years: the child then automatically wants to do things consistent with his or her gender. For boys this involves perception and acceptance of the male stereotype based on the male body image, which associates masculinity with activity, aggression, power and prestige, and leads to identification with adults who fit this stereotype and particularly the father. For girls this is less straightforward. The universal stereotype that girls turn to are those of nurturance and childcare, as well as a relative lack of activity, competence, power and aggression (that is the opposite of boys).

But as both boys and girls become aware of power and prestige, between the age of four and eight years, they will imitate adults 'who are valued because of prestige and confidence, and who are perceived as like self'. How then do girls reconcile this 'like self' identification (and her mother's lack of power) with (male) adult models of power and prestige?

Kohlberg maintains that during the age of five to eight years both boys and girls will identify with their father but girls will do so in a 'complementary way' which 'defines her femininity in terms of male acceptance and approval'. Girls also value 'niceness' and identify with this as having a subtle form of prestige (that is being a 'good girl'). Kohlberg's theory of development can be seen to based on the boys' and girls' relationship to power: in this way it does not take proper account of female development but merely treats it as something which occurs in relation to male norms. It also assumes male and female stereotypes are 'universal' and ignores differences due to culture and class. For example, what is the child of a low paid or unemployed father to make of the lack of power the father has in the outside world?

That girls see the freedom and power of being born male in our society and want that for themselves is neatly illustrated in this working-class woman's memories of a Lancashire childhood

I loved the streets; they were freedom. I had lots of adventures there, with my friends . . . I beat Malcolm Johns to a jelly when he said I had to be Maid Marion, a girl couldn't be Robin Hood. I showed him different. I wanted to be a boy. Not because I wanted a willy, or any such Freudian rubbish – on the contrary, I thought boys' dicks were daft; they reminded me of small worms or teapot spouts, and they looked to me as if they could get in the way of a good rough game. No, I wanted to be a boy because he could be Robin Hood, the Lone Ranger, Black Arrow, William Tell, Flash Gordon, and the rest, without a big battle beforehand. And boys weren't called in by their mums to wash up or dry up, tidy this, tidy that. It made me sick, being a girl. (Nickie Roberts, 1989, p. 47)

While the literature stresses the family influences on the child's socialisation it should not be forgotten that the parents and child are operating in a society which demands, reinforces and extends a particular 'norm' of socialisation.

Marianne Grabrucker (1988), a German lawyer, is one mother who has set about consciously trying to bring up her infant daughter differently. As the mother of a girl she was concerned and perplexed by the current idea that it is mothers who 'make' daughters and therefore mothers who through educating their daughters differently can undo the restrictive gender role in girls. To get a better understanding she kept a detailed diary of her days with her infant daughter from pregnancy through to three and a half years old – the results of which are written up in her book *There's a Good Girl*. From her own observations Grabrucker noted that 'Days teemed with role-enforcing events, concealed and obvious, for which I was only rarely responsible'. She concluded that:

An accumulation of such experiences provides the child with a pattern, in accordance with which it is bound to adjust its own behaviour within its environment. Only when I had gained this general view from three years of observing quite chance events, and grasped all the details as part of a whole picture, did I realise that I and the world around were building brick by brick a woman governed by patriarchy, and not

a human being with female or male components. (Grabrucker, 1988, p. 9)

Children are bombarded by stereotypical images of men and
women on the television, in books and comics and in the
'hidden curriculum' of schools, all ensuring that boys and girls
are prepared for their different roles in adult life and that
dominant social values are adopted (Sharpe 1976; Spender
1982; Spender and Sarah 1980).

It is likely that there will be a social class difference in the way
girls are prepared for their adult roles – we can recognise, for
example, a class bias in education where middle-class girls tend
to be given freer access to educational opportunities, and options
available to working-class girls are restricted fairly early on
(Sharpe, 1976, p. 143). This limiting of opportunities, as
Walkerdine and Lucey point out, has also been blamed on
mothers who are expected to prepare their daughters to get the
most out of schooling. What we see operating is

> a profoundly unfair and unjust social order which treats
> inequality and oppression as an effect of 'intelligence' (if you
> had it you could become middle-class, 'succeed') and nat-
> uralises inequality as a just system. On top of this, it lands
> mothers with the guilt of failing to produce a proper
> environment (the 80 per cent of the 80/20 hereditary/en-
> vironment couple) for development which would lead to
> educational success. Class then becomes naturalised, as
> though we all could potentially be middle-class with the
> right brains and the right mothers. (Walkerdine and Lucey,
> 1989, p. 178)

Mothers do not control their children's experience of school.
In what small influence they do have, mothers teach about the
world they know. Working-class mothers may have found school
so alienating that they encourage their daughters to pass through
it as quickly as possible and to rush out of the other end to
poorly-paid and largely manual jobs with domesticity as the
promise of escape. Or they may see education as the daughter's
way to a better life, not imagining that they may lose her to
middle-class values on the way.

CARING 'FOR' AND CARING 'ABOUT'

It can be seen then that the socialisation of girls into gender restrictive roles is much more than the mother's responsibility. The interaction of mother and daughter takes place within a familial and societal setting which is determined to shape girls and boys into the necessary mould for adult femininity and masculinity as it is viewed in our society.

The daughter's feelings of 'loss' may be as much about these restrictions – which appear to be imposed by her mother – than about an actual loss of care for her by her mother. Girls learn very early that being a 'good' girl and getting the approval and love they seek is about taking care of others in a selfless manner. They learn that this largely means taking care of father and brothers, as their mothers do. Girls then may not so much 'lose' their mother's nurturance as be expected to join mother in offering nurturance to the males in the family. Take this quote from Robbins

> Anna: "Dad was the center of attention in my family; all three of us 'girls', Mom, my sister and I, vied for his attention – you could never get enough of it. I remember how my mother would call us in from playing to change our clothes before he came home for dinner, so we would look pretty for him. And how we loved that! Dad was everything positive, he heaped a lot of love on us – he was a real King." (Robbins, 1985, p. 44)

One can imagine these 'girls' (one of them a grown woman with all the responsibility that entails) 'prettying' themselves up in preparation for their 'King's' return to his castle, his dinner ready, his clean shirt for the next day ironed, 'his' house immaculate. He comes home from a 'hard' day to 'heap love' (attention and approval) on his pretty and adoring wife and daughters, who (he fondly imagines) have been sitting pretty all day waiting for his return.

Jean Baker Miller has pointed out how women have to some degree internalised the belief that they are inferior to men and that their life should be dedicated to caring for men – after all we have all been raised as 'good' girls. Women also see the value in caring for others, and although this is not externally valued in society women feel better about themselves if they see themselves as caring people. As Miller rightly says

> It is extremely important to recognise that the pull toward affiliation that women feel in themselves is not wrong or backward; women need not add to the condemnation of themselves. On the contrary, we can recognise this pull as the basic strength it is. We can also begin to choose relationships that foster mutual growth. (Baker Miller, 1978, p. 100)

Caring can be seen as an activity in the serving of others' physical and emotional needs – caring 'for'; and as a way of feeling – caring 'about' someone. For women these two aspects of care are inseparable, that is, women are expected to show they care 'about' someone by caring 'for' them (Graham, 1983). As Dalley points out

> This blurring of the boundaries between functions typifies the woman's universe. In the domestic sphere, the menial tasks of family servicing are wrapped up and presented as part and parcel of her role as mother, and given the same affective value as the feelings she has about the family members for whom she is performing these tasks. (Dalley, 1988, p. 8)

Women describing their caring activities make the connection between looking after the needs of their family and their love for them – so for example cooking a meal for one's husband on his return home from work 'lets him know I am thinking about him' (Murcott, 1983). The physical acts of caring – preparing a meal, washing and ironing clothes and so on – therefore take on a special meaning in terms of how women show, and are expected to show, affection.

The work of care is not only physical but also emotional. It is women's work to 'charm . . . sympathise . . . flatter . . . conciliate . . . be extremely sensitive to the needs and moods and wishes of others before her own . . . excel in the difficult arts of family life . . .' (Woolf, 1931). Virginia Woolf's 'Angel in the House' is involved in all the emotional work of caring – work which has been shown to be very much women's work and is often about the upholding of men's egos. This can be seen every day when women act as supportive listeners to men (Fishman, 1978; Spender, 1980).

Tillie Olsen (1980) identifies a 'two-angel form', adding to Woolf's imagery 'the essential angel' who 'assumes the physical responsibility for daily living, for the maintenance of life' (Olsen, 1980, p. 34).

For women the concept of 'caring' for others is a complex mix of work, duty, love and identity. Girls learn of this at the sides of their mothers, and also by seeing and responding to their mother's need for help with the caring work and for care for herself.

'MOTHERING' MOTHER

We would all like to be taken care of, to have all our needs met unconditionally – in short to be mothered. So who mothers the mother? The myth has it that if you are a good girl you will get yourself a knight in shining armour (or even a King) who will 'heap' love on you. In reality this is less than likely – men are not taught to care in the way that women are, they often have trouble even understanding what a woman means when she says 'you don't show that you care for me'. Women themselves are wont to get confused over this – just what is it they do want? They are so used to looking after others, responding to their unspoken needs, that they may have lost touch with what they need, and in any case, if others' needs are met 'unspoken', why can't theirs be too?

Failing to find 'fulfillment' in their marriage, a woman may look to her children to offer what is missing. As Westkott says 'Mothers turn to other women and to their children to fulfil their emotional needs, not simply because men are not there for them, as Choderow argues, but because men *are* there – too much so – demanding to be cared for' (Westkott, 1987, p. 125).

Daughters then may learn – not only that they will care for the men in their life, but that mother is herself in need of care and may expect this from her. Our mothers are 'motherless daughters' too.

It is very important for me to have mothering, which is also important for her. She didn't get it from her own mother and she tried to get it from me, and I try to get it anyway I can. It's real hard to get. I think everybody wants it. It's a scarce commodity. (Arcana, 1981, p. 6)

Feeling that one has had to mother one's own mother is an added burden for daughters – not only do they feel they have lost out on being mothered themselves, but they feel that they have had to take on the responsibility of providing that 'scarce commodity' for their own mother.

In this early nurturance of her mother the daughter learns to put others' needs before her own, as her mother has done before her. Karen Horney, an early twentieth-century psychoanalyst, nurtured her mother Sonni, without (we are told) reciprocal nurturing, just as Sonni nurtured her husband and son. Karen Horney 'identified with Sonni's unhappiness in her marriage and expressed a protective, nurturing attitude toward "poor little mutti". She felt responsible for her mother, yet powerless to help her' (Westkott, 1987, p. 131). Westkott believes that although Horney spoke of her mother as her 'beloved', she was a daughter who was restricted and controlled by her mother, a mother who showed her preference for Karen's older brother and was absorbed in an unhappy marriage, and looked to Karen to nurture her. 'Karen Horney's need to nurture others . . . developed as a consequence of her mother's needs for nurturance, not from her mother's identification with her' (p. 133). Westkott sees the mother's expectation that the daughter will nurture her and the daughter's acquiescence in that expectation as a consequence of the devaluation of the female child and her needs. A mother then feels able to 'impose' her needs upon her daughter, and the daughter, already devalued and fearing further rejection, turns her anger inwards and devalues herself and her own needs while idealising the devaluing adult and behaving as they demand. For Westkott this explains Horney's 'idealisation' of her mother, her own feelings of being unloveable, and her need to offer others the nurturing she never had (by becoming a psychotherapist).

The daughter's feeling that she has to 'mother' her own mother may start in childhood (though we perhaps don't understand or articulate it until we are older), and as with women's 'caring' generally it is a complex mix of actual help with physical work and emotional support. Many daughters recall 'helping' mother when young, going shopping with her, helping around the house, running errands, looking after a younger sibling – helping with the work of mothering. For some this feels like taking over mother's responsibilities, for others it is a sharing exercise, a chance to spend time with mother, doing things with her (albeit mostly 'her' things, only sometimes yours).

The Newsons, in their study *Seven Years Old in the Home Environment* found that mothers stressed the companionship they shared with their seven-year-old daughters. This was mainly centred around the home and involved activities like knitting, sewing, housework, drawing, story writing, shopping, an interest in clothes and in discussing people and relationships. The Newsons noted a strong element of identification of mother with daughter which they felt sometimes impeded protectiveness 'as if the mother knew the child's weaknesses too well to be wholly sympathetic', they also saw this identification, particularly in working-class families, as taking on a feeling of 'feminine conspiracy which deliberately excludes men and boys' (Newson and Newson, 1976, p. 265).

Wodak and Schultz asked a number of twelve-year-old American and Austrian girls (and some boys) to write an essay on 'My Mother and I' in order to analyse the content linguistically. They found that while the boys wrote more objectively about their mothers, 'she gets me my breakfast' type thing, the daughters take a much deeper interest in the actual relationship between them and their mothers. Many of the American daughters in this cross-cultural study regarded their mothers as 'friends'. As one said, 'we have fights. Fear raising fights. But we always make up. I think we make up because, not for the reasons that we are mother and daughter, but for the reason that we are friends – best friends. She is my best friend' (Wodak and Schultz, 1986, p. 104). Wodak and Schultz regarded such statements as 'clichéd' reflecting, they felt, the American ideology of 'happy family'. Rather than taking the girls' statements of her love for and friendship with their mothers as given, their analysis, based as it was on psychoanalytic theories which stress conflict in the mother-daughter relationship, chose to see these as 'fairy tales', a good example of how a theoretical based determines research analysis and outcome.

Another of their American daughter respondents wrote

My mother and me do a lot of things together, like we go places together, and we clean our house together . . . When we shop together my mother gets a lot of things for me. So I do a lot of things for her to thank her for what she does for me. When my mom gets mad at my little sister, I help her to be calm, and I ask her to be nice. But when she gets mad, she is usually angry at someone (her sister, her mother, or her boss), but she gets over it because I help her to try not to be mean to them. So I ask her to say sorry to whoever she is mad at. When my mom is sick I feel sad for her. She gets sick a lot, too . . . When she is sick, I help out around the house and do my chores so when she gets better she will have a clean house to look at. So now you have heard things that me and my mom do. I hope that I can be just like my mom because we do things together and that I would like to do with my kids when I grow up . . . (Wodak and Schultz, 1986, p. 170).

Wodak and Schultz were surprised to find that the mother depicted here bore little resemblance to the confident, outgoing mother, sure of her mothering skills, who turned up for the interview with them. This mother worked outside the home and expected her daughters to help around the house, she believed that this has helped her daughters to grow, becoming more self-sufficient and independent of her. The daughter, however, clearly saw herself as the nurturer of her mother (in a reciprocal relationship?) – calming her, advising her as well as doing household chores.

Need the two scenarios be conflicting? We see caring 'for' mother (both in supporting her emotionally and in the physical tasks of care) intertwined with caring 'about', that is loving her. The acts of 'looking after' mother becomes proof of the daughter's love for her. The sharing tasks with mother and helping her in her caring work is not necessarily resented by the daughter, but is seen as a way of showing care and concern for a mother whom one loves.

Written and oral histories (Lewis, 1986) give us some idea of the extent to which young daughters were expected to give practical support to their mothers in their caring tasks in both middle-class and working-class households in the late nineteenth and early twentieth century. What is clear is that daughters, and not sons, were expected to help their mothers in the practical work of caring for the family, work which was often heavy and demanding before labour-saving devices and easily available contraception.

Jamieson's (1986) study of working-class mothers and daughters in Scotland (c. 1890–1925) gives some indication of the daughters' feelings about such expectations. Her data suggests 'that the willingness with which daughters accepted responsibility or housework varied according to their assessment of their mother's needs and intentions'. Of particular interest is that some respondents 'saw mother as having no choice but to ask' and 'recognised that demands made on a daughter were typically influenced by the overall burden borne by her mother, which in turn depended on many factors – the mother's health and energy, the size of the family, and the amount of other assistance she received'. Also

> Some daughters came to do housework willingly: they felt close to their mothers, sympathised with how much they had to do and regarded them as having no choice but to demand help when they did. A number of daughters explained the amount of housework they took on in terms of their affection for the mothers. (Jamieson, 1986, p. 61–2)

This doesn't seem to have changed drastically as one of Sue Lees' interviewees testifies:

> I don't mind 'cos my mum can't do it all herself. I've got my homework to do and half the time I don't do it. You wanna do your homework and you wanna help your mum, like you're sitting down doing your homework and your mum says 'Josie, can you do a job for me? (Lees, 1986, p. 132)

Neisser (1973), in her advice-giving mother-daughter book, does not question the care-taking which is the mother's, and therefore the daughter's 'lot':

> Direct and indirect benefits can accrue from a schoolage girl helping, in moderation, with the duties of running a house as well as with the care of younger children. A source of regret to mothers is that when their daughters are small, helping is regarded as a privilege, but when the girls reach an age and attain the degree of competence when they could take over tasks, they have to be repeatedly reminded, if not coerced, to get at the dishwashing, vegetable paring, or mopping that is their lot. (Neisser, 1973, p. 98)

She suggests that involvement in these tasks is important in the girls' development, which of course in terms of becoming a carer of men and children, it is.

As well as being expected (or expecting themselves) to offer help and support to mother, a daughter may bear the brunt of her mother's feeling unloved and uncared for. The burden of being a woman in our society can lead to chronic depression and being labelled mentally ill (Chesler, 1972; Rohrbaugh 1981, Part V). A daughter may then 'lose' her mother when she enters a mental hospital, or escapes from reality via alcohol or drugs. In some circumstances the daughter may have to look after her mother as a dependant, with no expectation of caring in return.

The mother may turn her angry feelings onto her less powerful children, as this extract from a poem by Alta suggests, when the love they desire is not forthcoming from other sources, and particularly onto a daughter where she may see her own neediness reflected:

> & all those years nobody loved me
> except her & I screamed at her & spanked her
> & threw her on the bed and slammed the door when
> i was angry & desperate for her fathers love,
> & I cant undo all those times i frightened her
> & she loved me, she still loves me, i cant undo needing
> &
> being tortured with loneliness until I cried out at
> her,
> who loved me even in my needy loneliness. & how
> do mothers, unloved, love their children?
> the wonder is that we do, we
> do not leave the little girls
> we cry out in our terror & we love our little girls
> who *must* have a better life . . .
> (Alta, 1974)

It is very difficult to cut through the ideological complications of the mothering of daughters to really see what the relationship between daughters and mothers is about. As Rich puts it 'Many of us were mothered in ways we cannot yet even perceive' (1977, p. 225). And yet we are left very often feeling unmothered.

The 'loss' of the mother can be felt in many ways. Mother may have, following the child-rearing fashion of the times, put her child out to a wet nurse; fed her to a rigid schedule; or not held her often enough. She may have taught her to be a 'good girl' and in so doing restricted her movements and her spirit. She may have been too concerned with the needs of others, particularly those of father and brothers, to offer her daughter the care she needed. She may have been trapped into employment which kept her away from her daughter, or worked so hard at ensuring the physical survival of her children that she had no time to show them affection.

As with Emily Dickinson a mother may not offer her daughter the role model of an assertive independent woman which she needs and this may be felt as another 'loss'. Or paradoxically, by being that assertive, independent woman, she may not be there for her daughter either: 'my mother was a liberated woman and I wanted a less liberated woman as a mother. Frankly, I would much prefer her home baking cookies' (Arcana, 1981, p. 6). She may have been so needy herself that the daughter feels she mothered her mother, or she may have 'deserted' her daughter by 'escaping' into alcohol or drugs, chronic depression or madness. Adrienne Rich again sums it up 'Few women growing up in patriarchal society can feel mothered enough; the power of our mothers, whatever their love for us and their struggle on our behalf, is too restricted' (1977, p. 243).

4 Doing It Differently

Adrienne Rich writes:

> I saw my own mother's menstrual blood before I saw my own.
> Hers was the first female body I ever looked at, to know what
> women were, what I was to be. I remember taking baths with
> her in the hot summers of early childhood, playing with her
> in the cool water. As a young child I thought how beautiful
> she was; a print of Botticelli's Venus on the wall, half-smiling,
> hair flowing, associated itself in my mind with her. In early
> adolescence I still glanced slyly at my mother's body, vaguely
> imagining: I too shall have breasts, full hips, hair between my
> thighs – whatever that meant to me then, and with all the
> ambivalence of such a thought. And there were other
> thoughts: I too shall marry, have children – but *not like her.* I
> shall find a way of doing it all differently.
>
> (Adrienne Rich, 1977, p. 219)

The mother-daughter literature suggests that daughters look to
their mothers to see what it means to be a woman – to see what
they can expect from that adult status – and more often than
not they decide that they will 'do it differently'. This does not
necessarily mean that the daughter believes that her mother
'got it wrong', but that she sees herself as different from her
mother.

The daughter may choose to make different life choices to
those made by her mother, which might involve, for example,
pursuing or not pursuing further education; her choice of job;
not becoming a mother; choice of partner and so on. Or it may
involve making similar life choices but attempting to carry
them through differently. In this the daughter is recognising
her basic connection with her mother, her shared gender which
can mean their common fate. Daughters are also recognising
that through their mothers they are learning how to regard
themselves and other women.

In that growing from adolescent girlhood to adult womanhood a young woman's identity and self-esteem will depend on
how she views women, and what she sees as necessary elements

for her own womanhood – how to look, how to behave, what to expect from life. A mother takes part in all of this in interaction with her daughter and usually as her daughter's most accessible model of womanhood.

The daughter's comparison of her own life to that of her mother's may start to be consolidated during adolescence. The theme reemerges at different stages of the daughter's life cycle, as she makes her choices regarding how she will live her life.

ADOLESCENCE

In Western culture adolescence, that period between childhood and adulthood, is seen as the 'second individuation' (Blos, 1967). It is a time of preparation for independent adult life, a time of searching for one's own identity and struggling against adult rule. Again – and more emphatically – the emphasis is on individuality, independence and autonomous development, and again the 'norm' is determined by male concepts – male subjects researched by male theorists, with female development added on as an afterthought.

So we see that Erikson's (1965) fifth stage of development (Identity vs Role Confusion) is about 'the celebration of the autonomous, initiating, industrious self through the forging of an identity based on an ideology that can support and justify adult commitments'. The development of an individual identity precedes the intimacy found in later relationships, an intimacy built on a strong sense of who one is, so that 'oneself' is not lost in this commitment to relationships with others. Men find themselves first and then look for an intimate relationship. But, says Erikson (1971), the course is different for a girl; she holds her identity in abeyance as she prepares to attract the man who will fill her 'inner space', and thereby confer identity on her as his wife, mother of his children.

Observing the relational development of women, it has been suggested by Iris Sangiuliano that 'shaping one's identity as a separate person is not the same process for women as for men'that women are 'late bloomers' and that 'in the woman's life journey, the striving for union precedes and postpones the labors of a personal identity, and sometimes sends it underground' (Sangiuliano, 1978, p. 43). Even here, though Sangiuliano makes it clear that she does not want to squeeze women 'under the umbrella' of male developmental theories, she still considers autonomy and independence as the major developmental goals.

Until recently (with the insistence of feminist theorists on the importance of connection in development) developing and maintaining connection with others has been translated into wishing to be 'one' with others, and has been rendered as oppositional and in conflict with individual identity. In this way we have lost the understanding that personal identity does develop within the context of connective relationships with others.

The connection considered so damaging to the adolescent girl's development is in the relationship she has with her mother, for again we find that it is the daughter's lack of separation from her mother which will prevent her from becoming 'her own person':

> During adolescence, girls are bombarded by several coalescing events that create feelings of helplessness. Adolescence is the time when *she* must begin to labor to earn her feminine identity. It is the time when she begins to separate from mother, a task for which she's ill-prepared, rarely having had to exercise those muscles of autonomy. Separating – being different, or 'better than' mother – she feels, will threaten an already ambivalent relationship. It is the time, as well, when her sexuality is beginning to burgeon, and being 'better than' can threaten not only her relationship to mother – the original competitor – but also her relationship to boys. Rather than meet these paradoxes of separating, of loosening those original ties, and achieving a personal identity, conflicted, too many women choose to remain little girls.
>
> (Sangiuliano, 1978, p. 25)

Here again we see that women are ill-prepared for 'growing up', which in essence means not only leaving mother but being her competitor and the victor. It seems that *only* in asserting oneself, as different to and better than mother, can the daughter be said to have become an adult woman.

Adrienne Rich when writing of 'doing it differently' was not, I think, referring to a competitive stance *vis à vis* her mother, she was not considering being 'better' than her mother, but was referring to the sense in which her mother took on her roles and fulfilled them as prescribed by patriarchy. In this Adrienne Rich recognises the constraints of mothering in a patriarchal society and what this means to the daughter and to the relationship between mother and daughter.

While learning about competitiveness and how to compete may be considered healthy and necessary for the daughter's development (Maguire, 1987), the emphasis in the mother-daughter literature on competition stems from the concept of mother and daughter as 'natural enemies'. This 'competition' is about who can best serve men, who can be the most 'feminine' as prescribed by patriarchy. This competition, seen as starting with the oedipal (mother-father-daughter) triangle, may be seen as continuing into the daughter's marriage (who is 'best' wife/housewife) and motherhood.

Competition and Power

Much of the anger and hostility said to exist between mothers and daughters is seen as having its roots in this phase of development, at the time when the daughter is becoming a woman. Simone de Beauvoir highlights the jealousy of a mother used to experiencing all other women as rivals

> many a mother hardens into hostility; she does not accept being supplanted by the ingrate who owes her her life. The jealousy of the coquette toward the fresh adolescent girl who shows up her artifice has often been noted; she who has seen a hated rival in every woman will see the same even in her own child . . . She who took pride in being the Wife, the Mother, in exemplary and unique fashion, none the less fights dethronement fiercely. She goes on saying her daughter is only a child, she regards her undertakings as juvenile games. . . . If allowed to do so, she condemns her daughter to eternal childhood; if not, she tries to ruin the adult life the other is bold enough to claim.
>
> (Beauvoir, 1972)

Hammer, in her book *Mothers and Daughters/Daughters and Mothers* dedicates two chapters to mothers and daughters as 'Friends and Enemies' and, 'Enemies and Friends' during the daughter's adolescence. Her main themes are consistent with the issues seen as paramount in the mother-daughter relationship at this stage and offer a quick overview. These are:

- the daughter's emerging sexuality and approaching womanhood, marked by menarche;
- the subsequent stepping-up of restrictions on the mother's part and the daughter's rebelling against them;
- the daughter's growing up and the mother's growing old, which may result in the mother having competitive and resentful feelings towards the daughter;
- the daughter's need to assert herself as different from her mother, with different expectations and dreams;
- the daughter's rejection of her mother's way of life and rejection of her mother, often experienced as hatred;
- the mother having to accept her daughter's separateness;
- mother and daughter competing for roles and domestic territory;
- daughter as source of mother's power and connection to world which with daughter's increasing autonomy mother will have to give up;
- the daughter's turning away from her own mother and looking for an 'ideal' mother.

Let us look at the first of these, the daughter's emerging sexuality. This raises a number of interacting issues, including the messages the daughter receives from the mother regarding how to view her body and her sexuality, the mother's own reaction to her daughter's development, and the mother's role as socialiser.

In teaching daughters to be 'good girls' mothers are expected to prepare daughters for heterosexuality whilst making them aware that it is their responsibility to control male sexuality. It is girls who get called 'slags' if they are seen as promiscuous, not boys, reflecting the continuation of sexual double-standards (Lees, 1986).

As the body changes in adolescence the daughter's relationship with her own body becomes more evident and this will be effected by how she has been taught to regard her body and sexuality generally. Adrienne Rich tells us that 'A woman who has respect and affection for her own body, who does not view it as unclean or as a sex-object, will wordlessly transmit to her daughter that a woman's body is a good and healthy place to live' (1977, p. 245). But can this 'transmission' remain 'wordless' when the daughter is daily faced with the objectification of her sex and the denigration of female bodies at home, on the streets and in the media?

The mother-daughter literature emphasises the mother's handling of her daughter's menarche as representative of her attitude to bodies and sexuality and to her daughter becoming a woman. In this we see how mothers often 'fail' to offer their daughters a positive image of being a woman. Perhaps we should not be surprised by this when the generally held view in our society is that menstruation is a 'a curse' and something to be hidden. This stems from the notion of female sexuality as corruptive of men, and menstruation as evidence of female impurity. In many religions a menstruating woman has been considered a polluter to be kept at a distance (Kitzinger, 1978, pp. 237–341). The literature suggests that at the onset of menstruation many mothers fail to tell their daughters what to expect, or to comfort them at this time of sudden and often frightening change. In this it is felt that they set the tone for the daughter's disownment of her body, her sexuality, her womanhood. So we hear that

> In the way she talked about our bodies, there was the sense that a woman's body was not nice; a woman's body was not OK to comment on. Breasts were not OK. Menstruation was certainly not OK. My God! The worst thing you could say about someone was that she had spots of blood on her clothes. I still have that icky feeling about myself. (Arcana, 1979, p. 58)

While Arcana found that 37 per cent of her respondents said their mothers never spoke to them about their bodies at all, there were some daughters who found their mothers informative and supportive.

> It was a big thing waiting to get my first period. We went out and bought Kotex; I had a special place in the medicine cabinet for all the stuff for when the day would come. Finally when it did come I got to stay up late and drink coffee, and stay home from school and be grown up. She told me a lot. It was all very positive. (Arcana, 1979, p. 58)

The daughter's menarche may be a fraught time for the mother as well as the daughter; here is proof that her daughter is growing up and will soon be a woman herself. Alongside her fears and excitement for her daughter will be the mother's changing perspective on her own role. How to keep her daughter a 'good' girl and prove herself a 'good' mother, how to protect her daughter from being ill-used and hurt, how to deal with her own feelings of 'lost' youth and prepare herself for the 'loss' of her child preparing to become an adult.

For a mother who herself has never been at ease with her own body and her sexuality it may be easier to try and ignore these aspects in her daughter, and to lay down explicit and rigid rules of sexual behaviour rather than to deal with the complexity of feelings and issues around emerging sexuality. Hammer points out that

> Most mothers do feel responsible for their daughters, and want them to experience their sexuality in a positive way. What is viewed by the mother as protection and concern for her daughter's welfare may however be felt by the daughter as undue restriction and an attempt to stop her growing up. (Hammer, 1976, p. 97)

Hammer also points out that those mothers who do cling to their daughters' childhoods and try to prevent them from taking charge of their own lives may be reacting in this way because they have grown up in a society which tells them that once their children are grown then they have lost their role in life. A 'clinging' mother is said to incite an extreme form of adolescent rebellion.

The daughter's adolescence is presented as a time of the mother's insistence and daughter's resistance; the mother growing old in the face of her daughter's youth; the daughter's need to assert herself as different from her mother whilst taking on her womanhood. The consequence of all this is hostile competition between them. This all suggests a fight for power – power which the mother is seen as having and which the daughter needs to take from her in order to grow up.

But what is this power actually about? It is the mother's 'power' over her daughter in the setting of restrictions and controlling her behaviour; the mother's 'power' over the family in terms of her responsibility to maintain stability; and the mother's waning and the daughter's increasing 'power' through youth and sexuality, her attraction to men.

The daughter seeking some control over her own life and her own body may respond by rebelling against her mother. Take for example Margaret Atwood's heroine Joan Foster in the novel *Lady Oracle,* when Joan's mother cries at the sight of her fat daughter dressed in a 'lime green car coat'. Joan is both dismayed and elated at her power: 'my only power. I had defeated her: I wouldn't ever let her make me over in her image, thin and beautiful' (Atwood, 1982, p. 88). Both the mother and the daughter's power here is rather dubious, determined by the roles assigned to women in a patriarchal society, potentially hurting both and benefiting neither. The dismay felt by the daughter relates to her need for mother's approval and validation, the desire to be accepted by her mother for the person she is, and to have the mother acknowledge and accept her different way of being, to be proud of her daughter and even impressed.

In a different kind of society where mothers can 'hand-on' their skills and knowledge to their daughters (as Smith-Rosenberg, 1975, has suggested has been the experience in Western history, and as may currently be experienced in other cultures); or where youth and beauty is not worshipped over age and experience; or where a woman is not considered useless once she has raised her children, there would be no need for a power struggle between mother and daughter, and no reason to feel that the daughter is specifically taking her mother's place in the world, other than in the sense in which generations do succeed generations. The daughter might also be free to move into adulthood maintaining the connections which offer her comfort, support and a positive reflection of herself.

The daughter's rejection of the mother is very often a rejection of the conforming female role. Seventeen-year-old Marian, a daughter in Terri Apter's (1990) study of mothers and adolescent daughters, hated her mother 'like poison' for being unable to understand her commitment to academic study. This daughter believed that her mother saw the 'nitty-gritty of a woman's life' as being 'family and home and all that' and believed her mother was unable to see that these issues 'just doesn't come into the picture' for her daughter. Apter comments

In the bloom of adolescence she wore her blue-stocking personality proudly, taking a stand as someone her mother would never understand. Therefore her interests were self-discovered, self-made. Their value was self-constructed, and was all hers. She was seeped in her individuality, and wanted to offer it to her mother, the gift of a valuable self. To show her appreciation the mother was expected to be bowled over by this new personality. The 'poison' was the mother who wanted her daughter to be something else. Or, more accurately, the poison was the mother who would not have minded if Marian had become something else. Proud of her new found interests and skills, to which she determinedly linked her identity, she could not accept that her mother did not value the particular direction she was taking above all others.

'I'm proud of her. So what does she want of me?' Marian's mother inquired without expectation of an answer.

(Apter, 1990, p. 64)

This scenario seems reminiscent of Emily Dickinson's denial of her mother who we assume was unable to offer her daughter the role model and possibly the support she needed to be a writer.

The daughter may see the mother only as a wife and mother and see her oppression and her seeming acquiescence in this: she may resolve to be different, stronger, not to be 'merely' a link in the motherhood chain.

But in surpassing the mother the daughter also needs somehow to stay connected. There is danger in surpassing the mother. The danger of the unknown (the mother cannot show the daughter how to be), and the danger of hurting the mother. These two fears can join together to impose an incredible burden on the daughter which she may 'resolve' by attempting to stunt her own development.

Kim Chernin writes of how she developed an eating disorder as she was about to enter college – an unfulfilled ambition of her mother. This she saw as a reaction to the dangers of 'surpassing' her mother, and in so doing betraying and abandoning their shared identity; and to entering a world that her mother could not fully enter with her and where therefore she could not offer her the support she needed. Kim Chernin's mother was a strong, independent woman who spent her life in an 'intensely meaningful struggle on behalf of the working class' (see Chernin, 1983 for her mother's story, and a wonderful account of three generations of women in this family). Yet Kim was going to be a different sort of woman, an intellectual, a poet and a writer, leaving behind (for a time) her mother's political concerns. But she was not only 'different' but was moving into an area of particular poignancy for her mother, for at the age Kim was to enter college her mother had 'dropped out of Hunter College and always, since then, had felt intellectually inadequate and extremely ambivalent about her capacity to absorb and understand culture, which she loved' (Chernin, 1986, p. 50).

Others have made the link between eating disorders and the mother-daughter relationship. Our earliest experiences of need fulfilment are via mother and food; feeding her child and making sure she grows is mother's primary responsibility, refusing food may be the daughter's first act of assertion and her first feeling of power. We are told to eat up and be big and strong, whilst with 'growing up' comes the message of losing mother's nurturance. Simone de Beauvoir eloquently sums it up:

> Eating was not only an exploration and an act of conquest – an acquired taste in the real sense of the phrase – but also my most solemn duty: 'A spoonful for Mama, and another for grandmama . . . If you don't eat anything, you won't grow up into a big girl.' I would be stood up against the door-frame in the hall and a pencilled line would be drawn level with the top of my head; the new line would then be compared with an earlier one: I had grown two or three centimetres: they would congratulate me, and I would swell with pride. But sometimes I felt frightened. The sunlight would be playing on the polished floor and the white-enamelled furniture. I would look at Mama's armchair and think: 'I won't be able to sit on her knee any more if I go on growing up.' Suddenly the future existed; it would turn me into another being, some-one who would still be, and yet no longer seem, myself. I had forebodings of all the separations, the refusals, the deser-tions to come, and of the long succession of my various

deaths. 'A spoonful for grandpa . . . ' I went on eating, all the same, and I was proud that I was growing; I had no wish to remain a baby all my life. (Beauvoir, 1963, p. 7)

Considering that eating disorders largely affect females (90 to 95 per cent of all eating disorders occur among women) and have their onset in adolescence (often resulting in disturbed menstruation and physical development) it would be surprising if the link with a struggle for identity and hence with the mother-daughter relationship were not made. Sheila MacLeod, who herself suffered from anorexia, says

> Anorexia nervosa may grow within the family context and be fed (overfed) by it, but to the anorexic, the most important member of that family is the mother. It is through her relationship – or lack of one – with her mother that her problems of identity and autonomy, as well as those relating to her own body, have arisen. In other words, anorexia nervosa is symptomatic of a (perhaps very early) failure of a one-to-one relationship. (MacLeod, 1981, p. 133)

While Marilyn Lawrence (1984) agrees that the daughter's relationship with her mother is a central concern for daughters with anorexia she does not see this as causal but as a *result* of the daughter's regression back to a state of almost infantile dependency on her mother. Lawrence notes that many of the daughter she has seen in treatment for anorexia have extremely close relationships with their mothers which they wish to be exclusive and in which they make tremendous demands on their mothers' time and energies, whilst feeling that they never have enough of mother. For their part mothers are often too frightened for the daughters' health to thwart them in their excessive needs: they often feel powerless, guilty and failures.

Other theorists have seen anorexia as a rejection of the mother (Crisp, 1967), and of the passive female role (Palozzoli, 1974); as an attempt by the daughter to gain control over her own body and assert independence (Bruch, 1978); and as a result of maternal deprivation both in the earliest mother-infant relationship and subsequently (Ehrensing and Weitzman, 1970).

Friedrich (1988) believes that women with eating disorders are 'acting out, via food, the dynamics of the dependent character solution' which Karen Horney proposed as the result of the devaluation and sexualisation of females in our society (see Chapter One). As a result of sexualisation the woman with an eating disorder has learned to see her body as her only source of power: she therefore uses it in the battle between appearing compliant (or ultra-compliant with the slender body ideal) and acting out her feelings of hostility. For Friedrich both compliance and hostility are in relation to the mother who has failed to nurture her daughter and the mother whose approval she is seeking, who she is 'merging' with for fear of abandonment. It is the mother who, through her own experiences of devaluation and sexualisation, leaves 'a legacy of self-contempt' for the daughter, whilst also looking to the daughter for both nurturance and perfection as a defence against her own feelings of worthlessness. Leaving mum means 'being nothing'.

Friedrich's analysis, like the feminist psychotherapists she quotes (for example, Eichenbaum and Orbach, 1983) not only takes account of the mother-daughter relationship in the aetiology of eating disorders, but puts this relationship centre stage and makes peripheral the very issues on which the analysis is based – that is, the devaluation and sexualisation of women in our society by men.

Father again becomes peripheral, even positive to some extent, and his sexualisation of his daughter is stated but somehow reduced in effect, for example when Friedrich says

> In the lives of many bulimics, the father has had a more active role. His added involvement leaves the daughter less vulnerable to merger with mother. In many cases, though, the father also exposes her to more experiences of sexualisation, thus devaluing her while increasing her reliance on the body as her expression of the false self. (Friedrich, 1988, p. 63)

Chernin is, I think, making a different point. She sees eating disorders in daughters as 'trying to tell us that their mothers' lives have impressed them through their suffering and devastation' (Chernin, 1986, p. 63). The daughter feels responsible for this in some way (since mothers are often seen to have lost some of their former independence and joy for life on the birth of their daughters) and so she seeks to make reparation to her mother, or at any rate feels tremendous guilt if she should be seeming to surpass her mother.

Seeing the difficulties that mother faces as an adult woman may also lead to the daughter's desire to remain a child. Marilyn Lawrence tells of a fourteen-year-old girl suffering from anorexia who stated a strong desire not to be like her single-parent, successful career-woman mother. Her reasons for this were that 'she works so hard. She has so much responsibility. I couldn't stand that. She's always tired and she's always guilty about *everything*' (Lawrence, 1984, p. 55). Perhaps if the daughter did not perceive that she would be alone in her adult responsibilities she would not need to try and remain a child by such dangerous means as starvation.

Connection and Identity

Karen Elias-Button believes that the daughter experiencnes difficulties in establishing an identity in adolescence in part because 'the mother's body comes to represent to her two mutually exclusive things: the childhood she must move away from, as well as the adulthood she must journey towards and eventually accept' (Elias-Button, 1980, p. 198). The confusion that results for the daughter may be experienced as a confrontation with her mother which feels potentially destructive to one or the other of them – either the mother must be 'killed', that is rejected, or the daughter herself will, as in the Medusa myth, 'be turned to stone', that is fail to develop. (But we see in the next chapter how women have a more complex relationship with the Medusa myth, which can be a source of creative energy for daughters.)

Caplan (1981, p. 100) sees the daughter as seeking 'the warmth her mother represents' but then being 'repelled by it, because it can seduce her back to the role of child or infant, inhibiting her emotional growth, and because it ultimately may arouse homosexual feelings'. Here we see the daughter having to give up her connection with her mother, and the nurturance which goes with it in order to fulfil society's definition of adult woman – that is someone who gives nurturance rather than receives it, and who is heterosexual. It is the preparation for adult womanhood, which was explored in Chapter Three, of a woman who cares for men but who can expect little care in return. Caplan goes on to say that

> The intensity with which the daughter may be attracted by her mother as an image of warmth and security depends to some extent on whether the mother was able to offer adequate nurturance during the daughter's infancy and early childhood. If she was, then the attractiveness of such security is not intensified by the fantasies the inadequately nurtured daughter feels – that perhaps someday her mother will be loving enough to make her feel finally secure and strong. An adequately nurtured daughter will have developed enough strength based on that early experience that she can look forward to further growth and development. (Caplan, 1981, pp. 100–1)

A distinction is being made here between those daughters who have been adequately nurtured as infants and those who have not. This needs emphasising since there is the danger of believing, as we have already seen, that *no* daughter is adequately nurtured as an infant and therefore all women suffer a developmental delay because of this.

We should also be cautious about assuming that adequately nurtured daughters can then go on without further (although qualitatively different) nurturing in adult life, the implication being that having had sufficient nurturance in childhood one can do without it in adult life. This is surely a mistaken belief, based on the idea that all important development is completed in childhood and that adulthood is only about individuality and being an independent person. It ignores the fact that we all continue to develop and we all continue to need some sort of nurturance from others. For men these needs are not declared but are on the whole met by women, thus supporting men's mistaken belief in their own 'ego strength', whilst women are classed as 'weak' if they declare these needs and often find it difficult to find someone who will nurture them.

Daughters, then, are expected to give up their mothers' nurturance in order to become adult women and look after others. The danger of seeking mother's 'warmth' is not of seduction back to childhood but of the rejection felt when the societal message is clear – as a woman you cannot have both care for yourself and adult status. Homophobia adds strength to this injunction to sever the connection with mother and take your place as an adult woman in a man's world. As Caplan points out, 'fear of homosexuality usually makes admiration and attraction for one's mother seem unacceptable' (Caplan, 1981, p. 102).

If we look briefly at studies of female adolescent development we can see the importance of maintaining connection for adolescent girls. Adolescent studies have tended to focus on peer group relationships as being most important, forming the stepping-stone from a family of origin to the setting up of a own family. Male peer groups have long been seen as important in the study of male adolescent development. Where girls have been studied, it has tended to be also from the focus of peer group relationships, but more emphasis has been given to a change of friends from girlfriends to boyfriends (Griffiths, 1987). It is suggested that only in moving out of what is seen as an immature relationship with female friends can the adolescent girl move on to more 'mature' relationships with boys in that search for the man who will offer her fulfilment of her identity through marriage.

In viewing the development of female identity in this way, we are denying and devaluing the importance of female relationships in this process. That Western adolescent girls are under cultural and ideological pressure to get a boyfriend is indisputable: it is after all viewed as proof of her 'normal heterosexuality' and 'grown-up femininity' (Griffin 1985, p. 59). What has been ignored, however, is the desire adolescent girls have to stay in intimate relationships with their girlfriends and the strategies they adopt to do this (Griffin, 1985; Griffiths, 1987). As Berzoff (1989a, p. 54) points out, 'peer relationships, especially female friendships, are valuable sources of self-knowledge and identity development of girls'.

While adolescent girls may tend to spend more time with their friends rather than their families, they may still maintain intimate relationships with their mothers. In keeping with the idea of connection, adolescent girls and their mothers may have supportive, confiding relationships, rather than hostile, angry ones (or more likely relationships which encompass all these aspects).

These quotes come from a study of working-class black and white pregnant teenage girls (Phoenix, 1988):

Any problems or that I could tell her if I feel like I wanted to tell her . . . Most of the time I did tell her . . . We're like sisters really . . . I wouldn't change her for anything in the world. She's a very good mother.

(Geraldine, a black nineteen-year-old living at home)

Me and my mum were always best friends . . . I never used to go to my dad with my troubles, I always used to go to my mum.

(Jan, a white seventeen-year-old living with her husband)

The fact that these girls were pregnant may have some significance here. It is difficult to be certain since, other than Apter's work, those studies of adolescent girls which give any attention to the adolescent girl's relationship with her mother tend to be those where the daughter is pregnant (Phoenix, 1988; Skinner, 1986) or has become a teenage mother (Sharpe, 1987). This in itself adds to the myth that unless the adolescent girl has been 'reconciled' with her mother through pregnancy and becoming a mother, her relationship with her mother is largely negative in her current stage of development. Pregnancy and becoming a mother may itself be the daughter's best adaptive attempt to remain in a connected relationship with her mother when separation is being culturally demanded.

There is, of course, a sense in which the adolescent girl and the young adult woman does strive to be different from her mother, which is about the healthy development of her own way of being. As Terri Apter (1990) found, this does not necessarily put the daughter in hostile competition with her mother. Neither need this development of one's own identity mean giving up connection to the mother – although it will mean renegotiating the relationship. Through interviewing sixty-five mother-adolescent daughter pairs living in Britain and North America, Apter found that

adolescent daughters continued to care deeply about their parents, and in particular retained a strong attachment to their mother which they very much wanted to preserve. The more I studied the relationship between mothers and daughters during adolescence, the more intricate and potentially positive it seemed to me. Daughters worked deliberately upon their mothers to get recognition and acknowledgement of the newly forming adult self. (Apter, 1990, p. 19)

The adolescent girl is striving to get her mother to respond to her differently whilst staying connected. The mother's role is one of being sensitive to the daughter's own self-image. Apter sees this as a more sophisticated form of the 'mirroring' of infancy as discussed in Chapter One. This mirroring may continue to present some difficulties for mothers in a society that itself fails to adequately mirror, and in fact distorts, women's experiences.

Apter's findings are in line with the work of Berzoff (1989). It is clear from these studies that the use of the concept 'separation' does not meet our need in understanding this process, Berzoff offers 'differentiation through attachments' as a more accurate description. The renegotiation which takes place between mother and daughter may be gradual or traumatic. It may involve a physical separation between mother and daughter, and/or a change in status of the daughter – say if she herself becomes a mother, or a wife.

The need for a physical separation between adolescent daughter and mother is stressed in the science fiction novel *Motherlines* by Suzy McKee Charnas. Here the community of 'Riding Women' arrange matters so that their daughters do not grow up in exclusive relationships with their bloodmothers, but are cared for by a number of 'sharemothers' until they take their place in the 'childpack'. On menstruation they are ejected from the 'childpack' back to the society of the women, and the tent of their 'sharemothers', including the bloodmother:

> The bloodmother looked at her child and saw her own image made young, her replacement in the world, Nenisi said. The child saw in her bloodmother the pattern of her own being. Women said it was best not to let this powerful connection unbalance all other relationships that guided their two lives, and so it was appropriate that the bloodmother and child be separated for a time.
>
> (Charnas, 1989)

Here the separation occurs within a community which does not encourage exclusive relationships but offers a kinship network which offers both mother and daughter other supportive relationships, and a sense of connection to and pride in their bloodline. The mother and daughter are fully expected to come together again as two women. Our own society, with its insistence on an exclusive relationship between a man and a woman, emphasises the negative aspects of the mother-daughter connection and encourages a separation that is difficult to heal.

Retaining connection does not mean that the relationship between the mother and daughter will not change. Of course it must as the daughter becomes adult, and they no longer face each other as adult and child but as two adults. Less obvious in our thinking about this stage of the daughter's development is the changes the mother also undergoes. Apter tells us that the daughters of her study expected their mothers to change in order to respond to them differently, and that mothers did in fact change themselves:

> Just as she has learned to empathise with her from childhood, just as she has felt her life to be extended by her child's vision, so the mother empathises with her adolescent's growth . . . Just as her daughter feels the pressure of choice and decision upon her, so the mother too may realise that she still has choices to make. (Apter, 1990, p. 157)

The daughter's critique of life may be infectious and the mother herself may begin to look at her life differently at a time when her energies are released from the care of a highly dependent child.

ADULT CHOICES

The renegotiation of the mother-daughter relationship is all important and necessary if both daughter and mother are to feel free to pursue their own lives whilst still maintaining connection with each other. In our society this seems to prove very difficult. Very often mothers have expectations for their daughters which the daughters have no wish to fulfil (or even if they do they need to do it their own way).

These expectations are usually about fulfilling the social role of women and becoming a 'good' wife and mother. This way, or so the mother has herself been taught, and is socially constrained to teach her daughter, lies happiness (or at least some degree of protection). The mother's responsibility is to be a 'good' mother, often with the added hope that her daughter will make a 'better' marriage than she did. In this way the mother may look to the daughter to fulfil some of her hopes and desires.

Elizabeth Wilson clearly remembers the occasion as a child when she thought that she was not going to be like her mother when she grew up. This was the time, she believes, that the unconscious conviction was formed never to be a mother. As a young adult she wrote to her mother to explain why she would never marry, her mother 'predictably . . . was horrified', Wilson tells us:

> she was bound to be horrified, for, like many women whose marriages have proved unhappy, and whose children have been ungrateful or unforgiving, she could imagine no other destiny for me than to repeat the song, but in a major, not a minor key, she was to live the story again through me, only this version was to be the one with the happy ending. As she used to say with satisfaction of a film or novel: 'it all came right in the end.' (Wilson, 1989, p. 12)

If these expectations are not fulfilled, the mother may feel she has failed. Certainly if her daughter 'turns out' promiscuous; homosexual; unmarried (read unmarriagable); or voluntarily childless (read unnatural), society in some way does hold her responsible. Again we may also be seeing the mother's wish to protect her daughter from the harsh realities of life as a 'deviant'.

The anger the daughter may feel at societal expectations and restrictions is directed against the one seen to have had these expectations and to have made these restrictions – that is more often than not, her mother. This anger has no easy outlet since 'proper' femininity does not allow for angry feelings, and so it may fester instead of being brought out and discussed, and possibly dealt with. The daughter may then reject her mother as confidant and model and look elsewhere for a 'mother' for whom she does not have these angry feelings. Adolescent girls may consider their friends' mothers as 'better', more approachable than their own.

But the mother is not so easily rejected and replaced as role model. There is a part of any daughter that she feels came from her mother. After all for the most part the mother has raised the daughter and taught her, loves her or does not: it is very difficult for the daughter not to look to her mother to see who she is and who she will become. A daughter who has not experienced a positive and nurturing relationship with her mother may wonder if she herself will be able to offer such a relationship to others.

> The barren landscape of my mother – it's so stagnant, infertile, nothing grows there. It's all gray and brown – actually those are colors I like – but it's not a nurturing environment. How I wish it were different. I want my mother to be a model for me. How can I be okay if she isn't? (Robbins, 1985, p. 43)

The daughter may decide that she can be OK by modelling herself on an ideal image of motherhood, giving what she always desired from her mother to others, as Westkott tells us Karen Horney did. Even so she will continue to doubt her abilities to nurture since such ideal relationships are unattainable and she is actually asking the impossible of herself. The daughter may on the other hand decide that she cannot possibly offer what she has not herself experienced and may decide not even to try.

It is unlikely that any mother will ever offer a clear-cut and acceptable role model to her daughter, for even in wishing to be like mother the daughter will also be aware of her need to be different from her. The daughter may indeed wish to be the very opposite of her mother, who she may view as a negative role model (Arcana, 1979, p. 10).

The difficulty for the daughter's identity has been seen to lie in her inability to separate herself from her mother, to be reliant upon how she perceives her mother for how she perceives herself, especially in these roles into which she follows her mother. But the answer is not to sever that connection and to deny the mother within us, but to recognise it in all its positive as well as its negative aspects. Dorothy West tells us that after the death of her mother, Rachel West, her family would criticise any who chanced to sound like mother and the speaker would be 'stung with shame and close to tears', until one day

> someone said with wonder, 'Have you noticed that those of us who sound just like her are the ones who laugh a lot, love children a lot, don't have any hangups about race or color, and never give up without trying?'

Dorothy West goes on: 'I suppose that was the day and the hour of our acknowledgement that some part of her was forever imbedded in our psyches, and we were not the worst for it' (West, 1982).

I do not, unlike Anne Sexton, believe 'A woman *is* her mother. That's the main thing' (Sexton, 1961, p. 48), rather I have much more sympathy with the varied possibilities offered by Joanna Russ

> I'm an I
> Sometimes I'm a she.
> Sometimes I'm even a he.
> Sometimes I'm vervvery I.
> Sometimes I'm my mother.

> (Russ, 1975)

Surpassing Mother

Surpassing mothers is very difficult for daughters who are aware of their mothers' disappointments and compromises in life and who wish to protect them rather than add to their pain. Mothers may well feel rejected when they see their daughters moving off into lives they can barely understand, let alone enter. 'We are a generation who, with every act of self-assertion as women, with every movement into self-development and fulfilment, call into question the values by which our mothers have tried to live' (Chernin, 1986, p. 42).

It may not be that mothers feel their daughters are rejecting 'their values' but that they feel a keen loss of the daughter whose main concerns are not now ones that the mother can share and discuss as an equal. No wonder then that mothers

feel more comfortable when their daughters themselves become mothers (after all they have been there) or choose the
same employment as them. They may then feel they have
something to offer as well as to share with their daughters.
Daughters who choose something different may experience
their mothers' uncertainty about this as their rejection of an
alternative way of life.

But not all mothers hold back their daughters from a different
way of life. Many encourage them to have something they have
not had, often against male opposition, as in the short story by
Helen Reimensnyder Martin (1923), 'Mrs Gladfelter's Revolt'.
Much against the wishes of her husband who says 'I don't favor
females bein' book-learnt! It's agin nature!', Mrs Gladfelter
arranges for her daughter's continued education, away from
their own community and without her father's knowledge. In
doing so she supports her daughter in her dearest wish and

> transfers to her daughter those elements of her own self that
> she most treasures. What she hadn't the opportunity to cher-
> ish or the foresight to protect in herself, she finds the cour-
> age to defend in and for her loved daughter. (Koppelman,
> 1985, p. xxi)

This is not to say that such mothers do not also feel the pain
of loss as their daughters move out into worlds they don't
inhabit. Valerie Walkerdine and Helen Lucey write of their own
ex-perience as working-class girls moving into the middle-class
world of academia

> And what of our mothers? When we didn't want to return
> home and get married, some of our mothers felt pain and
> envy: hurt that we wouldn't go back and give them children
> and envy that we didn't have to, that we had 'our freedom'.
> Some of us felt that our mothers were stifling us with de-
> mands we no longer wanted to meet. Other mothers were
> excited about our independence, encouraged and pushed
> us, warned us of getting 'tied down and having kids'. And yet
> they were at the same time confused and dismayed that we
> had changed so much, had so many ideas they didn't under-
> stand, and were frightened when they caught glimpses of the
> terrible alienation we felt, both at home and at work. A wall
> of misunderstanding grows up, fed by fear and ignorance

of 'what you actually do', of intellectual work and brainy
people. (Walkerdine and Lucey, 1989, p. 15)

While mothers may feel a sense of pride mixed with 'loss'
when daughters are upwardly mobile, for those whose daughters choose lifestyles which are neither understood nor re-
spected the mother may feel more a sense of abandonment and
failure.

The daughter may, for example, move away from her family's religion and culture by marrying 'out'. Mothers, who bear
the brunt of the outcome of their child's socialisation, may be
considered to blame for this, usually by the men in the family.
It is interesting to note that it is often fathers or brothers who
cut off the daughter from contact with the family and mothers
who try to maintain this contact (often without the father's
knowledge) or would do so if they themselves were not threat-
ened by the men in the family (Shaaban, 1988).

Lesbianism

Other choices may be made by the daughter which are even
more difficult for the mother to understand, being quite alien
to the mother's life experiences. The daughter's becoming a
lesbian may be one such.

Of the varied 'explanations' for homosexuality the most
acceptable one to the majority of the mothers in *Different
Daughters: A Book by Mothers of Lesbians* (Rafkin, 1987) is bio-
logical determinism which considers homosexuality as an inborn
trait, not a learned or acquired one. This is understandable
when one considers that socialisation is held to be mothers'
responsibility, and in our homophobic society, homosexuality
is not considered a positive choice.

For the most part a lesbian daughter is choosing a way of life
which is very different from that of her mother, and one that
the mother is unlikely to have envisaged for her daughter. The
majority of the mothers who appear in *Different Daughters* have
grown to accept their daughters' chosen way of life, although
some do separate out their love for their daughter and the life
she leads, and some would still change it if they could as with
Jane Ferguson:

I suspect that few parents, when presented with pink bundles by cooing nurses, have foreseen lesbianism as their daughters' sexual choice. I certainly was no exception, and while I think I can honestly say that I have accepted that choice on the part of both my daughters, I have to admit that I would wave a magic wand if I could and provide them with Prince Charmings, rose-covered cottages, and nuclear families, even in the face of all the statistics about divorce, wife-beating, and child abuse. This is where I came from, and what I have, perhaps ignorantly, imagined that I had in my own life. However, there is no magic wand, and my choice has been very clear: accept, learn, love. (Rafkin, 1987, p. 74)

Jane Allen, who has seen her daughters' choice as largely positive, sums up the negative side:

fear for their well-being and safety, concern about not having grandchildren, having to deal with other peoples' disapproval of them for the first time in my life, facing hurt and anger from their dad, and wondering at times if I had done something wrong in my parenting of them. (ibid, p. 52)

The mother's fear is not fear *of* her daughter but fear *for* her. Poet Jackie Lapidus's mother writes to her 'I am not afraid of her and you. I am simply afraid *for* you because I know the world better than either of you – or so it seems to me, with more than twice your years behind me' (Payne, 1983, p. 330).

Psychoanalytic theorists largely see homosexuality as a form of retarded emotional development in which the primary love object, the mother, has not been relinquished. This can be because the daughter had insufficient love from the mother in childhood, or because she was not 'allowed' to leave the symbiotic relationship with her mother, or enabled to do so by father. It is not surprising then that those mothers in *Different Daughters* who looked for advice and understanding from psychiatrists about their daughters' homosexuality, had their feelings of guilt confirmed. Darlene was told that 'you and your husband have done something in the family home that has made her this way' (Rafkin, 1987, p. 99); Jane was warned that she was raising independent daughters 'that no man would want to live with' (ibid, p. 56), and Constance read that 'lesbians are endlessly searching for the love their mothers denied them in infancy' (ibid, p. 143). In terms of expectations the mother's concern about her daughter not having children was a general one (although more lesbian women are now choosing to become mothers).

For one mother, Ann Landau, 'the hardest thing to accept was that she probably wouldn't have children', this daughter had been born as her family were learning of the mass extermination of the Jews by the Nazis. Their whole family, outside the few in the United States, had been slaughtered. 'The thought that my beautiful, intelligent daughter would not continue our family was difficult.' The 'loss' was also a very personal one:

> I love being a mother. Of all the things in my life – and it's been interesting and exciting in many ways – my relationship with my children has been perhaps the most rewarding. Even as a child, my lesbian daughter had always been 'parental' and I'd assumed she would become a mother. I know she would have been a wonderful one. (Rafkin, 1987, p. 70)

Despite their concerns and feelings of loss, many of the mothers in this book came, through continuing relationships with their daughters and increasing their own understanding, to accept, support and even enjoy their daughters' choice of different lives to their own.

Marriage

Choosing a more socially acceptable life style – getting married and having children – does not mean that the mother and daughter relationship does not alter, or that the mother does not experience a sense of loss. This loss may be made more profound by distance or different life styles but may also be felt even if the daughter remains physically close to her mother after marriage. Changes in the relationship between mother and daughter are likely to be a gradual occurance, although it is more often the daughter's marriage, as the acceptable route to leaving home in our society, which heralds these changes.

Although a girl may physically leave home without going into marriage, it is often not until she is married that her parents consider her no longer their responsibility. The idea that the father gives his daughter over to the safe-keeping of her husband is still prevalent. Even after having been married, a divorced woman may find herself the subject of her parents' concerns until she is being 'looked after' again by her next husband. Susan, a thirty-one year-old woman, has been divorced several years. Her parents (especially her father) see her as 'more helpless' than when she was married: 'It's like I'm going to have troubles if they don't watch out for me . . . I think they'll just keep on going until . . . someone takes care of me [I get married]' (Greene and Boxer, 1986).

The expected effect of getting married is that the daughter will 'finally' separate from her mother and transfer her feelings of connection to her husband. This is based on the assumption that the task of young adulthood is to separate from the family of origin, to become independent and establish one's own family, and that within this women find their identity through marriage (Erikson, 1956). It suggests an abrupt severing of familial ties which Greene and Boxer point out is based on

> a rather odd assumption about the nature of intergenerational attachments, that is attachments between parents and their young adult children are assumed to have an implicitly dichotomised quality. Successful transition to adulthood and separation from parents is presumed to entail disruption of, if not an end to, attachments between generations (Bettleheim 1965; Mead 1970). Conversely, the maintenance of strong and cohesive parental attachments is thought to be suggestive of an inadequate or unsuccessful transition to adult status. (Greene and Boxer, 1986, p. 130)

In analysing relevant research in this area, Greene and Boxer however, suggest that the child's young adulthood is characterised by a reciprocal renegotiation between parents and child of the interdependencies that bond and bind them. They recognise that 'the task of young adulthood is not the achievement of familial autonomy, but rather familial interdependence – a state of differentiation rather than separation, in which the maintenance of parental bonds and independent functioning are dual achievements'. That women have more often maintained involved relationships with their mothers has in the past been seen as a weakness and lack of development; perhaps we can now begin to reinterpret this in the light of a less dichotomised view of development.

The renegotiation that takes place between mother and daughter on the daughter's marriage is highlighted in this quote from Molly, a twenty-four year old newly-wed. It seems to suggest that the mother sees marriage as 'the' status passage to adulthood – at least for her daughter:

> My mother really treats me differently now . . . before she would want to know what I was doing, who I was with . . . you know . . . personal stuff. Now she starts to do it and stops and says, 'oh . . . you're a married woman, I can't say that anymore. You have your own life now'. Wasn't it my life before? (Greene and Boxer, 1986, p. 141)

It also makes one think of the mother's readjustment to no longer feeling responsible for her daughter – a responsibility that mothers give up more willingly and with greater relief than the 'empty-nest' theorists would have us believe (Glenn, 1975).

The idea that women 'find themselves' in marriage and have to transfer their affections from mother to husband in order to do so still has an effect, however. A daughter may feel disloyal towards her husband at her wish to spend time and share things with her mother, especially if her husband accuses her of being 'like a two year old baby . . . always running home to mother' and admonishes her to 'cut off from her mother' as does husband Gerald in Tess Slesinger's (1935) short story 'Mother to Dinner'. Koppleman tells us that this story is about 'how daughters love, honor, fear, hide from, and long for their mothers – and how the mother-daughter knot is invisible to men' (Koppleman, 1985, p. 142).

For me the story is rather about the wilful breaking of that knot by men, both through the husband's anger at the daughter's connection to her mother, and through the daughter's socialisation into the belief that he is right to be angry and that she has no right as an adult to the warmth and care she receives from her mother. Feeling loneliness surround her 'like a high black fence', Katherine felt she should not contact her mother and that she dare not contact her husband (who would see such an interruption in his working day as 'an imbecilic waste of time'). The effect of such a marriage can be isolation from the 'private language and priorities of the women's culture she has lived in until marriage' (Koppleman, 1985, p. xx).

But marriage does not always have this effect. Young and Willmott in their study of East London working-class families in 1958 found that married daughters tended to live close to their mothers and to maintain a high frequency of contact. While strong mother-adult daughter links have been viewed as rather an oddity in Western life, it is likely that such connections have merely been ignored by researchers biased in their view of adult development and ignorant of women's lives and experiences.

It may instead be easier for working-class women to maintain and admit to such links than it is for their more educated and more mobile middle-class sisters. The economic basis which segregates the classes cannot be ignored, since although middle-class women may have the educational opportunities to have independent incomes, they may also be more dependent economically on their husbands and have 'more to lose' than working-class women who sometimes have more control of their families (albeit scarce) resources. Middle-class women may also have been educated into believing that they should not maintain close relationships with their mothers following marriage.

That marriage can often be a disappointment to a woman looking for a close, confiding and nurturing relationship with her husband, has, in the therapeutic literature on marriage, been blamed on the woman's loss of nurturance as a child and her (unrealistic) desire to have those needs met. The couple mentality of Western society and the romantic notion that all needs should be met within the couple relationship, cuts off women's sources of care for herself other than from her husband, who as a man is often ill-equipped to meet those needs. But rather than accept women's needs as valid, the therapeutic literature has blamed women themselves for having these needs (for not being adult enough) and of course blamed their mothers for not having given their daughters enough nurturance as a child so that they would have no need of it as an adult. When a woman finds herself trapped in a marriage with a partner who not only fails to offer nurturance but also belittles and derides her, and when (accepting society's devaluation of women) she keeps her rage in and develops phobias, she is considered a 'dependant personality' in need of a great deal of therapeutic intervention to overcome their 'phobic reactions' to the 'ordinary stresses' of marriage (Symonds, 1973; Fodor, 1974).

Hammer considers that women who 'lose themselves' in a relationship with a man are reenacting their lack of separation with their mother.

> And because she has not separated from her mother, she becomes dependant on the man, needing from him all the reassurance of her own worth that she needed from her mother, and perhaps never got. Or, she may express toward men on hostility she really feels toward her mother. (Hammer, 1976, p. 132)

Again we see that nothing negative in the male-female relationship is attributable to men: women are seen to create their own dependency on men and any hostility is misdirected. If a relationship with a man embodies a battle for possession of oneself, this is, according to Hammer 'really a continuation of a daughter's battle with her mother.' But I think these two issues are quite different. The retaliation of a man faced with an assertive woman can be quite different from the feelings between a mother and daughter when the daughter asserts herself as a separate woman. The possibilities of renegotiation of the relationships are different, as is the effect of the outcome on the woman herself. A woman is unlikely to be economically dependant on her mother or, in adulthood, under threat of violence from her.

Hammer points out that today fewer women feel the need to suppress the effects of marital conflict (as in becoming phobic). They may rather divorce, or change the structure of their marriages, as they develop a sense of themselves as persons (although the difficulties inherent in both these options are not explored), they may even flee heterosexuality altogether. For Hammer this latter option is an extreme and negative step. She does not consider homosexuality as a positive choice for women, a more healthy resolution being a strong sense of selfhood while remaining sympathetic towards and interested in husbands' or (male) lovers' activities. However, she does say that

The strongest sense of selfhood and of mutual respect that I observed in the mother-daughter relationships I explored appeared most often in situations in which the mothers either had established themselves outside of a marriage, generally by getting divorced and deciding not to remarry, or had managed to structure a marriage that freed them from traditional role expectations. (Hammer, 1976, p. 137)

There is a danger in ignoring the strength and resources needed to do these things in our society, and in again blaming the mother if she does not offer us this model of independent womanhood. Adrienne Rich says 'As daughters we need mothers who want their own freedom and ours' (Rich, 1977, p. 247). But let us not once again set the mother up only to knock her down by insisting on a way of being that for many (most) is difficult to achieve.

The overvaluing of autonomy and independence, 'going it alone' as a sign of adult status rather than the acceptance of our connection to others, has led to psychological theories which favour separation over connection and indeed insist on the young adult's separation from their family, and especially the daughter's separation from her mother, as a sign of the daughter's growth and healthy development. The mother is expected to hold the child close and then let her go whilst offering her daughter a model of how to be an independent woman. If the mother cannot do this she has 'failed' and the daughter is encouraged to seek out, either in someone else, or in herself, an 'ideal' mother who will offer nurturance, offering unconditional love and care, encouragement towards independence and a model of how to be autonomous. Just what that 'ideal' involves and the effect it has will be the subject of the next chapter.

5 In Search of the Ideal Mother

Mother, according to Nancy Friday, is the person who should give you a self and then let you go. Friday tells us that

> We get our courage, our sense of self, the ability to believe we have value even when alone, to do our work, to love others, and to feel ourselves lovable from the 'strength' of mother's love for us when we were infants – just as every single dyne of energy on earth originally came from the sun. (Friday, 1977, p. 55)

If the daughter does not measure up to this then it is presumably because her mother did not love her enough. Before giving us this image of the power of mother's love Friday has already pointed out the dangers the daughter faces in the idealisation of her mother – seeing mother as 'perfect' binds the daughter to her, the mother telling the daughter that she alone loves her in this way keeps the daughter from growing up.

There is a difference here in idealising mothers and idealising mothering. Mothering should be 'perfect', but if the daughter actually views her mother as 'perfect', or the mother imposes such an image onto the daughter, then the daughter becomes forever beholden to the mother, forever in her debt and unable to separate from her. If mother love is wholly responsible for the development of the daughter's sense of self and her self-esteem, then any deficiencies the daughter has in this area must be mother's fault. The message is that the daughter has to denigrate her mother in order to be 'free' of her. In this influential work (more than three million copies in print) Friday sets up expectations of the perfect mother and then, finding a real mother cannot measure up to this, demonises her. In this she is following the patriarchal psychological traditions of the idealisation of mothering, and mother-bashing.

THE LOVING AND TERRIBLE MOTHER

Consider these two quotes

> Mother's love is bliss, is peace, it need not be acquired, it need not be deserved . . . Mother is the home we come from, she is nature, soil, the ocean . . . Motherly love . . . is unconditional affirmation of the child's life and his needs . . . Mother love . . . makes the child feel it is good to have been born; it instills in the child the *love of life,* and not only the wish to remain alive . . . the happiness in being alive. (Erich Fromm, 1956)

> Who can look fairly at the bitterness, the hatefulness, the sadistic cruelty of Adolf Hitler without wondering what Hitler's mother did to him that he now repays to millions of other helpless ones? We must remind ourselves again and again that the men by whom women are frustrated are the grown-up sons of the mothers who were chiefly responsible for the personality of those sons. (Karl Menninger, 1942)

The idealisation of mothering sets the scene for the demonisation of the mother. The mother who fails to live up to the promise of the idealised version is blamed for whatever ills befall her children and whatever evil there is in the world. Such idealisation may be considered a male device borne out of men's fear of women's power of procreation, and of women's 'otherness'. Jung says

> The mother has from the onset a decidedly symbolic significance for a man, which probably accounts for his strong tendency to idealise her. Idealisation is a hidden apotropaism; one idealises whenever there is a secret fear to be exorcised. (Jung, 1972)

The very splitting of mothering into 'good' and 'bad' can be viewed as part of the patriarchal tendency to dichotomise reality; to ignore women's lived experience and to devalue women. The isolation of mothers in Western society (bridged by women with tremendous effort) ensures the perpetuation of the myth of the 'perfect' mother and the feelings of individual failure for those mothers who believe in it and don't see themselves as living up to it.

Mothers not only have the social construction of mothering to deal with, but also the mythological and religious images of the 'Great Mother', which according to Jung have a part to play in the collective unconscious. Jung brings together the images of the Great Mother: mother-goddess, mother nature, bearer of life and of the witch mother, evil and devouring, in the mother archetype, 'the loving and the terrible mother'. The great goddess/great mother may be viewed as the bringer of life and death in the cyclical mother of creation (as with Demeter). Life and death go together, represented by woman, but the patriarchal tradition has split this image, to emphasise the ineffectuality of the 'good' mother and to promote the evil intent of the 'terrible' mother, using distorting myths and selective knowledge (Eisler, 1987; see Introduction).

The story of Demeter and Persephone (explored in Chapter Two) continues to be interpreted as a story of an evil mother intent on holding back her daughter's development (Herman, 1989), whilst our own culture continues to perpetuate images of the 'evil' mother in Fairy Tales such as Cinderella, Snow White and Rapunzel. The mothers of these stories are all 'evil' stepmothers, the 'real' (idealised, good) mother having died. The stepmothers lock-up, attempt to kill, or put their adolescent daughters to sleep to prevent them from meeting their Prince. As Chesler points out

> In a sense, many of the evil stepmothers are Mother Goddess figures who, like the Greek goddess Demeter, are essentially protesting the loss of their own Persephone-like daughters to patriarchal marriage and motherhood. Such goddesses equate their daughters with themselves as virgin adolescents. They protest mortal woman's fate (death in childbirth, being replaced by younger women, aging, menopause, etc.) Perhaps the goddess-stepmothers are protesting the loss of their virgin priestesses to patriarchal monotheism. (Chesler, 1990, p. 139)

One would certainly not think so, given the patriarchal presentation of these tales.

The embracing, loving mother becomes the terrible mother in her power to hold onto her children, not allowing them to separate from her to become autonomous people, rather, like Medusa she turns them (developmentally) to stone. Medusa has come to represent 'within male mythology and psychology, the grasping (female) unconscious whose power to fascinate, and ultimately castrate, must be permanently destroyed by the (male) hero' (Elias-Button, 1980; p. 202). Through today's distorted patriarchal knowledge, which has 'no powerful image of a great mother or indeed of any strong female symbol' (Chaplin, 1988, p. 29), women have lost touch with the creative image of the great mother. Some choose the patriarchal way of debasing the image, as does Nina Herman who finds the graphic image of the great goddess 'horrific, with those accentuated buttocks, sedatary thighs and breasts'. Others are searching for ways to bring back the whole image and to seek the creative powers in the representation of the terrible mother, as Elias-Button shows us in her analysis of contemporary women's poets confrontations with Medusa. I find this best expressed in her study of May Sarton's poem 'The Muse as Medusa' which she says is

an encounter with the dark 'mother' to which she came in fear, 'as naked as any little fish / Prepared to be hooked, gutted, caught'. Having looked Medusa 'straight in the cold eye', however, she finds that instead of being turned to stone, she has been released into a 'world of feeling / Where thoughts, those fishes, silent, feed and rove . . .'. And she realises, at the end of the poem, that the 'frozen rage' Medusa represents is really the necessary concomitant of the world of creative feeling:

I turn your face around! It is my face.
That frozen rage is what I must explore –
Oh secret, self-enclosed, and ravaged place!
this is the gift I thank Medusa for. (Sarton, 1974, p. 332)
(Elias-Button, 1980, p. 204)

Here a woman, taught by patriarchy to fear the great goddess/ great mother, finds the power of the goddess to be her own which by confronting she can incorporate 'those matriarchal powers which are both ancient and her own' (Elias-Button, 1980, p. 202).

Returning to Jung, we see how the archetypal image of the Great Mother interacts with how the real mother is experienced within the child's psyche:

> Although the figure of the mother as it appears in folklore is
> more or less universal, this image changes markedly when it
> appears in the individual psyche. In treating patients one is
> at first impressed and indeed arrested, by the apparent sig-
> nificance of the personal mother. This figure of the personal
> mother looms so large in all personalistic psychologies that,
> as we know, they never get beyond it, even in theory, to other
> important aetiological factors. My own view differs from that
> of other medico-psychological theories principally in that I
> attribute to the personal mother only limited aetiological
> significance. That is to say, all those influences which the
> literature describes as being exerted on the children do not
> come from the mother herself, but rather from the arche-
> type projected upon her, which gives her a mythological
> background and invests her with authority and numinosity.
> The aetiological and traumatic effects produced by the mother
> must be divided into two groups: (1) those corresponding to
> traits of character or attitudes actually present in the mother,
> and (2) those referring to traits which the mother only seems
> to possess, the reality being composed of more or less fan-
> tastic (i.e. archetypal) projections on the part of the child.
> (Jung, 1972, p. 17)

The 'mother archetype' of 'the loving and the terrible mother'
depicts the contrast between the all-giving, all-loving mother
and the controlling, withholding, wicked, witch mother. But
where do these split images come from and how do they come
to be related to the person of the real mother? Following
Melanie Klein (1959), many psychoanalysts relate this splitting
back to the infant's earliest experiences of the mother. The
mother is experienced by the infant as sometimes fulfilling
all needs, and at other times as frustrating and withholding.
In order to protect the image of the 'good' mother from
the infant's angry and destructive feelings about the 'bad'
mother, the infant treats them in her imagination as two separate
mothers.

As the infant develops and learns to better tolerate frustration, the two mothers can be merged again and experienced as
one person. The extent to which the infant does re-merge the

twin aspects of the mother is said to depend on the actual experiences in the mothering. If the mother has not offered the infant, on balance, a satisfying experience of mothering, then she will continue to feel the need to hold onto an image of a perfectly satisfying mother.

But it is not only in the 'imagination' of the child that this 'perfectly satisfying mother' exists but in the expectation of mothering in our society. As the child grows, she learns how mothers are supposed to be, and indeed is taught that she herself should strive to be (or rather should 'naturally' be) the 'good' mother. The idealisation of mothering lies not only in the child's imagining but in the surrounding culture (see Chapter One).

As children our mothers can never really be good enough for us, there will always be times when we feel frustrated and hard done-by, and hold the belief that we are entitled to a better mother. Which child has not at some time wondered if her parents are really her parents, if she was not somehow meant to be in some different, 'better' family? As a child I remember vividly (probably after my mother had frustrated me in some aim) searching my parents' bedroom for my birth certificate, convinced that it would reveal that I had been adopted. Did I feel disappointed or relieved when it did not? I think a mixture of the two. When Jean Radford's adoptive daughter says to her 'You are not my real mother' she thinks beyond the 'truth' of this:

> I did not feel either that my mother was my real mother, perhaps every daughter, every child, has this doubt. There is always the fantasy of another, more perfect, reality, of other possibilities reluctantly, if ever, relinquished. But what my daughter says to me is true, in a sense it was not for me. The gap between the ideal Mother, and the mother we actually have, is perhaps always there. If the Mother is the fixed perfect image of the ideal, a mother (small m) is always what falls short of this image. For me and my adoptive children, this gap between Mother/mother can be represented as the difference between the mother(s) who gave birth to them, and the mother who now looks after them. But if this way were not available, they would find other ways of representing the shortfall, as I did. (Radford, 1989, p. 143)

Arcana (1979) suggests that as adults we demand much more of our mothers than we did as children, this can include loving (not always reciprocated), emotional support, child care, financial aid, mutuality of interests and so on. She also points out that we learn to make these demands on our mothers in childhood, when they themselves teach us that motherhood requires such services and sacrifices of them, to be met with dutiful obedience from the daughter. Our demands and expectations may also increase as we learn the ideology of mothering current in our society.

The image of the 'ideal' mother has not only been imposed but has also been internalised. We can view with admiration this mother's reflection on her ideal of motherhood, and wonder at what cost to herself she maintains this balance of love and support

> I like to think of my love for my only daughter as the 'slack net' spread beneath a performing aerialist. I hoped that she would not view it with alarm or undue apprehension the necessity for its being there, but rather climb as high as she might care to go, secure in the knowledge of its support. It was frightening to know that pulling the corners too tightly could send her bouncing off into oblivion and leaving the knots too loose might plunge her into certain disaster.
>
> What I wanted most for my daughter was that she be able to soar confidently *in her own sky*, wherever that might be, and if there were space for me as well I would, indeed, have reaped what I had tried to sow. (Helen Claes quoted in Payne, 1983, p. 6)

The strength of our expectations of mothers as first-line nurturers and protectors shows itself when we consider children who have been abused. Abuse (whether physical, sexual or emotional) is seen as much more damaging to a child's psyche when it comes from the mother. In a society where individual mothers are wholly responsible for the care of their own children, to be abused by one's mother is to lose *all* protection, and to be abused by someone other than mother is mother's fault.

The idealisation of mothering may actually lead to abuse, as Westkott (1987, p. 169) says: 'beneath the attempt to live up to the idealised image of the perfect mother can lie the deep hostility toward having to give unconditionally to others when one feels herself to be deprived'. This also applies to the child (and especially to the daughter) who in response to the 'perfect' mother has to try to be the 'perfect' child. The anger felt at suppressing one's own needs and looking after others has to be repressed by both mother and daughter if they are to live up to the image of passive and caring femininity.

While it is easier for men to continue to believe the myth of the perfect mother, women come face to face with it firstly when they are expected to be perfect daughters in response to their own perfect mothers and secondly when they are themselves expected to offer perfect mothering to others. The guilt and shame they feel at not measuring up is then referred back inside themselves as well as out on to their own mothers.

The conflict created for the daughter when she is pulled towards being a perfect daughter and a perfect mother, and the distance created between mother and daughter because of this can lead women to seek a better understanding of themselves and their mothers in therapy. Women may or may not go into therapy with the goal of better understanding their relationship with their mother, but it is likely, as Arcana points out, that the issue will arise and will turn out 'to be pretty important'. This reflects the fact that therapists of all persuasions see the relationship with the mother as crucial to the woman's psyche.

THERAPY

The outcome of therapy can depend to a great extent on the values and beliefs of the therapist and her or his approach to the difficulties of the client. This can be extremely important for a woman who may be faced with a misogynistic interpretation of her experiences. Therapy operates within, and is strongly influenced by its societal context. It is difficult for it to escape its roots in patriarchal, middle-class and white knowledge.

The concept of mothering and the person of the mother has always held a particularly important place in the understanding of the psyche and particularly in the aetiology of disturbance – as noted by Jung. Whatever the therapeutic approach and theoretical base, the effect of the initial and the continuing mothering is more often than not viewed as crucial.

Marianne Walters (1988) points out that mother-bashing is a favourite sport of psychological theorists and therapists, where 'hysterical, overinvolved, enmeshed, intrusive, clutching, clinging, dependent, needy, smothering, selfless, selfish, covert, overemotional, unreasonable' mothers abound. The powerful, all-giving, all-loving mother is responsible for all the emotional ills of her children. The 'experts' tell the daughter this and the daughter believes it and blames her mother. In order to mature the daughter must separate from this imperfect mother, to do so she may first need to experience better 'mothering', the experience of being nurtured and then 'let go'.

Therapy as Remothering

Therapy with a feminist perspective has a lot to offer women in terms of developing self-esteem, valuing and developing strengths and (unlike orthodox therapy) accepting and respecting women's needs for nurture without viewing this as weakness. It also holds out the possibility of 'good' mothering. Here you can expect caring without strings, someone who accepts you as you are, helps you to understand yourself, to 'grow' and then lets you go. It would seem to offer the mothering that we all hold as an ideal – the unselfish and non-judgemental nurturing that we all crave.

For some feminist psychotherapists (Eichenbaum and Orbach; Flax) as we have seen (Chapter Two) women's psychological make-up is significantly related to that very first relationship with mother where the daughter was seen to be incompletely nurtured. Eichenbaum and Orbach describe women's psychology as

> a psychology that means we frequently do not feel whole, we feel undeserving, and fraudulent in significant ways, we feel exhausted with all the giving that comes of being emotional antennae, we feel that our real selves have either not emerged or if they were to do so they would be unattractive, and so on. (Eichenbaum and Orbach, 1987, p. 56)

In psychotherapy the earliest mother-daughter relationship becomes a central focus in working on these issues rather than the denial of their own feelings and experiences that women face daily.

This may be approached differently depending on whether the psychotherapist is a feminist or not. As Eichenbaum and Orbach point out, orthodox psychotherapy has concentrated on the issue of mother-daughter separation – or rather lack of it – and has made 'separation from mother the *sine qua non* of the therapeutic endeavour' (ibid., p. 61). In this the woman's needs are seen as invalid and developmentally immature, and she is encouraged out of such 'neediness' and led to 'resolve not to want'.

Feminist psychotherapy, as Eichenbaum and Orbach describe it, anticipates ambivalence in the mother-daughter relationship, and difficulties in the separation, but 'speaks to the issues not in the separation *per se* but to the difficulties that have occurred in the original merger and the subsequent impact these have on the achievement of *intimacy and connection*' (p. 63). For them 'the task of feminist therapy is to address the original not-getting and to provide an experience of consistent caring that can be ingested in the present'.

Nurturing
In an earlier work, 'Understanding Women', Eichenbaum and Orbach explain in more detail the actual process of therapy: here is how they describe the middle phase

> All the women we have seen in therapy have come with problems and confusions about their sense of self because they did not embody enough of mother to allow them to separate . . . The therapist is aware of the ways in which the early nurturance was inconsistent, and in being consistent herself she offers a new kind of psychological umbilical cord. She creates a circle of care and attention that surrounds the therapy relationship. . . . Being respected and related to precisely and rhythmically the woman slowly lets down her defences as she begins to feel the care of the therapist. Now she can begin the process of embodying the goodness of the therapist inside herself. As she internalises the caring, she

feels more secure and more sure of herself. This taking in of caring from the therapist heals the hurt of the little-girl. When we say *heal*, we mean that the therapist allows the woman's previous pain and loss to be acknowledged and validated. In allowing pain, anger, and regret to emerge, the therapist and the client are transforming deeply rooted internal experience. The therapist acknowledges the pain as legitimate: the girl wanted to be loved and accepted: this wanting, not met, was turned against the girl herself in her psyche, so that she blamed herself for not getting what she wanted. As the pain is exposed and tolerated, this formulation dissolves. The woman puts her anger and despair more outside herself and allows the therapist to come in with the love, nurturance, and attention she so badly wants. She is beginning to have a new experience of relating. (Eichenbaum and Orbach, 1985, pp. 96–7)

Although not claiming that the therapist can 'make up' for the loss the woman carries with her, Eichenbaum and Orbach clearly do see therapy as in some way reworking the early mother-daughter relationship with a more 'perfect' mother replacing the defective original one.

Letting Go
When the woman is feeling more confident in herself, when she has accepted her needs and feels worthy of having them met, it is time to begin the process of leaving the therapy. This stage echoes the separation from mother and again the therapist offers a different model from the original mother

The client may be hesitant about bringing up the idea of leaving and extremely tentative when she first broaches the subject. She may be afraid the therapist will not support her autonomy and her strength and may fear her disapproval. In addition, the client may imagine that she is stirring up feelings of competition and envy in the therapist, who will then in some way try to hold her back. She may anticipate that somehow her good feelings about herself will threaten the therapist.

The starting point for working on these feelings is that women, because of the ambivalences in the mother-daughter relationship, have not had the experience of feeling their strength and separateness supported. . . . The client needs repeated experiences of being supported in her strength. She needs to feel that her successes and her autonomy are truly appreciated and that the therapist's support is not a one-time fluke. (Eichenbaum and Orbach, 1985, pp. 104–5)

Whilst making some extremely good points – especially in relation to women's needs and the validation of these rather than their suppression as part of adult status – Eichenbaum and Orbach are in danger of suggesting that the 'ideal', all-nurturing, selfless mother is a possibility which women could have expected from their own mothers and which, their own mothers having failed to provide, they can experience in the therapy relationship.

Eichenbaum and Orbach are clearly aware of the constraints of patriarchy on the daughter's sense of herself, for example they say

Feminist therapy is about learning to love the little-girl inside that patriarchy has taught us to fear and despise; it is about allowing her to grow up and become part of an autonomous woman; above all, it is about being loved by another woman and helped by her to grow and become separate. (Eichenbaum and Orbach, 1985, p. 107)

But they also imply that this 'being loved by another woman and allowed to grow' could and should have been offered in that first relationship with mother, and that therefore mother (albeit herself a victim of patriarchy) has let the daughter down.

Jocelyn Chaplin, a British feminist counsellor, does make a distinction between symbolic 'mothering', as offered in the therapeutic relationship and the actual person who bears the label 'mother'. She stresses the importance of mothering as a particular kind of relating which can exist between lovers, friends, colleagues as well as between parent and child. She also points out that 'mothering' is undervalued in our society which has a 'deeply damaged relationship to the "mother" archetype'.

Having said all this, however, it is very clear from her case studies that it *is* the actual mother who, more often than not, is seen as deficient in her mothering and put in contrast to the 'better' mothering offered in the therapy. Although the client may come with 'the opposites of "perfect" mother and "bad" mother etched deeply into their unconscious' and may initially see the therapist as totally 'bad' and her actual mother as totally 'good' the aim is that the client will 'accept the rhythmic ambivalence of life' and eventually see both good and bad in both her mother and the therapist.

However, in helping her to do this the therapist *is* aiming to offer a particular kind of mothering that the client has *not* received from her own mother. This sort of mothering Chaplin describes as 'holding', 'letting go' and 'non-judgemental acceptance', and these terms relate to the idea of what 'good' mothering is about in our society. Chaplin assesses which type of 'mothering' her client needs from what has been deficient in the client's early experience of mothering from her real mother, so, for example, she says 'Louise need to be accepted as she is, not judged or criticised as she was by her real mother, who had been so affected by patriarchal attitudes' (p. 87). Or again, with Julia, 'I realise I will have to provide some remothering of a much more containing nature than the mothering she had in real life' (p. 31).

As with Eichenbaum and Orbach, mothers are held responsible but are seen as victims of patriarchy which they were not strong enough to resist in the way the therapist is:

> Throughout this stage and for the whole process of counselling, I am always aware that the real mothers our clients talk about were themselves given an impossible role. It is hardly surprising that most of us did not get the mothers that we needed. We did not have mothers who were comfortable with all sides of themselves, who were assertive and confident and, at the same time as demanding space for themselves, gave us space to be ourselves. Often we did not have clear boundaries between ourselves and our mothers, or between our needs and those of others. In the fifty-minute sessions counsellors, male and female, are trying to provide a different, more balanced, kind of mothering; a mothering with boundaries. (Chaplin, 1988, p. 43)

Because mothers are seen as not giving daughters enough nurturing and then letting them go the relationship with mother is seen as the cause of mistrust between women. Joan Hamerman

Robbins, an American feminist therapist, describes therapy as 'a delicate and complex working through of old, painful, long repressed feelings from childhood that have been denied and devalued because they are reminders of one's femaleness'. The new female-to-female bond, she tells us, can become a reworking of the mother-daughter arrangement, at the heart of which is the mistrust of female closeness.

Where does this mistrust come from? We have been led to believe that it comes from the experience of a mother who won't let her daughter grow up. Nancy Friday quotes Robert Robertiello as saying 'What makes symbiosis hard to break through is that it is endorsed by society. This sticky, gooey closeness between mother and daughter is seen as some idyllic, wonderful thing. In fact past age one and one half or two, it's absolutely terrifying' (Friday, 1977, p. 387). Here speaks a man himself terrified by an intimacy between mother and daughter, not because it is developmentally hazardous for the daughter but because it is hazardous to male power. The closeness between women has not been 'endorsed' by society as he says (except in an impossible idealised way), but on the contrary has been denigrated and denied in an attempt to weaken the power which evolves from that closeness.

Fantasy Mother

The Women's Therapy Centre in London offers a very popular workshop where daughters consider their relationships with their mothers in depth. Tricia Bickerton describes one session which concentrates on the daughter's images of a perfect mother. This begins by asking participants to write 'a fairy tale about their ideal mother'. Stories are constructed of 'abundance, of nature, flowers and fields and the sun shining; a happy picture of mother and daughter entranced in each other, in love. There is no domestic routine and rarely an intervening father or other children with whom to compete' (Bickerton, 1988, p. 23).

This should not surprise us – the symbolic mother is related to mother nature and is devoted only to our well-being. Bickerton goes on to say that 'almost every woman in the group can produce an ideal mother in comparison to whom her actual mother seems enormously inadequate' and she asks 'how does this wish for a perfect mother come about?' Her answer, as a psychotherapist, is to look to the early infant relationship with the mother and the splitting I described earlier. She implies that as daughters we all to some degree carry that splitting into adult life and hence experience problems in seeing the mother as a real person with both good and bad aspects, which leads to difficulties in separating from mother and in 'growing up'.

The ability to imagine an 'ideal' mother here becomes a device for unearthing the real mother's deficiencies and the daughter's coming to terms with what she missed out on in her childhood. The stated aim is to bring to light 'the discrepancy between the ideal and the reality, the difference between the desire for the perfect mother and the daughter's inevitably mixed experience'. It is about forgiving the ordinary mother for not being perfect, and allowing the daughter also to be less than perfect. While this is all well and good, all too often the positive aspects of the mothering experience play a peripheral role. Only the 'bad' aspects seem to be brought into reality with any force, the 'good' being largely reserved for the current experiences in the support of the therapist or group members.

Role Model

As well as offering nurturance, enabling separation and allowing the daughter not to be perfect, 'the feminist model of therapy also stresses the function of the therapist in serving as a role model for female clients' (Sturdivant, 1980, p. 82). As Ballou and Gabalac point out

> Role-modelling is an important part of the process. In feminist therapy, overt use is made of the person, experience, behaviours and attitudes of the therapist. The goal is not to have the client become just like the therapist, but rather to set an example of a competent woman dealing effectively with her life. (Ballou and Gabalac, 1985, p. 32)

Having experienced nurturance and development of self-esteem in the therapy relationship, the client is ready to take her place in the world as a mature woman. She is expected then to look to the therapist as a model of how to be a strong, but caring, woman. This again of course is a role the mother should (but probably did not) fulfil, for even if the mother herself is an assertive, confident woman, she may not have given the daughter enough nurturance for her to feel self-confident enough to model herself on her mother.

Indeed, what qualifies the therapist to offer such a model? In therapy there is the danger of idealising the therapist and of seeing in her a model of 'perfect' womanhood – a woman who can be both assertive, self-confident and caring of others, all the time, an image of 'superwoman' to live up to and measure our failure by.

A Different Emphasis – the Devaluation of Women

It must be clear that a fifty-minute session, once a week (or even once a day) between two adults, bears no resemblance whatsoever to the mother-child interactions over the years of the child's growth. Whilst the therapeutic relationship may be considered as symbolic 'mothering' it seems highly dubious, and damning to the mother, to consider therapy as 're-mothering' and able to offer what the client failed to get from her real mother.

If we believe that it is mothers (and only mothers) who make us into or prevent us from being the sort of women we want to be, and that we can only be that sort of woman if she is too, then we are ignoring both our own agency and the influence of all our other interactions.

Even if we understand the difficulties mother has faced under patriarchy and therefore 'forgive' her for not being what we needed her to be, then we are still imagining that the 'ideal' mother can exist in reality (albeit under different societal conditions, which she should have been fighting for). We are seeing the mother as all-powerful and as able to be all-giving or all-withholding. We are in fact confusing the reality of a flesh and blood mother with the infantile fantasy of an all-powerful mother (Choderow and Contratto, 1982).

It would be in total agreement with the argument that *any* kind of therapy is potentially detrimental to women, grounded as it is in a misogynistic psychology (Daly, 1979; Masson, 1989), were it not for the fact that some women have benefited from therapy (notably, in print, incest survivors such as Jacqueline Spring, 1987 and Kathy Evert, 1987), and that there are some feminist therapists who tackle the issue of women's oppression and devaluation head-on, rather than concentrating on the 'faulty mothering' of the past (Miller, 1978).

Enabling a woman to value her own strengths, and recognise and respect her own needs does not have to entail 'remothering' – which implies a devaluing of the original experience of being mothered and an offer of a better one. Rather, the therapeutic or counselling relationship can offer a space where the woman is valued for herself, where she can gain a better understanding of her own experiences of devaluation and sexualisation and relate this to the experiences of women generally (including her mother).

Jean Baker Miller, on being asked about the experience of mothering that women bring to the therapy, agreed that women often recount big difficulties with their mothers who may be deemed 'bad'. To underscore her own approach to this she recounted an experience told to her in therapy:

> A little girl, about three, was walking with her father and they went into the side door of a theatre. The male manager immediately scolded the father telling him he shouldn't be there, and told him to leave, the father was compliant, said he was sorry and left. The daughter remembers being so shocked to see her adored father treated in this way and responding in this way. On the other hand her father treated her mother like this all the time. Somehow it just didn't become a question in the same way . . . it was so normal . . . We are all so used to having women treated in that way in one way or another that little girls then would much rather stay stuck with seeing the problem around their mother, these days . . . than to really question the whole role of the father, and the mother-father relationship . . . Women patients can go on and one forever about their 'bad' mothers and blaming their mothers and you have to find ways to get past that, which is much harder. (Miller on 'Voices', Channel 4)

What Jean Baker Miller seeks to impress upon us is the position of women as subordinates in our society and how daughters grow up to see that mothers not only lack the power of their fathers but are also continually degraded and their knowledge and skills devalued. The difficulties of then identifying with that mother are obvious. Girls are also taught that they cannot identify with their father's power but can gain some small part 'on approval' by serving father's (men's) needs.

It is not through a process of 'remothering' but by the help a woman receives in exploring her experiences of devaluation, of denial of her feelings, by the validation given to her needs and the encouragement given to her strengths, that she can be helped towards an 'authentic sense of a fully valued self' which Woodward rightly tells us is the 'core of good mental health' (Woodward, 1988, p. 123).

Mother-Daughter Interaction

There will be times when the mother-daughter relationship is a necessary focus in the therapy. In working with the daughter (there is little written about work with women as mothers of daughters) on her internalised image of her mother, the therapist seeks to help the daughter to some better understanding and acceptance of herself.

Whether or not this gets taken up with the actual person of the mother is up to the daughter, and we may speculate on the usefulness or otherwise of this in terms of enhancing the current mother-daughter relationship. Some daughters may wish to share their insights with their mothers. Others may not consider it appropriate, having come to the view it is something they needed to work out just for themselves.

Some women may feel the need to tackle current issues in their relationship with their mother (or their daughter) and so may seek a more interactive therapeutic approach. In working with the real-life current mother and daughter relationship, feminist family therapist Marianne Walters seeks to enable the renegotiation of the mother and daughter relationship as both parties grow and change. She explores new ways in which mother and daughter can relate to each other while supporting and encouraging their attachment as well as their individual sense of self and self-esteem (Walters, 1988).

An interactive approach need not be confined to the adult relationship of mother and daughter. Choderow and Contratto suggest that we should be rethinking theories of child development within an interactive perspective. This could open new doors of understanding to the mother-infant relationship by according agency to the child as well as the mother, by recognising collaboration and compromise as well as conflict, and by stressing relational capacities and experiences. We may then be able to 'move beyond the myths and misconceptions embodied in the fantasy of the perfect mother' (Choderow and Contratto, 1982, p. 71).

SEARCH FOR SELF

The search for the ideal mother is also a search for oneself. A belief in the dominant ideology of mothers as selfless and nurturing leads a daughter to seek those qualities in herself and to condemn herself if she fails to live up to the image. The daughter has been encouraged to develop such qualities as part of her socialisation.

But self*less* is not only the opposite of selfish, it is the loss of self. Learning to care for others, as females do from a young age, means putting the needs of others before her own and this, it is said, can lead to women losing touch with what their needs actually are. One's own needs and wants are not so easily 'lost', they may rather be actively and painfully suppressed. This may be first practiced in relation to the mother.

Looking for the mother who will love us whoever we are, whatever we do, is looking for acceptance of our self rather than approval of our behaviour. It is saying that we have value in ourselves and not because we service other people's needs. The mother in Tillie Olsen's story 'I Stand Here Ironing', knows that we all need someone for whom we are a miracle: the expectation, and the likelihood, is that that person will be our mother. But as with this mother, who was left alone with no support, emotional, practical or financial, to care for her child, the constraints of everyday life, of sheer survival sometimes, can intervene.

One does not get the impression that Joan Foster's mother in Margaret Atwood's *Lady Oracle* regarded her child as 'a miracle. Rather, she was largely ignored except when her mother was attempting to make her over in her image (slim and attractive). In this 'monster' mother one gets the image of a woman who

has lost out on the dreams promised to her in her beautiful youth. The trouble she takes over retaining her beauty and keeping her house ready and socially acceptable for entertaining, is not repaid with an exciting and romantic life. The husband returning from war after five years' absence 'brought nothing and did nothing, and that remained his pattern'. The daughter feels herself unwanted and unloved, the 'embodiment of her [the mother's] own failure and depression'. The daughter, then, can have little sense of her own value and must battle against her mother to try and find her self.

In this, as in much contemporary women's literature, we see the daughter's struggle to find herself in opposition to her oppressive mother. Whereas the daughters of the Victorian novel were largely motherless (as often were their authors), more recent women's novels portray embattled mother-daughter relationships, signifying the daughters need to rid herself of her mother in order to become herself.

One such daughter is Martha Quest of Doris Lessing's 'Children of Violence' series. Martha has no wish to be like her mother (who represents traditional, passive motherhood), but having no other model of womanhood her only way to be different is to set herself in complete opposition to what her mother represents by being a 'nonmother'. In so doing she also has to rebel against her mother's expectations of who she should be. Lessing portrays the symbolic nature of the mother quite forcibly. Mrs Quest is described as 'the eternal mother, holding sleep and death in her twin hands like a sweet and poisonous cloud of forgetfulness' (Lessing, 1952). She is, as Fishburn (1980) points out, 'the projection of Martha's inner turmoil, the physical manifestation of Martha's archetypal fears'. Mrs Quest is the source of the restrictions and social expectations against which Martha is rebelling; it is she who is experienced as the obstacle to Martha's maturation and finding of her true self. Martha uses the traditional scapegoat provided by society for this purpose – the myth of the evil mother. Martha's fear of becoming her mother becomes the determining factor in her search for herself, she is as Fishburn says 'always [moving] away from and never toward. She is moving away from the one fate that she knows absolutely she would not choose given the chance: that of motherhood. She is terrified of repeating the pattern, of

becoming her mother.' She sees in her mother not someone she wishes to emulate, but a loss of freedom which is terrifying. For Martha her mother comes to represent the restriction and oppressions of patriarchy on women: only through ridding herself of her mother will she finally be free (Fishburn, 1980).

The difficulty lies in the daughter's close identification with her mother. For if, as patriarchy has taught her to do, the daughter constructs an 'evil' mother in order to aid her separation, then she carries both the burden of guilt at betraying her mother, plus the fear of what she herself will become.

If in searching for herself back through her mother the daughter takes Nancy Friday's route – listening to and believing male theories of mothers and daughters – then the daughter can only find herself by denigrating and denying her mother. This perpetuates women's oppression since what daughters feel about their mothers is too closely tied up with they feel about themselves.

'Learning to love yourself' sang Whitney Houston 'is the greatest love of all' but for women it is not 'easy to achieve'. Women have been taught to put others' needs before their own and to seek approval and love outside of themselves, to the extent that loss of that love may be experienced as 'loss of self' as Jean Baker Miller points out:

> women stay with, build on, and develop in a context of attachment and affiliation with others. Indeed women's sense of self becomes very much organised around being able to make and then to maintain affiliations and relationships. Eventually, for many women the threat of disruption of an affiliation is perceived not as just a loss of a relationship but as something closer to a total loss of self. (Miller, 1978, p. 87)

Loving yourself is about being aware of your own needs and wants, valuing yourself enough to feel entitled to have those needs met, feeling worthy of the love and nurturance of others, having confidence in yourself and control over your own life.

It is not the mother who denies the daughter her value, her rights and control over her life, but a system which treats women as subordinates, taught to service men, devalued and sexualised for men's needs. Daughters may learn to value themselves and fight for their rights by looking back through their mothers,

but not in the patriarchal way of denigrating mother and wrest-
ing 'power' from her, but by valuing her strengths and understanding her needs – which are also the daughter's.

Karen Horney's 'female hero' lets go of the idealised image
of how she should be in the 'triumph of the ordinary', she
believes that 'she herself is worthy of care and that the world is
her domain. She practises an empowered caring that risks
conflict to change the world so that women and the socially
necessary need to care for one another can no longer be
devalued'. She does not criticise herself but 'opposes the conditions under which she is devalued and sexualised' (Westkott,
1987).

While mothers may be experienced as part of those conditions, we must also recognise the strength of the connection
between mothers and daughters and the ways in which the
devaluation of women has affected them both.

6 Mother to Mother

Stephanie Dowrick's mother died when Stephanie was eight years old. She speaks here of changes in her internal relationship with her mother.

> She has danced in my dreams, my mother. The space she vacated on one side of me was balanced by the waiting space on my other side, waiting for my child not yet born. We have danced together in my dreams, my mother, my self, my child. When my child is visible, real in the world's understanding of the word, then my relationship to my mother will change again. I do not want to *become* her by becoming a mother, but I expect to increase my knowledge of her; I would welcome that. (Dowrick and Grundberg, 1980, p. 73)

For any woman becoming a mother will effect some changes in this internal relationship, whether or not the mother is alive. Becoming a mother may lead the daughter to view her own experience of being mothered in a different light, and to an adjustment in her internalised image of her own mother.

If the mother is alive it will also effect changes in the actual interaction between mother and daughter. Sharing as they now do, the common status of 'mother', they may feel that they have more in common with each other and therefore may begin to regard one another differently. The daughter may find that during pregnancy and on becoming a mother she feels the need of a close relationship with her own mother, one that she may have previously spurned, or which has never been on offer. The mother also has to adjust her perception of her daughter. She is likely to begin (if she has not already done so) to see her daughter more as an adult and an equal, someone with whom she has shared experiences on an adult to adult level. The level of contact between mother and daughter may also be altered, with them having or desiring more or less involvement in each other's lives with all the issues this raises.

The daughter becoming a mother is likely then to be a time of change in the mother-daughter relationship. In psychoanalytic theory it is seen as a time of potential reconciliation

156

between mother and daughter after the separation of the adolescent and young adult years.

DECISION TO BE A MOTHER

As we have already seen in Chapter Four, a woman's desire to become a mother may be closely tied up with her own experience of being mothered and her perception of her own mother. We recall that Elizabeth Wilson decided at an early age that she did not wish to be like her mother, leading to a further decision not to be a mother, while Adrienne Rich thought she would be a mother but she would 'do it differently' to her own mother. Helena Kennedy tells of how her own experience of being mothered by a mother 'who felt good about herself as a producer of babies and carer of children' left her in no doubt that she too wanted 'the experience which had made her life so worthwhile' and like her mother 'to be good at it' (Kennedy, 1989, p. 2). Anna Wileman was proud in her early childhood to be described as 'the motherly sort' and regarded this comparison of her with the person she loved the most, her mother, as perhaps the moment when she began to regard her life as 'inevitably filled with children' (Dowrick and Grundberg, 1980, p. 214).

Of course the decision of whether or not to become a mother is a complex, possibly biologically and certainly socially related one which cannot be reduced to a woman's own experience of being mothered and her relationship with her mother. But when a woman first contemplates motherhood, during her pregnancy, at the birth of her baby and after, a woman's feelings and thoughts are very likely to be tied up with her own mother.

The daughter's experience of being mothered and her observations of the life of her mother is bound to lead to certain expectations of what motherhood will hold for her. Where the daughter has experienced a somewhat exclusive relationship with her mother, cut off from the influences of other mother figures, and of a mother cut off from the support of other women, as encouraged and endorsed in our Western nuclear family structure, a daughter may have little knowledge of other possibilities of motherhood, seeing only how her own

mother has experienced it. Such a situation may give a daughter little chance of envisaging a different sort of motherhood
for herself. Brook D'Abreu found little of use when she looked
to her own childhood to supply the answer to the question 'why
children?' She found

> no evidence of the possibility of meaningful relationships
> between people of different ages, apart from the limiting
> and overdependent mother/child relationship; no experi-
> ence of the process of birth which might provide some in-
> sight into my own participation, either as a child or as a
> potential mother; no acquaintance with motherhood in any
> form other than the prolonged hysteria caused by impris-
> onment in a meaningless marriage 'for the sake of the chil-
> dren'. (Dowrick and Grundberg, 1980, p. 96)

Nancy Choderow considers such isolation as causal in her
proposed lack of psychological separation between mothers
and daughters and as being perpetuated through generations
as the mother's 'overinvolvement' in her children. She says

> Girls who grow up in family settings which include neither
> other women beside their mother nor an actively present
> father tend to have problems establishing a sufficiently
> individuated and autonomous sense of self. They in turn
> have difficulties in experiencing themselves as separate from
> their own children. (Choderow, 1978, p. 212)

In the body of her work Choderow's 'answer' to this lies in the
more active involvement of fathers, although in her 'Afterword'
she does suggest that this repetition can be avoided if the
mother is surrounded by supportive women. Whatever the
'answer', the question seems to be based on unsubstantiated
overgeneralisation. Choderow neither interviewed mothers and
daughters or observed them in the situations she talks about.
What may be a simple relationship between the mother's lack
of emotional sustenance and practical support from other adults
and her intimate relationship with her daughter becomes in
this scenario a cause of psychological difficulties for generations of daughters to come. The presence of fathers who mother
(where are they going to come from?) will lead to the development of women and men who can mother, and (in similar vein

to Dinnerstein, 1976) to the end of male domination and women's oppression.

The presence of other women who can support the mother in her role is also taken by Choderow beyond its simple outcome of more relaxed and less conflictual mothering and alternative models of mothering for the child, to the production of 'daughters with capacities for nurturance and a strong sense of self' (Choderow, 1978, p. 213).

While a mother who feels supported and sustained in her role is likely to feel better and present a more positive image of motherhood to her daughter, to say that an unsupported mother will create daughters with no separate 'sense of self' who in turn will also prevent their children's autonomous growth seems to me to be taking one step too many in the analysis.

This is not to say that mothers who are unsupported will not experience stress which may be communicated to the daughter, but the outcome of this will depend on the particular people involved. Brook D'Abreu, as mentioned above, seems to have experienced being a 'separate' person who could clearly see the negative aspects of mothering as experienced by her mother. This is not to say that she does not have the capacity to nurture but that she has chosen not to exercise that capacity in motherhood. Kathy Kea, who as a child was continually abused by her mother, learned at an early age that 'wife and mamma makes you crazy', a situation to be avoided at all costs (Kea, 1987, p. 213).

A daughter then may grow up with positive or negative expectations of motherhood which have been strongly influenced by her observations of her own mother's life and her experience of mothering within that. The varied possibilities of motherhood are likely to be best understood where the daughter has grown up with a number of different models, for example in an extended or communal family setting where childcare is more shared. The opportunity to observe and experience different 'styles' of mothering may give the daughter more options and a better understanding of the possibilities as well as the restrictions of motherhood.

For some daughters their childhood experience is actually of 'being a mother' by looking after their siblings and sometimes their own mother. They may then feel as adults that they have had enough of mothering (for example Melba Wilson, in Dowrick and Grundberg, 1980, p. 105) or they may see their identity as strongly linked to the mothering role.

Wanting a child may be related to feelings about one's mother. A baby may be, to some extent, a replacement of one's mother – someone to share an intimate relationship with along the lines of that experienced with mother. Alternatively, it may be seen as a chance to offer the sort of mothering which was not experienced but craved. Jane Lazarre, whose mother died when she was seven years old, found on becoming a mother herself that she was 'becoming the mother I had been seeking for twenty years' (Lazarre, 1987, p. 44). Becoming a mother may also be seen as offering the chance to repeat the relationship with one's mother but this time of having some control over it.

The decision on whether or not to become a mother may not be one that is easily discussed with one's own mother. The mother herself will have some thoughts and feelings about her daughter becoming or not becoming a mother. A daughter who chooses to remain 'unchilded' (to use Adrienne Rich's value-free term) may be seen by her mother as rejecting the mother's way of life, and as a direct criticism of that way of life and of her mothering (which clearly sometimes it is). This will not make it easy for the daughter to talk to her mother about her decision.

On the whole mothers do seem to wish to see their daughters become mothers, sometimes putting their daughters under some pressure in this direction. The mothers of lesbian daughters who contributed to *Different Daughters* (Rafkin, 1987) largely shared a common disappointment and sadness that their daughters, in all likelihood, would not have children. A mother may be viewed by her daughter, correctly or not, as embodying the social pressures upon her to bear children.

As previously noted, although mothers are often seen as the major socialising force of their children, this is in fact not the case. The external pressures a daughter feels to become a mother will come from a variety of (sometimes covert) sources but may be seen as being represented in the wishes of her mother.

Mothers do not, in any case, always express a wish that their daughters become mothers, even though this is a strong social expectation. Some mothers may prefer their daughters not to become mothers – perhaps if they themselves have found mothering difficult, or where the mother is dependent on the daughter and fearful of being 'replaced' by a dependant infant. They may not however directly express this to the daughter since to do so flaunts the expected desires of 'normal' mothers.

PREGNANCY

Pregnancy is seen as a time of psychological as well as physical change. It is a stage of transition for the family and for the mother, as the family prepares to welcome a new member and the mother contemplates the changes in her own life and identity which will come about with the baby's birth. The extent of the changes will differ depending on whether or not this is a first baby, but with each baby there is likely to be some adjustments to be made both within the family as a whole and for each of its members. Pregnancy is a time of preparation for these changes, and for the mother in particular it is a time during which physical, psychological and relational changes interact to affect her identity.

Internalised Mother

Because much of the psychological work of pregnancy is related to maternal identification, the internalised relationship between the pregnant woman and her mother is very likely to be in evidence.

This may show itself in the vivid dreams of the pregnant woman. Jane Lazarre recalls how her mother returned to her in dreams when she was pregnant with her first child:

> She came as a wise priestess offering love and encouragement. She came as herself, but with a vividness I had not experienced in my conscious life for eighteen years. Her face would be there, looking at me in the darkness, just the way it had been when I had known her. I saw aspects of her features that I had forgotten so long ago, articles of her clothing, the texture of her hair. One night she came as a witch. She seemed to be warning me. She seemed to know something I didn't. (Lazarre, 1987, p. 10)

The psychoanalytic texts are generally negative about the possible effects of the mother-daughter relationship on the daughter's pregnancy. Pregnancy is regarded as a 'transitional crisis', a time to 'resolve primary conflicts with the woman's mother' (Zuckerberg, 1980, p. 154), a time when issues of ambivalence, autonomy and dependency are revived (Ballou, 1978; Bibring et al, 1961). This is related back to a reworking of oedipal themes 'centering on competition, guilt and retaliation' (Zuckerberg, 1980, p. 156). The pregnant daughter is said to re-experience feelings of envy and anger towards the early fertile and 'baby hoarding' mother (Kestenberg, 1976; Deutsch, 1947).

The woman is once again seen as in competition with her internalised mother by becoming a mother herself, to the extent that physical problems in the pregnancy are taken as signs of conflicts in the mother-daughter relationship. Zuckerberg tells us that

Experimental research has pointed to hyperemesis gravidarum (undue nausea), habitual abortion, infertility, toxemia (hypertension), and pseudocyesis (false pregnancy) as the five core psychosomatic conditions, the gross warning signals of a maladaptive pregnancy. Problems in conception and then difficulties in holding one's baby may be physical in nature but the research seems to indicate the presence of psychological issues. The above physical states have been associated with conflicts regarding one's relationship to one's mother, and rejection of the female role . . . If there is residual immaturity, dependency, or hostility toward the mother, the pregnant woman may have a high incidence of psychosomatic complaints manifested as 'warning signals'. If a problematic relationship to one's mother is not counterbalanced sufficiently by growth–promoting forces present in the woman's life situation and marriage, then this problematic identification with the mother will have a greater likelihood of evidencing itself in psychosomatic warning signals. These problems also may be displaced unconsciously onto the obstetrician/midwife, the woman's body, the husband and marriage, or the self . . . Further displacement onto the woman's mother, father or finally onto the future child may occur. This displacement may be the beginning of a family neurosis . . . (Zuckerberg, 1980, p. 159)

It is the woman's internalised relationship with her mother that is here being blamed for some major physical problems of conception and pregnancy and ultimately for 'family neurosis'. This internalised relationship – we must remember – can be traced back psychoanalytically to the earliest mother-infant daughter relationship and the mother's handling of this (Chapter One). Even possible problems with the obstetrician/midwife, or in the marriage, can conveniently be related back to this early mother-daughter relationship. Any problems (regarded as pathologies) are neatly focused in the psyche of the woman herself and related to an unsatisfactory early relationship with her mother.

The husband is usually seen as playing both a nurturant, maternal role and a protective oedipal father role towards his pregnant wife (Ballou, 1978). The wife is only able to accept her husband's help (and later that of midwives and obstetricians) if she has resolved her dependency conflicts (her feelings of 'guilt, envy, rivalry and fears') with her internalised mother (Raphael-Leff, 1983). A woman who is able to do this is likely to be what Raphael-Leff calls a 'facilitator', and this has implications for the kind of mother she will be. A 'facilitator' is able to trust her 'intuitive knowledge' of mothering, will be confident in going with her body in giving birth and will bond early with her baby.

On the other hand the pregnant woman who Raphael-Leff terms a 'regulator' will try to maintain her familiar identity for as long as possible. She is therefore 'unlikely to 'indulge' in introspection and hence to work through her ambivalent feelings towards her mother . . . Feeling unable to identify with her 'split' internal mother, she either confronts her defiantly or is determined to hold her at bay and withhold grandparenthood from her'.

This affects not only the pregnancy but also the labour (and of course the subsequence bonding with and handling of the baby). 'Facilitators' practice natural childbirth and stay at home longer at the onset of contractions practising their breathing with their husbands at home, while 'regulators' 'avail themselves of drugs and epidurals . . . appear to have longer labours in hospital . . . seem to have more technical interventions'.

In early motherhood 'facilitators' are empathic and responsive to their babies' every need, while 'regulators' 'restrict communication' in order to increase their own confidence of understanding. The 'facilitator'

> having utilised the period of pregnancy to achieve a 'reconciliation' with her mother . . . is now able to accept her own dependency needs and tends to establish a 'hierarchy of mothering' during the early months, whereby she is mothered by her own mother or husband, which enables her to mother the baby in turn.

Whatever it is Raphael-Leff is trying to say about different 'styles' of mothering (her judgements are implicit rather than explicit), it is clear that she, along with other psychoanalytic analysts of the daughter's relationship with her internalised mother, views the ability in the daughter to deal with the conflicts in this relationship as very important in terms of what help and support the daughter is able to accept in child birth and after.

This implies that the support is available to the mother and her use of it depends upon her own psychological abilities. It denies the reality for many women of the lack of acceptable help and the conflicts which may exist between the various people concerned. In giving birth, for example, the labouring woman may quite justifiably feel that the 'help' on offer from the obstetrician or midwives is not of the type she actually needs. Again, suggesting the mothering of the new mother comes from either her own mother or her husband oversimplifies the complexities of interactions which can occur around this issue. For example, the grandmother's help may not be accepted because this is seen as disloyalty to the husband (who may not actually offer adequate replacement care); or neither of these people may actually offer what feels like help and support to the new mother.

Although Raphael-Leff seems at pains to withhold any judgement on the 'types' of mothering she depicts, it seems clear that in terms used by contemporary (middle-class, white) child development 'experts', the 'facilitator' appears to be a 'good' mother (that is, she devotes herself totally to the baby, she is a 'natural' mother empathic to baby's needs who bonds early and well and stays at home to look after her child), while the 'regulator' is deemed 'bad' (that is she is determined to hold onto her own identity and not to 'fuse' with baby, and is likely to return to her career). The suggestion seems to be again that good early experiences with one's own mother leads to an ability to deal with the conflicts with one's internalised mother and subsequently to become a 'good' mother oneself.

The daughter's ability to resolve the conflicts she carries with her internalised mother during her pregnancy is certainly seen as a sign of psychological health. In doing this it is considered that the daughter will then be able to accept her relationship with her mother in reality in a less ambivalent way.

The progression through dependency, separation and re-conciliation is rather too neat. The age of the daughter and the mother, the ongoing changes in their relationship (which may be provoked as much say, by, a daughter's career choice or a mother's change in life-style as by the daughter's marriage and pregnancy) are not accorded due consideration. The daughter's pregnancy, while provoking psychic changes for her, is only part of the story, and it cannot be possible to say this will necessarily lead to a 'reconciliation' between mother and daughter, or even that such a reconciliation is necessary.

While I would agree that pregnancy is a time of reworking the internal image of motherhood and the internalised rela-tionship with mother, the suggestion that the outcome depends on the psychic health of the daughter (and by implication of the mother as it was she who helped create that internalised image) ignores the complexities of the external relationship of the mother and daughter and the agency of mother in this as well as daughter.

Daughters have been led to believe that all will be well in their relationship with their mother once they become a mother themselves: for some this is one of the reasons for deciding to become a mother. The 'failure' in this reconciliation merely adds to the patriarchal myth of conflict and competition between mothers and daughters (and between all women), just as the cultural messages of competitiveness between mothers themselves can lead to the loss of potential support between mothers.

Mother-Daughter Interactions

I could find little in the literature on the actual interactions between mothers and daughters during the daughter's pregnancy. Arcana's chapter on the daughter becoming a mother shows, in a way totally ignored by the psychoanalytic literature, how the varied relationships which exist between mothers and daughters up to this point may effect the giving and taking of support, as well as influencing renegotiation in the relationship when the daughters becomes a mother. Of course, as usual in the mother-daughter literature the voices are those of the daughters and their interpretations of their mother's feelings at this time. One wonders, for example, what the mother of the daughter who tells us that her mother took care of her a lot during her pregnancy and who enjoyed it, really felt when that same daughter also tells us that her mother now looks back on it and tells her 'not to have another baby because she can't go through all that again' (Arcana, 1979, p. 185).

The small amount on the mother-daughter relationship in teenage pregnancy (Phoenix, 1988; Skinner, 1986) and motherhood (Sharpe, 1987) offers differing views which seem related to the teenage daughter's stage of pregnancy/motherhood and attitude to it. Skinner's adolescent girls – most of whom were seeking abortions – had distant and unhappy relationships with their mothers. Phoenix found that in her sample 21 per cent were mainly negative about their relationships with their mothers in late pregnancy, while Sharpe, talking to adolescents who had already become mothers, found that on the whole the girls had good relationships with their mothers who had been supportive both in a practical and an emotional sense.

The findings of Sue Sharpe's study seem to indicate a positive renegotiation of the relationship between daughter and mother, many of the daughters finding that they could now share more with their mothers because they had been through the same experience, as one respondent, Helen, says:

> Mum and I are much closer now. I can talk to her in a way I couldn't before and she's been a great help over the past year. I wouldn't have got through it without her. (Sharpe, 1987, p. 50)

Pregnancy is a time when the mother-to-be may feel particularly vulnerable emotionally, experiencing a wide spectrum of emotions like excitement, anxiety, elation and sadness, sometimes quite intensely and in quick succession. It is likely then to be a time when the woman feels particularly in need of some mothering herself. As one woman in a TV discussion of mother and daughter relationships said, pregnancy was the time 'when I needed my mum most'. This daughter found her mother was able to meet her need, but for many daughters it will not be so simple.

GIVING BIRTH

The daughter's understanding of being pregnant and giving birth will be strongly influenced by her own mother's experiences. She may as an elder daughter have been around at the birth of a sibling, she most certainly will have picked up some message from her mother about the experience of pregnancy and childbirth, if only from her silence on the subject. This is obviously tied up with issues of sexuality and regard of the body, which were explored in Chapter Four.

A prospective mother may be told very little about pregnancy and childbirth, which can leave her blissfully unaware or generally fearful. Again the culture in which she grows up will affect this. Advertisements of dreamy pregnancy and blissful motherhood will serve to enhance the romantic image of the process; being around when a woman is enduring the pains of labour and the fatigue of early motherhood may make the daughter more sceptical of such images and prepared for a more mixed reality. Mothers may share with their daughters as honestly as they can their own experience in this area – but that does not mean the daughter will believe that her experiences will be the same. The pregnancy texts (for example Bourne, 1972) warns the mother-to-be of the 'old wives' tales' they may hear. Thus is the received wisdom of women's experience denigrated.

The supportive relationship which may exist between mother and daughter during the daughter's pregnancy, labour and early motherhood has been largely dismissed and devalued in our culture which emphasises male-female interactions as of primary importance, and in which childbirth and understanding childhood development has been taken over by male 'experts'.

John Bowlby (1988) notes with some surprise the practice on a South Sea Island of a mother-to-be being attended both during and after the baby's birth by a couple of female relatives who cared for her throughout the first month, leaving her free to care for her baby. Bowlby advocates the presence of a female companion during the labour and childbirth as a way of aiding childbirth and promoting early and positive contact between mother and baby. What he fails to note is that until childbirth was taken over by male surgeons this was actually common practice in our society. It is only with the growth of technology in childbirth and the wish to see this as a male domain that women attenders have been ousted, to the extent that midwives, long since put under the 'rule' of (largely male) doctors, are currently fighting to maintain their role (Kitzinger, 1988). The once female territory of labour and childbirth has become more and more the domain of male 'experts' (Ehrenreich and English, 1979; Kitzinger, 1978). Women's expertise and role in the Western birth chamber has been denigrated and devalued to the point that having one's mother, sister or female friend present during labour is most unusual. The support that women have generally offered other women at this time seems to have been blanked from our communal memory.

Fathers, on the other hand, once restricted to pacing up and down outside, are now actively encouraged to be present during labour and birth, providing they don't faint or generally get in the way of the medical staff. The experience of Yasmin Alibhai, an Asian woman giving birth in Britain and caught between two cultures, highlights the transition of birth from an all-female activity to a largely male and technologically led process

> It felt so strange in the hospital that night. My husband, well oiled by then in the ways of modern childbirth, had done all the right things, and was anxiously awaiting the results while playing a game of scrabble which the forward looking hospital had provided for him. I had to have my mother there too, because it just did not feel right without her. The two did

not mix well at all. Unease rapidly set in. None of us knew what to do. My husband was, officially, on female territory. I did not know if I wanted to be a modern young miss or creep back into the folds of what I knew and loved best. My mother, whose suspicions about men were still red-ripe, saw his presence as an infringement of our basic rights as women. I found myself playing a part for the first time against my real instincts, falling in too willingly with the expected norms of this society. Meanwhile, my mother waited outside for seven hours, with no role to play. It was a painful birth, and the pain added to the general feeling that I was somehow not performing in the right way, washed up between so many different expectations. (Alibhai, 1989, p. 38)

Attempts to regain this territory are underway and may not necessarily include the exclusion of men – but rather increase the element of choice in birth companions and the context of delivery.

That home births, a normal enough occurrence in the 1950s in Britain, have now to be strenuously fought for, indicates an increasing level in the technology of childbirth, as does the increase in caesarian deliveries. Midwives fighting to maintain their role and status, and the conspiracies against Wendy Savage and Pauline Bousquet, two of the small number of female consultant obstetricians in Britain and both proponents of choice for women in childbirth, points to the power which male doctors fear they will lose if women actively have a say in the conduct of their own labours (Savage, 1986). A comment to a newspaper by a senior obstetrician on the Wendy Savage case is instructive:

She should have been a good and agreeable girl and made sure she got on with her colleagues. If she had played her cards right she would have found being a woman was to her advantage and her male colleagues might have been prepared to do her more favours. (Savage, 1986, p. xv)

The issue centres around male and female control of this area, and is reflected in the choice of birth companion(s) to the labouring woman. It would be interesting to know how many women in our society would choose to have their mothers present at this time. My guess is that the distortion of the

mother-daughter relationship would not be very easily overcome. For some daughters the worst possible scenario is to have
their mothers present at this crucial time, this could be for a
number of reasons. If the daughter's relationship with her
mother has always been one of conflict she is unlikely to want to
bring it into the birth chamber. If the daughter is used to
protecting her mother from her pain and problems who will
look after her mother at this time when the daughter is too
occupied elsewhere? What if the mother worries too much or
fusses too much – how will the daughter control this or bear it?
Will the mother offer support or be a burden? If she is supportive will the daughter be reduced to a childlike dependence on
her, and how can she allow this at a time when she herself is
about to become a mother? If the mother can offer the daughter
the support she needs at this time and the daughter can accept
this, then the problem may lie in how the daughter's partner
feels about the mother's presence and the daughter's split
loyalty. Finally, how are the medical staff likely to react?

The daughter may find herself trying to orchestrate relationships to maintain harmony at a time when she does not
have the energy to do this. A mother who is used to being
present during other women's labours will be more clear about
her role, but even so will find it difficult to assert her authority
if medical staff and societal norms are against it.

Perhaps, like Adrienne Rich, we cannot admit, even to ourselves, how much we do want our mothers at this time:

> I wanted her to mother me again, to hold my baby in her
> arms as she had once held me; but that baby was also a
> gauntlet flung down: *my son*. Part of me longed to offer him
> for her blessing; part of me wanted to hold him up as a badge
> of victory in our tragic, unnecessary rivalry as women. (Rich,
> 1977, p. 223)

ADJUSTING TO MOTHERHOOD

As well as adjustment to pregnancy, British psychotherapist
Dana Breen has related the woman's internalised image of her
mother to her adjustment to motherhood. She found that
those women who adjust well to the birth of their first child

tend to perceive their own mothers positively and through this are able to value themselves as mothers. She says

> It may be that the truly adaptive processes of the birth of a first child involve a woman being able to call on a positive image of her mother postpartum and identify with her and view herself more positively as a mother. This is in line with the psychoanalytic notion of an 'identification with a good mother image'. (Breen, 1975, p. 114)

She also found that

> The most striking feature amongst the women who experienced most difficulties, was the split between a very idealised picture of what they felt a mother should be like (often opposed to the bad mothering they felt they had received) and the way in which they saw themselves after the birth of the baby. (ibid., p. 192)

The idealised image of mothering that permeates our culture did affect most of the women in Breen's sample, in that during pregnancy they all tended to focus on this image. However, Breen found that after the birth of the baby the 'well-adjusted' group, who held positive images of their mothers, were more able to relinquish the idealised image and modify their picture of what a good mother should be. Those women having no 'good mother' reality to fall back on tended to continue to view perfection in mothering as possible and desirable.

While I do agree that the image a woman carries with her of 'a mother' is very important in her own relationship with mothering, it is dangerous to reduce the complexities of this relationship to her own positive and negative experience of being mothered (especially as psychoanalytically defined). Adjustment to motherhood must also be related to the actual circumstances and context of that mothering. This will include all the socio-economic variables as well as the woman's intimate ongoing relationships which may or may not offer her adequate support in her new role. This can include her actual relationship with her mother which, because of the concentration on the psychic world tends to be ignored and devalued in the psychoanalytic texts.

After the confused expectations of the birth chamber, Yasmin Alibhai and her mother had little difficulty in their shared care of Yasmin's son from the age of six weeks. Yasmin says she felt 'no jealousy at all' when her mother moved into the role of primary caretaker to her son, rather she felt freed to 'love and spoil and know him' (Alibhai, 1989, p. 39). Mothers offering practical support after the birth of the daughter's baby are much more common in our society than their presence at the actual birth. Ann Oakley, in a study of London women having their first baby in 1975–6, found that three-quarters had help from their mothers after the birth, this involved learning to care for the baby and domestic tasks (Oakley, 1979). Women will vary as to how far they welcome this help from their mothers and it will of course depend on the previous relationship between mother and daughter and their renegotiation of this. Some of the women interviewed by Vivienne Welburn for her study of postnatal depression certainly found their mothers' support necessary and useful. One says:

> I've been very much closer to my mother since I've had children than I was before. I just felt a terrific need for her – because I thought possibly she was the only person who would be able to tolerate my acute involvement with myself both before the baby was born and after. There were also overtones of being able to lean totally on somebody else's shoulder. (Welburn, 1980, p. 177)

There is an expectation in our society that the one to lean on and look to for support will be the father of the child. Donald Winnicott (1960) refers to the mother and baby as the 'nursing couple' who need to be supported and protected from the outside world by the father. Although fathers are now much more involved in childcare than they were expected to be by Winnicott, this is still limited (Lewis and O'Brien, 1987).

The expectation that the maternal grandmother will come and stay to look after the new mother for the first few weeks seems currently to be clashing with our expectations of 'new' fathers who offer this support to their wives and take their shared child care seriously. Sometimes the new mother will be caught up on the conflict caused by these differing expectations, for example one of Vivienne Welburn's interviewees who was really glad to have her mum around after her baby's birth says

'The only thing that marred it was the fact that my husband didn't want her to be there' (Welburn, 1980, p. 178).

The lack of provision for paternity leave in the UK means that many fathers can take only one or two weeks away from work to look after his partner and baby. If the grandmother's stay is prevented, limited or curtailed, then for many new mothers the isolation of motherhood can begin at this point, particularly if her relatives live at some distance and previous full-time work has meant that she has made few friends locally.

Post-Natal Depression

Carol Dix in her book *The New Mother Syndrome* on post natal depression was at first reluctant to relate this condition to the mother-daughter relationship, but halfway through her research (and halfway through her book) she found the need to confront this issue. What she concludes is that women may become depressed after the birth of a child because of their identification with their mother.

Becoming a mother oneself the daughter may no longer be able to avoid identifying with her mother, having spent much of her life so far trying to be as different as possible from her. Dix herself confesses that the sense of becoming like her own mother 'was terrifying and had dragged me down'. She puts this down to the daughter's need (for psychological health) to separate from her mother with the emotional distress this induces often contributing to PND (Dix, 1986, p. 135). Here I think Dix is a little confused, what causes the distress and hence the depression? The feeling of being like her mother or the 'need' to be psychologically separate from her? She confuses her need for her mother with a lack of adult independence, in a way in which we have all been taught to do. She sees herself 'reduced' to 'a mother', in keeping with the way in which we have been taught to devalue motherhood.

What is depressing is the way mothers are treated in our society and a mother's depression is directly linked to this. Ann Oakley points out that some degree of depression after child birth is deemed 'normal' in our society, rather than being seen as a response to the abnormal treatment of mothers (Oakley, 1981b). That our mothers have shared this abnormal treatment links the depression to the mother-daughter relationship. Also, the support and emotional care we need to get over depression is likely only to be on offer from another woman, possibly our mother. That some mothers fail to recognise and accept their daughter's post-natal depression is likely to relate, as Dix points out, to the fact that for the mother's generation it was unthinkable to admit to any unhappiness in being a mother.

Dix does refer to the change of identity taking place for the daughter which gives her a common identity with her mother and with all mothers; the understanding this may evoke in the daughter for her mother; the desire to be mothered oneself at this time, a need to receive back some of the nurturance she is giving to her baby. How difficult it is to accept this, or even for mothers to offer it, if the daughter is caught up in an angry conflict (internally or externally) with her mother over what she did and did not do for her.

The utter exhaustion of caring for a baby, the feelings of total responsibility and the guilt felt when one 'fails' to be the perfect mother; the general lack of status associated with motherhood, and the lack of facilities for mothers and babies must surely all add to the feelings of depression which affect many mothers (see Chapter One). If one adds to this the feeling that as an independent adult you should not at this time need your own mother (or at least some mothering), it is clear how the idea of the daughter's post-natal depression can be linked with the mother-daughter relationship, and how once again mothers carry the blame for societal impositions and neglect.

In a society that isolates mothers and children, a mother will find that at the time when she most needs the support of other adults, she is expected to take on all the work and responsibility alone. As Welburn says 'the new mother exhausts herself caring for her baby, her children, her husband and her home and caring less and less for herself. So who mothers mothers?' (p. 179).

Dix was surprised to hear many of the women she interviewed reject with vehemence 'this significant woman in her life'. Considering the way the mother and daughter relationship has been distorted and that these distortions have been passed on to daughters, I do not find this surprising. Perhaps more surprising is the number of mothers and daughter who *do* maintain supportive and caring relationships through it all, like the mothers and daughters of Ann Oakley's and Vivienne Welburn's studies, who offered help and emotional support which was gratefully accepted.

BEING A MOTHER

The ideology of motherhood is a strong influence over how women plan to mother. It may operate in such a way that a daughter whose experience of being mothered is largely negative may attempt in her own mothering to be much closer to her idea of the 'perfect' mother as culturally construed. For this daughter the expectations of mothering may be strongly dichotomised between 'bad' (as she has experienced it) and 'good' (as she hopes herself to give).

A daughter may remember certain aspects of her own childhood and determine not to repeat these with her own children. For Jane Lazarre the memory of her mother leaving her with a maid while she went to work became permanently confused with her final leaving – her death. Jane the mother then decided she would never leave her baby with a stranger. My own memory of being a 'latch-key' child, while less devastating, is probably just as potent in how I intend to mother my child. I have little doubt that our children will remember something quite different about their own childhoods which they will endeavour not to repeat with their own children.

How a daughter regards herself as a mother may also be tied up with her childhood experience and may be reinforced in the ongoing relationship with her mother. Jane Price, a feminist psychotherapist, describes a woman who felt herself to be an inadequate mother to her baby son. A dream alerted her to the notion that her relationship with her own mother was not as good as she had consciously believed it to be. In psychotherapy she began to understand how her mother had turned to her for mothering and how deeply buried in her own psyche (and shared by her mother) was the feeling that she had failed to mother her mother adequately. When she now turned to her mother for support in her mothering role her feelings of inadequacy as a mother to her baby were reinforced.

This woman's anger at her mother's expectations and her realisation that her mother 'should mother' her is probably a common one, and I believe relates in part to the feelings many women have of being inadequately nurtured – particularly when they are in that 'all-giving' stage of early motherhood.

Child Care

> The modern mother takes for granted that she will have the advice of experts and will not have to rely on the advice of her mother. The previous generation of mothers may not necessarily be the best advisors of the present generation. This is not to belittle the enormous support which grandmothers can give . . . But the modern mother is less convinced than her predecessors that her mother knows best. (Jolly, 1981, p. 1)

The message is clear – 'experts' not mothers know best, and for women becoming grandmothers their 'experts' may have taken a completely different line to that taken by 'experts' today. The conflict is not as stated by Jolly between modern mothers and old-fashioned grandmothers – but between two sets of conflicting 'expert' advice, the more rigid schedules of Truby King, the permissiveness of Dr Spock and the current child-centredness of Jolly (1981) and Leach (1977).

What is lost in all of this is the lived experience of yesterday's mothers and today's mothers. Of course not all mothers will lose out on this as they turn to their own mothers as well as to their contemporaries to discuss their concerns and learn more about the shared experiences of motherhood. The attempt by 'experts' to denigrate and devalue women's experiences as mothers does not always work. But it may help us understand better what is going on, for example when a mother 'fails' to give her daughter the advice and support she is seeking, or the daughter rejects the mother's advice as wrong.

Ideally it is not advice which new mothers need but a chance to share and compare experiences with their mothers and their contemporaries, leading to ideas which can be taken up or ignored to suit the new mother without feelings being hurt. The competitive stance set up by 'experts' is a source of confusion to the new mother and a barrier between her and her own mother's experiences, denigrating as it does the experiences of both.

Accepting practical help seems less contentious – as Jolly implies – the support a mother offers her daughter at this time can be of a practical nature, although I would doubt that two women could share childcare without them working out some basis of shared values. Perhaps this is where problems do set in with mothers being expected to offer their daughters' practical support, but their own experience of childcare being ignored and dismissed – another example of 'unselfish mothering'?

We seem so well-trained in accepting what 'experts' have to tell us and in denying the value of experience (even our own), that when mother's advice does actually concur with that of an 'expert' we make it clear it is the expert's advice we are following. For example, a respondent in a study by Urwin says

> When she [Anna] was little I couldn't bear to leave her to cry. But my mother said, you know, leave her. It's only *natural* for babies to cry. But I always felt I couldn't. Although I must admit I gave in at night, but that wasn't anything to do with my mother. It was only because the doctor suggested it – I would never of naturally left her to scream. It seems cruel. (Urwin, 1985, p. 181)

Here the woman seems to have followed advice against her own 'instincts' (more likely her internalisation of current child-care values) but that advice had to be the permission of an 'expert' rather than from her own mother.

This quote is interesting in that it highlights two different generations of 'expert' opinion, that which sought to regulate babies and saw picking up a crying baby as 'spoiling', and the current philosophy which seeks to understand and respond to the baby's communications. The transmitter of the former culture is not the literature of that time but the generation of women who took that 'expert' knowledge on board, the current grandmothers, making it easier to dismiss not only that former 'expertise' but also the adapting of that philosophy through the grandmothers' own experience. By dismissing the grandmother's experiences as old fashioned and denigrating her knowledge as 'old wives' tales' the daughter is in danger of losing a potential source of support, and the grandmother is liable to be left feeling she has no role to play in support of her daughter's mothering.

It is likely that this issue of 'expert' advice may have class connotations. Many of the women interviewed in Urwin's study had gained their own contemporary knowledge of child-care in their training for the 'women's professions' of teaching and nursing: they were then well versed in current child-care values, they had sought out other women of like values to share their concerns and everyday activities with. Urwin suggests that the child-centred approach may only gain hold where there is some minimum level of material security. One is reminded of the imposition of middle-class values onto working-class culture, as when a middle-class social worker attempts to 'teach' a working-class mother how to play with her children, and how irrelevant and insulating this may seem to that mother when other concerns are so pressing. For the working-class mother it may be her own mother who offers her real help and support of a kind relevant to her, for example childminding while she works.

Such practical help is indeed a norm amongst working mothers in the UK where grandmothers constitute the largest percentage of child-care arrangement of children under five whose mothers work full-time (Martin and Roberts, 1984, p. 39). The most acceptable form of childminding where mothers work part-time, after the children's father, also appears to be the grandmother.

It may, of course, not always be the case that grandmothers wish to look after their grandchildren for any length of time or in any regular way. They after all may have their own work to attend to and indeed may feel that they have 'done their bit' when it comes to raising children. Cohler and Gruhnbaum (1981), on finding from their sample of American mothers that some were seeking help with childcare from grandmothers who were not forthcoming with this, concluded that the life-cycle stages of the mother and daughter meant that the daughter was seeking more closeness from her mother at a time when the mother was wishing to separate herself more from her daughter. I think this psychoanalytic explanation, based on the theory of lack of earlier separation between mother and daughter, is a rather tortuous way of explaining what could basically be a desire for daughters to have help with their role at a time when their mothers are feeling they deserve a rest from the exertions of child care.

RECONCILIATION OR RENEGOTIATION?

It seems unlikely that the daughter can herself become a mother without some alteration in the relationship between mother and daughter. For the daughter's part there is the work of processing her new identity, an identity in which she comes to share the role of mother. Whether her mother is living or dead, close by or miles away the daughter will have some psychological work to do on her internalised image of her mother and what this means to her as a new mother. If the mother is close by and offering or being asked for help with the mothering of the new baby, there is a practical level at which the mother-daughter relationship has to be reworked, taking into account the new status of both parties.

The wish for a transformation in a previously conflicted relationship is unlikely to be fulfilled, but there may be some new ground for sharing and for considering compromises. A previously close relationship may be the foundations for a mutually satisfying continuation of this relationship, or may be the scene of instability and new conflict.

Whatever the circumstances it may be expected that some renegotiation of the relationship will have to take place (if only in the daughter's psyche). The literature suggests that the new mother becomes reconciled with her own mother after the separations of adolescence and young adulthood. A daughter who has made every effort in adolescence and young adulthood to move out of an intimate relationship with her mother may, during pregnancy or early motherhood, feel the need to regain that relationship and may look to be reconciled with her mother.

This may not be easy, since although the ideology of motherhood decrees that mothers will 'be there' for their children whatever, the mother herself has feelings which she has to cope with. She may have felt rejected and angered by her daughter's moves away from her, and used by the daughter's newly-expressed need for her.

If the communication between mother and daughter has been ongoing, then it is unlikely that the strict separation between mother and daughter will have happened in the first place, although culturally this is the expectation as shown in developmental theory. We have already seen why this might not be the case (Chapter Four), but rather a process of negotiation around the parent-child relationship will be ongoing. The daughter's becoming a mother will present a further reason for negotiation and may bring about more or less changes depending on the current state of the relationship.

Lucy Fischer (1979; 1981) in her small study of American mothers and daughters found that there was a tendency for them to re-evaluate each other and become more involved with each other when the daughter herself became a mother. There was increased mutual understanding, a reduction in conflict, and an increase in identification by both mother and daughter. A working-class respondent to the British study by Willmott and Young (1960, p. 74) put it thus:

> A daughter alters when she marries and has children of her own. She seems to feel closer to her mother than before. They understand each other more.

Or as Jane Price puts it:

> However the daughter has perceived her mother in the past, a new breeze of reality sweeps through her assessment when she becomes a mother too. She begins to understand much that has previously hurt and confused her, and, perhaps most important of all, she begins to know that mothers are only ordinary people. As one woman said to her own mother in family therapy marking this reassessment, 'Mothers are normal, doing their best in a difficult job. They're just like you and me . . . in fact they are you and me!' (Price, 1988, p. 119)

While this positive reassessment may be the norm for many women there will be some who find the experience of motherhood takes them even further away from an intimate relationship with their mother – either through their mother's choice or through their own. A woman who had been abused by her father as a child told me that until the birth of her own children she had not blamed her mother for her difficult childhood, however once she had children and realised how easy she found it to give them the physical affection she had craved as a child she realised that her mother had not given her what she could have had. Rather than reconciling her with her mother her own experience of motherhood had served to sever the tie with her mother completely.

Despite this, there is still an important issue in the shared identity of the mother and her daughter turned mother. Here is the potential for intimacy between mother and daughter based on shared experience and mutual support, which can be positive for both of them.

7 Thinking Back Through Our Mothers

So far I have concentrated on how much of the literature on mothers and daughters has offered a distorted view of this relationship, seeped in patriarchal ideas and concepts. This distortion has led to an emphasis on conflict and encouraged the erection of barriers between mothers and daughters as patriarchy attempts to erect barriers between women generally. In this chapter I will be looking at how these distortions are being overcome, how women are voicing their own experiences and strengths, making connections with other women through sisterhood and shared daughterhood, and consequently looking back to their mothers to see and value their matrilineage.

In contemporary women's literature this trend is evident, particularly in the writings of 'minority' women. Davidson and Broner point out that a 'new matrilineage' is to be found in the writings of Black writers such as Alice Walker, Margaret Walker, Gayle Jones, Nikki Giovanni, Lucille Clifton and Carolyn Rodgers. They say that

> One important theme running throughout all these writings is the sense that the daughter is no longer alone. The lost mother is found. One consequence of the women's movement is a new emphasis on sisterhood, on shared daughterhood. As Maglin states, there is a 'need to recite one's matrilineage, to find a ritual to both get back there and preserve it.' 'The sudden new sense the daughter has of the mother; the realisation that she, her mother, is a strong woman; and that her voice reverberates with her mother's' – all this is part of the new matrilineage.'
>
> (Davidson and Broner, 1980, p. 254)

SISTERHOOD, FOREMOTHERS AND MATRILINEAGE

There are several strands to the connection between women that women are increasingly writing about. Firstly there is

182

'sisterhood' – and certainly, at least in the written word, there has initially been a concentration on the connection between contemporaries, looking at shared experiences of women within patriarchy.

Then came the looking back to women's history, and to our 'foremothers' as political activists in the earlier women's and civil rights movements, and as pioneers in the arts and sciences opening the way for women into public life.

Finally, probably with more difficulty and only now in its early stages (particularly I think for white, middle-class academics) women are beginning to 'think back through our mothers' in the true sense of valuing the strengths and creativity, however expressed, of the mothers who gave birth to us.

Of course all of these strands are interwoven and ideally involve women valuing themselves as women, and their heritage both globally and personally. But things are not so simple. The sisterhood which forms the foundations of the feminist movement has been found to be flawed in both its theoretical and its practical application in that it often fails to adequately take account of differences between women.

The combining forces of patriarchy, imperialism and capitalism mean that women of different races and classes do not experience sexism within our society in the same way. White, middle-class feminist academics have largely failed to understand this and have assumed white, middle-class woman as the norm (Hooks, 1982). So, for example, we find popular feminist writers like Australian-born Dale Spender ignoring race and class issues in her feminist analysis (Segal, 1987, p. 23); whilst influential North American feminist Mary Daly (1979) envisages a 'Race of Women' which appears to exclude all but a select few (Segal, 1987, p. 21). On a practical level we find women's activism fragmented by the differences between them:

> We witnessed bitter confrontations between Israeli Jewish women and pro-Palestinian women, between political lesbians and heterosexual women, between mothers and non-mothers, we heard the anger of working-class women, Irish women, disabled women, and others. (Segal, 1987, p. 59)

Much-needed feminist conferences are still in danger of failing to address the needs of Black and working-class women, for example at the First International Feminist Bookfair held in London in 1984 (Parmar, Kay and Lorde, 1988, p. 121–31). The power differential between white middle-class, white working-class and Black women conferred on us by a racist and classist society continues to split women off from each other in some sort of struggle which is in danger of creating a hierarchy of oppressions.

The desire to value differences as well as connections, and to work together to fight all oppressions, is too often thwarted by women's own oppressive ways of behaving. If we speak only of sexism and ignore the interaction of multiple oppressions some women are subjected to, then, as Audre Lorde says, 'we distort our commonality as well as our difference' (Lorde, 1981). The answer lies not in ignoring our differences but in celebrating them and using them to learn from each other. But this also demands a relinquishing of power on the part of some women.

In a similar way, if mothers and daughters are to recognise and value their differences, be willing to learn from each other, and gain from their connection, this requires some understanding of the power relationship between them. The different experiences which split women from varied backgrounds may be the very experiences which unite mothers and daughters. Shared oppressions through poverty and racism, for example, may enable mothers and daughters to be more tolerant of their individual differences so that they look to each other to also share their strengths and offer each other support.

Sometimes it is easier for women to value and look for their heritage in a woman or women other than their mother. Women need to know of and have pride in the lives and work of our 'foremothers', and the restoring of women's history has been an important move in understanding women's oppression. But even this can be barbed if it leads to a denial of personal matrilineage. In taking respect and admiration for a talented woman who has been an inspiration to the point of saying 'I wish I had had a mother like that', is to confuse two very different areas of influence and in the process the daughter denies not only her mother's strengths but her own.

Our foremothers are not only those 'great' women whose achievements extend to the public sphere but also all those 'ordinary' women who have struggled and won through in their own way. It is a pleasure to see the experiences of these women being made public, like the Jewish women in London Group's exhibitions and book *Generations of Memories* (1989) and Susan Hemmings' *A Wealth of Experience* (1985).

It seems easier, somehow, to value the experiences and heritage of women who are not our mothers. The process of recognising and reciting one's matrilineage is complicated by the very essence of the reality of the mother-daughter relationship. This is reflected in the interconnecting themes which appear and reappear in the literature of matrilineage. As Nan Bauer Maglin points out these are:

1. The recognition by the daughter that her voice is not entirely her own;
2. the importance of trying to really see one's mother in spite of or beyond the blindness and skewed vision that growing up together causes;
3. the amazement and humility about the strength of our mothers;
4. the need to recite one's matrilineage, to find a ritual to both get back there and preserve it;
5. and still, the anger and despair about the pain and the silence borne and handed on from mother to daughter. (Maglin, 1980, p. 358)

Points two and five seem to cause daughters the most difficulty and are not easily overcome in a relationship which is not freely chosen.

By 'choosing' each other in adulthood, Simone de Beauvoir and her adopted daughter Sylvie le Bon de Beauvoir avoided the difficulties caused by growing up together, and Sylvie reserved the anger and despair for her own mother (Beauvoir, 1989, pp. 125–6). While Simone de Beauvoir chose not to be a mother, being very clear that this could only offer restrictions to her life's work, her choosing a 'daughter' in later life seems to have been more a desire for an intimate female friendship, based on intellect and love, satisfying both heart and head. Sylvie for her part is very clear that the relationship she had with Simone was not that of mother and daughter. Her clarity on this rests on the stereotypical idea of a conflicting and unequal mother and daughter relationship which she considered formed the basis of her relationship with her own mother. This appears to me as a denial of the possibility of a good and strengthening relationship between a mother and daughter, just as, for Simone de Beauvoir, motherhood itself had to be denied if a woman wished to be something more than a mother.

Alice Walker, herself an inspirational 'mother' to many Black women, exemplifies the idea of matrilineage – the recognition of the strength and creativity of one's own mother – whatever form it took. Her paper 'In Search of our Mothers' Gardens' explores the need for Black women artists to understand their maternal heritage and the creativity passed to them by mothers often unable to express this in conventional artistic ways themselves. Alice Walker tells us how her mother created beautiful gardens wherever they happened to be living, so that even her 'memories of poverty' were 'seen through a screen' of beautiful flowers. As she says

> And so our mothers and grandmothers have, more often than not anonymously, handed on the creative spark, the seed of the flower they themselves never hoped to see: or like a sealed letter they could not plainly read. And so it was certainly with my own mother . . . no song or poem will ever bear my mother's name. Yet so many of the stories that I write, that we all write, are my mother's stories. (Walker, 1984, p. 240)

The heritage from mother to daughter is not denied even where their creativity takes a very different form, as we find with Nigerian born writer Rita Anyiam-St. John

> I am now
> like mother like daughter
> a regular rattler
> me with pen and sheets of paper
> you with scissors, machine and cloth
>
> (St. John, 1987, p. 84)

Sometimes the creativity is more obviously passed-on as with writer Gayle Jones whose mother would write stories to read to her and her brother. Gayle Jones did not connect with the stories heard in school. 'But my mother's reading the stories –

I connected with that.' (Jones, 1977)

In exploring the literary works of Black women, women from varied ethnic groups, working-class women, lesbian women we can see beyond the issue of problematic mother-daughter relationships and the possible reasons for that to something more like the complexity of those relationships. Here we see 'ambivalence' in all its glory. Rage and love; autonomy and connection; a recognition of the hurt, and a pride in one's heritage. This literature speaks of the connection between mothers and daughters and the legacy of strength between them without denying the anger, guilt and difficulties in communication which can also exist, and the fact that connection and anger can in fact co-exist. Paula Marshall's (1959) novel *Brown Girl Brownstones,* about a Barbadian family in New York, vividly portrays the complexity of a Black mother-daughter relationship, circumscribed as it is by the racism of white society.

Carolyn Rodgers (1969) in her poems at the beginning of *Songs of a Blackbird* clearly shows the conflict between herself, a 'revolutionary poet', and her mother 'a Christian of the highest order' (Parker-Smith, 1985, p. 397). Mother and daughter have quite different ideologies, the mother does not understand her daughter's politics, she fears for her psychological and moral health and for her physical well-being, and she blames the education she worked so hard to secure for her daughter for her 'going astray'. But this mother has no difficulty saying 'If yuh need me call me' and when her concern rises at her daughter's phone being disconnected the mother 'slipped on some love' and went to see about her 'baby'. The daughter acknowledges and accepts this act of love for what it is, she sees and values their connection

> My mother, religious-negro, proud of
> having waded through a storm, is, very obviously,
> a sturdy Black bridge that I
> crossed over, on.
>
> (Rodgers, 1969, p. 13)

Maya Angelou also shows a great pride in her inheritance from her mother. An inheritance which others may translate as entirely negative, Angelou relates to positively as being about personal strength and independence:

By no amount of agile exercising of a wishful imagination could my mother have been called lenient. Generous she was, indulgent, never. Kind, yes; permissive, never. In her world, people she accepted paddled their own canoes, pulled their own weight, put their own shoulders to their own plows and pushed like hell . . . (Angelou, 1974, p. 7)

In *I Know Why the Caged Bird Sings* Maya Angelou writes 'to describe my mother would be to write about a hurricane in its perfect power. Or the climbing, falling colours of a rainbow' (Angelou, 1984, p. 58).

Daughters can be proud of their mothers and the heritage they pass on without having to deny their humanness and their weaknesses as this poem by a white working-class woman, Kate Hall, shows:

MY MOTHER
I am
the daughter
of an amazon
she
survived
violence
pain
abuse
worked
hard
all her life
no
she's not
a six-foot-tall
warrior queen
she made
mistakes
felt weak
even
collapsed
occasionally
but always
rose again
phoenix-like

from
her life's
disasters
'life goes on'
she says
and
so it does
I am
the daughter
of an amazon
I
have
her
blood
in me.

                                (Hall, 1989, p. 289)

In *Watchers and Seekers* (1987), an anthology of creative writings
by Black women in Britain, the editors point out that

> Many of the writers whose work is included in this anthology
> explore the cycle of emotional and material interdepen-
> dence between mother and daughter, grandmother and
> granddaughter, aunts and nieces, cousins, sisters, friends.
> Their perspective may be critical, nostalgic or celebratory,
> sentimental or distanced. But repeatedly there emerges a
> sense of sisterly solidarity with mother figures, whose strengths
> and frailty assume new significance for daughters now faced
> with the challenge of raising children and/or achieving artis-
> tic recognition in an environment hostile to the idea of
> female self-fulfilment. (Cobham and Collins, 1987, p. 6)

Of course the relationships between mothers and daughters
under the added oppressive conditions of racism, classism,
homophobia and so on are not free of distortions. Rather it
may be that the struggles for survival enable the mother and
daughter to see each other as allies and co-supporters in that
survival rather than as enemies and rivals.

We need to increase our knowledge about these relationships, knowledge which has been hidden and subverted by
white, middle-class male ownership of knowledge bases. As Mary
Helen Washington (1975) has pointed out, 'the relationships

of black mothers and daughters can only be discovered as one comes to terms with history' (Washington, 1975). We will not begin to understand the full complexity of mother and daughter relationships until we understand much more about the distorting effects of oppressive social constructions and the different ways in which these relate to the experiences of women.

The importance for women of tracing back and reciting their matrilineage is becoming increasingly evident. We see this in a number of works published in the 1980s – for example in the collection of letters between mothers and daughters brought together by Karen Payne (1983); in the collection of prose and poetry about the mother-daughter relationship by mothers and daughters complied by Tillie Olsen (1985); as well as in biographies and autobiographies.

Matrilineage is not only about the daughter's need and desire to know about her heritage, but also about the mother's and grandmother's need to pass this knowledge on through her daughter and granddaughter so that it will not be lost. Kim Chernin's mother did this in the telling of her mother's story and her own story, as a Russian immigrant to America, to her writer daughter. The daughter then continued the tale through reflections on her own life and her relationship with her daughter. The resulting book – *In My Mother's House* (1985) – gives us some insights into the lives of four generations of women in one Jewish family through changing social conditions.

Similarly Margaret Walker remembered the tales of slavery in Georgia heard at her grandmother's knee and later fulfilled her promise to her grandmother in writing the story of her great-grandmother in her novel *Jubilee* (Walker, 1966). In telling their mothers' stories daughters are reclaiming the past and their own heritage and through it seeking to understand their mothers and themselves, their commonalities and their differences, more completely.

It is probably not coincidental that much of the literature of matrilineage comes from women who experience more oppression than sexism. When Davidson and Broner (1980) talk of the daughter finding her 'lost' mother they use the literary work of 'minority' women to evidence this. Here again we have to be careful about overstating the commonality of women's experiences. The literature used to illustrate the 'loss' of the mother (see Chapter Three) is that of white, middle-class, Victorian women. The experiences and the stories of women who are subject to added oppression through being Black, working-class, Jewish, lesbian and so on have until recently remained within their own cultures or have been rendered invisible by racist, classist, homophobic society. Because of this it may be wrong to assume that the matrilineage we discover now in the writings of 'minority' women is 'new' as assumed by Davidson and Broner, but that it is now slightly more accessible.

What may be 'new', however, is the breaking out of white, middle-class women from the traditions, values and theoretical constraints of white, middle-class men. Perhaps it is through listening to the experiences and values of 'minority' women (who have had much less to gain from the upholding of white, middle-class, male values) that more women generally will feel able to pursue their maternal heritage and gain a better understanding of their own mothers; their strengths, their difficulties and their legacies to their daughters.

So we see that there is more than one herstory to be considered here if we are to look at how mothers and daughters have been 'lost' to each other through patriarchy and have only recently begun to 'find' each other via the sisterhood of the women's movement. The white academic feminist tradition which has so far had most to say publicly, because of its relatively easier access to the published written word, may have experienced the mother-daughter relationship differently from those who are only just beginning to make their views publicly known.

Women whose life experiences have differed from those of white, middle-class women and who have found it necessary to challenge other forms of oppression interacting with sexism may be closer to an understanding of shared reality with their mothers and their 'sisters' than are those women who have more to gain from 'standing by their man'.

MULTIPLE OPPRESSION

Looking at the family forms of women who suffer multiple oppressions can give us more insight into the potential connections between women and between mothers and daughters.

Apart from novels there is relatively little written about the experience of the mother-daughter relationship in, for example, Black families or working-class families.

I have taken what literature is available to me to try and look at this area. What I can offer is a fairly superficial look at the family situations and possible effects on the mother-daughter relationship for Asian, Afro-Caribbean, African-American, white working-class, and lesbian women living in Britain and North America.

Asian Women

In trying to summarise a number of varying cultures under the heading of 'Asian', I am aware of the danger of misrepresentation, especially as this covers experiences I am not personally acquainted with (see Matsui, 1989). However, I feel it is important to look at the very general aspects of Asian family life for daughters and mothers and its effect on the mother-daughter relationship, even though in specific areas this may differ considerably. I rely here on the interpretations given in the various studies used.

One major drawback is a lack of concentration on the mother-daughter relationship within the literature. To read about the family life of Asian girls and women is to see again the female as second-class citizen, as owned and ruled by men. At birth a boy is to be celebrated, a girl to be tolerated with a 'better luck next time'. A girl is taught very early to take care of the menfolk and in particular to protect the honour of the family. But the messages are inevitably mixed, and probably depend on whether you are considering the dominant, and more public, male view or the more private female view of family feelings. Ranu, a Sylheti woman, tells how a baby girl will be celebrated with the same joy as a son by the women in the family; a daughter will be loved by and grow close to her parents, particularly her mother, but when she marries and goes to live in her parent-in-law's home they will hardly ever see her (Wilson, 1978).

The heritage bestowed on the daughter may also be very mixed. Indira Parikh speaks of the 'dominant, assertive and capable women [in her family] who sowed the seeds of aspiration, courage and a set of values and ideals based on self-respect, grace and dignity' on the one hand, and on the other:

a legacy of the idealised traditional role of being a woman which encourages helplessness, a giving up of aspirations, being bound by role definitions, living for others, glorifying in the sacrifice of self, and learning to live without any legitimate space for the self in the system. (Parikh and Garg, 1989, p. 25)

The growing daughter may also see her mother's experiences within this system as confusing. It is likely that within the maternal family she will be accorded respect, love and affection and will find emotional support, while in the paternal family she may be seen as alien, a threat to the order of the family to be controlled and judged within her role.

The mother and her growing daughter may have a very close relationship but there is the danger that this will be transient, for on marriage the daughter becomes very much a part of her husband's family and may be cut off from her own kin. Indira Parikh and Pulin Garg tell us that one message 'prevalent in India is that the daughter is *paraya dhan* (somebody else's property, held in trust)'. They summarise the basic import of definitions prevalent across different regions of India thus;

'You have some freedom here. Enjoy it with constraints. Once you are married beware of the in-laws;' or 'you will have a hard time'; or 'Your fate is to be subservient to fathers and brothers before marriage and husbands and in-laws after marriage, and to sons if you survive your husband. Your destiny is to live for others. This you can only do by denying yourself.' (Parikh and Garg, 1989, p. 65)

The daughter's marriage can, particularly for a Hindu or a Sikh women who is expected to marry outside her own community, mean an 'uprooting' and a total loss of her relationship with her mother, especially since by tradition the bride's parents must not accept the hospitality of the groom's parents. For the daughter this can mean being completely cut off from her family of origin and having to accept a low status in her husband's family under the rule of her mother-in-law. As Brown et al. point out:

New brides pose a threat of potential breaches of family solidarity – they have to go through the dangerous process of aligning their interests with those of strangers and breaking the ties with their natal families. A mother in her turn must let go of her daughter. There are many Punjabi proverbs and sayings about daughters which illustrate the point: 'she is a bird of passage', 'Another's property', 'A guest in her parents' home', 'A thing that has to be given away'. (Brown et al., 1981, p. 129)

The loss is also felt by the mother. Amrit Wilson spoke to a Sikh woman from Jullunder recently arrived in Britain, who described her feelings when her daughter married six years ago

Yes, I wished I could see her. I felt so sad but if I had gone there and seen her, how would I have felt? At home she was a queen, I never liked her to do the heavy jobs. There she is a slave, I know because my life was the same. But to see her like that would hurt my feelings and hurt our *Izzat* (pride). (Wilson, 1978, p. 5)

The separation of mother and daughter is in this case very real, and in order to survive one imagines that the daughter will need to forge new relationships with the women in her husband's family, possibly with her mother-in-law. Indira Parikh (1989, p. 24) tells how she carried the unresolved issues in her turbulent childhood relationship with her mother into her relationship with her mother-in-law to be enacted and lived through until the original socially desirable conformity worked through defiance and rebellion to emerge as mutual understanding, deep trust and respect.

Within this oppressive patriarchal system women look to each other for practical and emotional support; this is possible because there is no nuclear family ideology to prevent it. Child care and household tasks are shared by the women of the family, and women take care of each other, giving each other physical and emotional support (Wilson, 1978, p. 27).

Asian women who have moved to Britain (particularly those who have come here to marry) may find themselves cut off from the female care and support they received in their own family. Their subsequent isolation and depression is likely to be misunderstood in a society where the nuclear family is seen as the norm, and where racism presents barriers to the seeking and offering of appropriate help (Wilson, 1978, pp. 25–9). Things have changed somewhat since Wilson described this state of affairs in 1978. Asian communities have grown in Britain, despite the deliberate attempt to split families by British immigration legislation. Asian women themselves have come together to form organisations and groups, offering services in their own communities, some on religious lines, or, like the United Kingdom's Asian Women's Conference (UKAWC), on issues of particular importance to women's daily lives (child care, care of elderly, health, immigration and so on).

While there has been a growth in support groups and services for Asian women in Britain, this also has not been without its problems. Rahila Gupta points out the

> gulf that exists between those Asian women who consider themselves part of the wider Black feminist movement (and in this context, accepting the description 'Black' as opposed to 'Asian' is significant) and the vast majority of Asian women on behalf of whom they campaign. The ideology of feminism, concepts of patriarchal oppression, and women's liberation have to be constantly played down in order to foster the atmosphere of trust to encourage women to come forward and use the services provided by women's groups and centres. (Gupta, 1988, p. 26)

The struggle for connection between women, wherever we look, is constrained by the patriarchal culture in which we operate.

Whilst we can see Asian women coming together, despite their differences, to offer each other support, the literature tells us very little about the experience of Asian women within mother-daughter relationships. Signe Hammer believes that 'the basic psychological mechanisms in the mother-daughter relationship are common to almost all women [whatever their race, ethnicity or class] in our society' (Hammer, 1976, p. xii). But the 'proof' for this lies in her own interpretation of her findings from interviews with a few mothers and daughters from different ethnic and class groups within American society. In her generalisations she fails to see that her own analysis of these 'psychological mechanisms' is based wholly on white, middle-class theories and understanding. How a relationship such as that between mother and daughter is experienced cannot be divorced from its social context.

Women of African Descent

The literature on women from African, African-American and Afro-Caribbean families gives us quite a different picture. Here we find the dangerously stereotypical 'strong, black matriarch', female head of household who has been blamed in the racist and sexist literature of white supremacy for the breakdown of 'the black family' and the emasculation of black men. One must wonder at the fear the Black female, who for the most part has struggled to raise her family in the face of poverty and oppression, must induce in both Black and white men who thus castigate her (Bryan, Dadzie and Scafe, 1985, p. 213). Or perhaps it is just another twist in the story of mother-blaming.

Of course there is truth in the image of Black women raising families without the support of a man, but as Bryan, Dadzie and Scafe point out

> We do not raise our families in this way because we are superwomen or 'sturdy Black bridges', but because we have been compelled to accept this responsibility both historically and as a result of the internalised sexism of many Black men today. There is no power or respect to be gained from performing such a task, particularly in a society which invalidates any family structure which does not conform to the nuclear model, with men as the providers and decision makers. The fact that Black women are often prepared to raise a family without a male figure around does, however, attest to a different kind of strength, and an independence which the pervading oppressive sexual stereotypes have not undermined. (Bryan, Dadzie and Scafe, 1985, p. 221)

Growing up as a daughter in a female-headed household must mean that some lessons are learnt about the independence of womanhood. Carol Stack (1974) in her study of family life in a poor Black American community found that 'Women's own accounts of their situations show how they have developed a strong sense of independence from men, evolved social controls against the formation of conjugal relationships, and limited the role of husband-father within the mother's domestic group'. The resulting attitudes of daughters may be reflected in Julia's comment that 'a woman has to have her own pride. She can't let a man rule her' (Stack, 1974). This respect, self-reliance and independence is exhibited by mothers and admired and emulated by daughters (Joseph, 1981).

Black mothers have offered their daughters the skills necessary to resist oppression, from the Black slave mothers who 'taught their children to trust their own self definitions and value themselves' (Collins, 1990, p. 51) to the Black mothers of today who teach their daughters 'to survive the interlocking structures of race, class and gender oppression while rejecting and transcending those same structures' (p. 124). As Collins points out

> Understanding this goal of balancing the need for the physical survival of their daughters with the vision of encouraging them to transcend the boundaries confronting them explains many apparent contradictions in Black mother-daughter relationships. Black mothers are often described as strong disciplinarians and overly protective; yet these same women manage to raise daughters who are self-reliant and assertive. (Collins, 1990, p. 125)

Whilst providing for their children may leave many Black mothers with little time or patience to show their daughters affection, Joseph's (1981) study shows that 'most Black daughters love and admire their mothers and are convinced that their mothers truly love them' (Collins, 1990, p. 127).

Black motherhood within racist countries has always been denigrated and devalued. There is a history of Black women being used to care for white people's children, often at the expense of their own born or unborn children. Here again we see the 'good' mother, 'bad' mother split in the controlling stereotypes of Black 'mammy' (the faithful, obedient servant of white families) and 'matriarch' (the dominant, castrating mother of her own family). Black mothers are only allowed to be seen as 'good' when they are caring for white families. As Collins points out

> By loving, nurturing and caring for her white children and 'family' better than her own, the mammy symbolises the

dominant group's perceptions of the ideal Black female relationship to elite white male power. (Collins, 1990, p. 71)

'Mammies' are certainly not expected to have any influence
over the white children they care for, although some did as
Adrienne Rich tells us:

> My black mother was 'mine' only for four years, during
> which she fed me, played with me, watched over me, sang to
> me, cared for me tenderly and intimately.

> 'Childless' herself she *was* a mother. She was slim, dignified,
> and very handsome, and from her I learned – nonverbally –
> a great deal about the possibilities of dignity in a degrading
> situation. (Rich, 1977, p. 254)

It is not surprisingly that Black women academics studying
the role of Black mothers find neither 'matriarchs' nor
'mammies' but complex individuals coping with great tenacity
under oppressive conditions (Hale, 1980; Dill, 1980; Ladner,
1972; McAdoo, 1985) who offer protection and pass on survival
skills to their daughters (Joseph, 1981; Collins, 1987).

White Working-Class Women

The so-called matriarchal nature of Black families is also to be
seen in studies of white working-class families. In the studies of
the 1950s by Young and Willmott (1958) in the East End of
London, the strength of the mother-daughter tie was com-
mented on by these male middle-class sociologists as some sort
of aberration. This was related to the 'power' of the mother
over the daughter, the daughter's 'inability' to move away from
this relationship into a more 'adult' one with her husband and
the subsequent exclusion of the husband.

The interdependency of working-class mothers and daughters is highlighted in a more recent study in the same area of
London by Jocelyn Cornwell. Whilst finding similarly close relationships between mothers and daughters, Cornwell's interpretation of this bond is quite different.

Cornwell found a great deal of sharing amongst the women,
especially of housework and childcare but not to the exclusion
of husbands, rather taking place in the daytime when the men

were at work. She also points out that

> whilst the relationship between the women are based on a mutual exchange of services, the quality of their relationships is very varied. Some relationships are based on shared skills and practical activities and that is all; others involve some degree of emotional intimacy and the mother and daughter are each other's confidante; still others are based simply on family loyalty and a sense of duty. In some cases, of course, the relationship between a mother and her daughter involves all these different dimensions. (Cornwell, 1984, p. 112)

The difference between these two sociological studies of East London family life is instructive. When Young and Willmott 'discovered' a close mother-daughter tie in this working-class community, they viewed it as an aberration of nuclear (middle-class) family life and expected its disappearance with the increasing affluence of the working-class families involved. Cornwell, thirty years later, found similarly strong ties between mothers and daughters but could see the connection between this and the woman's shared positions in the sexual division of labour. Whilst Young and Willmott studied what Cornwell calls the 'public' accounts of these families, Cornwell drew a distinction between the material she collected which was 'public' and 'private'. The 'public' accounts highlight the interdependency of mothers and daughters whilst the 'private' accounts speak to the variation in emotional relationships that one would expect to find within the structure of service and skills sharing.

It is tempting to romanticise the mother-daughter relationship in both Black and white working-class families, but this is as much a disservice as to suggest that all mother-daughter relationships are basically antagonistic. What we are talking about is real relationships between different people, with all the variety of emotional contact this implies, and taking place within the context of other relationships, not in exclusivity.

We can see how a patriarchal interpretation of the mother-daughter bond, such as that by Young and Willmott, can once again be used to blame women for the lack of marital cohesion that Young and Willmott thought they saw. Just as the Black 'matriarch' was blamed for the break-up of the Black family and emasculation of the Black male, so the white working-class 'matriarch' was blamed for the 'failure' of the working-class couple to establish a 'proper' (husband dominant, wife isolated) marriage.

But the term 'matriarch' implies a social and economic power that these women certainly do not have. Perhaps what Black and working-class women have in common is that their difficult circumstances highlight for them their own resources as women and how the combining of their resources may be necessary for their survival and the survival and betterment of their children. For power read guts.

Lesbian Existence and Female Intimacy

The ideology that offers us a distorted view of the mother-daughter relationship setting daughter against mother and mother against daughter in jealous rivalry is part of the overall attempt to keep women separate from each other and looking only to men for relationships.

This is the myth strongly sold to adolescent girls – give up your female friendships, put away childish things, you and your girlfriends are now rivals in the struggle to get a man who will meet all your needs. But girls don't give up on their girlfriends so easily and women have always come together to offer each other love and support, even if historians and theoreticians try to tell us otherwise. Because of men's fear of women's connection with each other the history of women's shared intimacy has been 'distorted, dismantled, destroyed' (Raymond, 1986, p. 4), particularly when it is seen as a threat to male domination. Sheila Jeffries (1985) tells us that

> in the eighteenth and nineteenth centuries many middle-class women had relationships with each other which in-cluded passionate declarations of love, nights spent in bed together sharing kisses and intimacies, and lifelong devo-tion, without exciting the least adverse comment.
>
> (Jeffries, 1985, p. 102)

Mothers and daughters were also unashamedly close, as with Frances Power Cobbe speaking about her mother:

She was the one being in the world whom I truly loved through all the passionate years of youth and early woman-hood; the only one who really loved me . . . No relationship in all the world, I think, can ever be so perfect as that of mother and daughter. (Cobbe, 1894, p. 99; quoted in Levine, 1990, p. 68)

Carroll Smith-Rosenberg (1975) informs us that in nine-teenth-century America women formed emotionally satisfying relationships with each other, and that 'An intimate mother-daughter relationship lay at the heart of this female world'.

These intimacies between women were permitted by men since they did not form a threat to marriage and to male supremacy, but as Celia Kitzinger points out:

Male indulgence of love between women ceased abruptly with the first wave of feminism, which brought a political analysis to sexual relationships. . . . As feminists increasingly challenged male dominance in all areas, and as new social and economic forces . . . presented middle-class women with the possibility of choosing not to marry and to be financially dependent on men, women's friendships with other women became a real alternative to marriage (rather than an ad-junct to it), and as such came to be seen by men as a threat. (Kitzinger, 1987, p. 41)

The response was to pathologise lesbianism, to set it apart from the normal, and to use it as a stick to beat women back into line. Feminists (women who dared to challenge men) were labelled lesbian, lesbians were labelled sick.

Embracing lesbianism can be very difficult when the word has been used by others and sometimes by yourself to denigrate and devalue, as Mo Ross described it on moving out of a con-ventional marriage into a lesbian existence:

I found the word lesbian very hard to say, very hard to claim. I couldn't attach it to myself. It sounded harsh. It sounded like those negative things that I'd heard all my life; like the negative things I'd said or talked about – *lezzie friends* – when I was growing up. (Ross, 1988, p. 175)

Not only was lesbianism pathologised but the blame for this 'sickness' was, of course, largely laid at the mother's door (see

Chapter Four). Psychoanalysts have referred to lesbianism as a 'repressed longing for mother' (Deutch, 1947); 'emotional incest with mother' (Wolff, 1977); the 'idealisation' of the mother and the projection of bad feelings onto the father and men generally due to the daughters 'almost symbiotic relationship' with her mother (McDougall, 1979). The mother is blamed for not giving the daughter enough affection, or for giving her too much, not allowing her to separate and develop emotionally by giving up her primary love object (the mother) in favour of firstly the father and then other men.

In our homophobic society the 'threat' of lesbianism becomes a useful antagonistic device between mother and daughter which may begin early in childhood with the daughter's loss of her mother's physical affection (see Chapter Three).

While in psychiatric circles attempts to pathologise, 'treat' and 'cure' lesbianism may have to some degree given way to a 'live and let live' approach, societal and political forces still ensure that lesbians for the most part remain invisible. Women are still persecuted in their everyday lives for proclaiming themselves to be women who love women, and mothers are still held responsible for their daughter's 'deviancy'.

MOTHERS AND DAUGHTERS AS FRIENDS

Women's close friendships can be empowering and related to high levels of self-esteem. Berzoff (1985), for example, found that 'for many women friendship plays a central role in the articulation of self and identity' and those women who described very close friendships with other women also had high levels of ego development. In recent studies of adolescent development using a 'connection' rather than a 'separation' model (see Chapter Four) psychologists have found this is also true for daughters in relation to their mothers (Grotevant and Cooper, 1983). The notion that a daughter staying connected to her mother results in her remaining a child and lacking a 'sense of self' is perhaps beginning to lose ground.

For it is not mothers but the woman-hating culture in which we grow that threatens our sense of self: it is in trying to play the role of 'real woman' as defined by male culture that a woman loses touch with what is her real self, whilst women are also being taught to hate their 'original Selves' (Raymond, 1986, p. 6), and other women. Raymond suggests that 'if we were confronted with the mother as a female friend who puts women first in her life' then women would feel quite differently about themselves and other women. The obvious danger here is again seeing the solution to some extent in the mothering, which on the one hand holds out some hope that women can grow loving themselves and other women, but on the other condemns the mother who does not 'produce' the desired effect in the face of all the mitigating factors in our society. In loving ourselves and other women we must also not forget that our mother is a woman equally worthy of our affections.

Mothers and daughters can and will be friends – perhaps not always the 'perfect' friendship which existed between Crystal Eastman and her mother Annis Ford Eastman, as described here by Crystal's brother Max:

> The great love of Crystal's life, never replaced by any man or woman, was our mother. I have never seen or heard of a friendship more perfect than theirs. They asked no greater happiness than to be together; in separation they wrote to each other constantly, as often as twice a week; and yet, each rejoiced with admiration in the outgoing career of the other. No wish to retain, no glimmer of possessiveness, filial or parental, ever marred the sweet, tranquil, confident, life-enhancing flow of their friendship. (Quoted in Payne, 1983, p. 140)

What is often possible is something like the mutual concern, support and companionship which exists between many mothers and daughters (Baruch and Barnett, 1983), and which can help the mother to develop as much as the daughter. As Ann Gabriel's story shows us mothers and daughters can learn from each other:

> So at 55 I came to make the decision to retire, but strangely with no real idea of what I was going to do. What followed came as much as a surprise to me as it did to my friends. I retired at more or less the same time that Susan [her daughter], now finished her training, went to London to live. She was becoming more and more interested in radical fem-

inism. Our discussions continued, and I found myself very interested for the first time in my life in something that seemed to be entirely positive; women not depending on someone else's approval, or someone else's decisions, but living and working together to support each other in developing each other's strengths as well as our own. As the months passed my relationship with Susan began to change again. She did not try to influence me, but just by being herself I began truly to realise all that I owed her from the past. For me, feeling close again to her and her ideas brought me great joy, one that has gone on growing, a deeper joy than I have ever known before in my whole life. . . . At last, in my wonderful new relationship with my daughter, and through the interest and bond I feel with her in our commitment to women through feminism, along with forging a new set of beliefs, I seem able suddenly, to be me. (Gabriel, 1985, pp. 68–9)

The mother here relates to her daughter as an adult, an equal, they are able to have a new mother-daughter relationship and through this the mother regains her self.

Of course not all daughters want their mothers to be their friends, they may consider mother/daughter relations and friendship to be mutually exclusive and mother's attempts to become a friend may prove an embarrassment. For some daughters the feeling that they have missed out on mothering brings the response in adulthood that they do not want their mother as a friend but as a mother, presumably as someone to care for them unconditionally and without expectation of reciprocated care.

An equality in the relationship between mother and adult daughter requires some changes in the power imbalance which existed between the adult mother and child daughter. The daughter grows and the relationship must change both on the daughter's part and on the mother's.

The daughter too must be willing to see her mother as a woman, a perception too often denied in a society which fails to see beyond the mother to the woman she is. This will be explored further in the final chapter.

Note

Some of the work cited in this chapter is American in origin and therefore uses the term 'Black' as meaning of African descent, Asian, Latina and Native American women being known as 'Women of Colour' (see Audre Lorde, interviewed by Parmar and Kay, 1988). In British works 'Black' is used to encompass people of African and Asian descent.

8 The Final Loss

There is little attention given in the mother-daughter literature to the potential for a mutually dependent and supportive relationship between an adult daughter and her mother. Rather it moves on to the so-called 'role-reversal' of later years where the adult daughter takes on the role of carer to her elderly dependant mother, or to that final separation – the death of the mother. In this way the literature continues to emphasise the themes of one-way dependency and the struggle for separation.

The daughter's emotional dependency on the mother and the effect of this on her ability to 'grow up' and separate can be seen in the literature to exist side by side with the elderly mother's physical dependency on her adult daughter. The daughter's taking care of her elderly mother is not seen as proof of her adult status but ironically as proof of the opposite. The daughter in this sense can only be 'freed' to develop as an individual when the mother is dead – and even then there will be problems. The possibility of mutual caring and interdependency gets lost within the narrow constraints of the polarised concepts of dependency and independency.

In the social policy literature on taking care of adult and elderly 'dependants', the person who needs to be 'taken care of' is very rarely portrayed as a person in their own right who also has much to give. Rather the so-called dependant is portrayed, as Lois Keith (1990) points out, as 'passive, feeble and demanding'. This is done in order to highlight the very real plight of carers who are often 'coping alone'. But as Keith points out this leads to the disabled person being presented as 'the other', a non-person. The images presented in the social policy literature are of active carers and passive recipients of care, the one-way image again of dependency. For mothers and daughters this has meant that we hear the voice of the daughter but not that of the mother (which as we have seen is also largely the case at other life stages), and we concentrate on dependency and ignore, and therefore never really find out about, the possibility of interdependency and mutual care.

In ignoring the mutuality of care we are also in danger of negating the real effects of the mother's death upon the daughter and seeing the daughter's grief as at times going beyond the limits of the acceptable. A daughter's profound grief may then be explained in terms of the theory of separation, the daughter is seen as having failed to separate adequately from her mother and so has real problems 'letting go' of her when she dies. Within this theory the daughter also has now to face the world alone and as an adult which she has not been practiced at doing.

DAUGHTERS WHO CARE

Although not all daughters will take on the role of carer to their aged mothers, recent social policy literature has highlighted the fact that many do. Let us first then look at this scenario.

We will not be surprised to find that what the literature tells us is that women's caring roles extend from being a 'good' and obedient child, through being a 'good' wife and unselfish mother to being a 'good' and dutiful adult daughter to her elderly parents. If the daughter has not taken on the traditional roles of wife and mother she is seen as being particularly available to care for elderly dependant relatives since she is considered to have no other commitments (Pulling, 1987; Allen, 1989).

Qureshi and Walker in a study of elderly people and their families ask 'which relative was the one most likely to be providing care?' and answer

> As in all similar studies, daughters were predominant (see for example, Hunt, 1978; Nissel and Bonnerja, 1982). Over half (52 per cent) of elderly people receiving help (and just under one-quarter of all elderly people) had at least one daughter helping. One in four people with helpers were being helped by a lone daughter. (Qureshi and Walker, 1989, p. 120)

What studies of carers has shown is that there is a hierarchy of care, both in people's expectations and in practice, in that where there is no spouse able to care for an elderly dependant person the most likely person to be doing so is a daughter (especially if she is single and has no children), or where there is no daughter available, a daughter-in-law (Qureshi and Walker, 1989).

Throughout the life-cycle women are expected to show that they care *about* someone by caring *for* them (Graham, 1983), and so it is for adult daughters and their elderly parents. Since on average women live longer than men (in the elderly population in Britain their are five women to every three men), this parent is often a mother.

Because the emphasis of this research has been to effect changes in social policy with regards to improving matters both for elderly people and for their carers it has, appropriately but in a limiting way, concentrated principally on the physical, psychological and social effect of caring on the main carer (Ungerson, 1987; Hicks, 1988) who is often a daughter (Lewis and Meredith, 1988), and to a lesser extent on the feelings evoked in both the carer and the cared for by this 'dependant' relationship.

While we currently know very little about the daughter's perception of her relationship with her mother at this stage, we know even less about the mother's. It is likely that their perceptions will differ, for example Lucy Rose Fischer (1986) found that in interviewing mothers and daughters the daughters used the term 'role-reversal' about their relationship with their elderly mother, while the mothers did not.

Helen Evers (1984; 1985), in a study of fifty women aged seventy-five and over, found that older women's perceptions of their own dependency did not necessarily correlate with the degree of care they needed from others. Evers says of these women that

> their health and physical capacity for leading autonomous and independent lives did not, however, bear a straightforward relation with the women's perceptions of the extent to which they were actually 'in charge' of their own lives, as opposed to dependent on others to organise things for them. (Evers, 1984, p. 307)

Evers distinguished two broad categories of response, those women who 'see themselves as being in control of their own lives despite in some cases very considerable reliance on others for help with the basic activities of daily life' who she calls 'active initiators'; and those who 'see themselves as being largely dependent on others to organise and structure their lives for them, despite in some cases apparently having the capacity for relatively autonomous living' whom she calls 'passive responders'.

The use of labels such as 'active initiator' and 'passive responder' implies that the woman's response to her situation and perception of herself within it is wholly dependent on her personality. It should be considered, however, that the relationships that she has with others and their perception of her will also have an effect on her response. Freda, for example, in Janet Ford and Ruth Sinclair's 'Sixty Years On' (1987) talks of how her position within the household has been so eroded by her family's attitude that she is no longer 'capable', her daughters complain about her standards of cleaning, and along with her husband, Frank, make all the decisions, effectively rendering her passive and dependent. She says

> One of my girls is at the house now, cleaning. She makes me cross really. She interferes too much. She says I don't look after things well enough and they will smell . . . I resent it. I know I have diabetes, and as well sometimes I don't always get there in time, but it's not how she says. I can still look after my house. I'd rather they didn't interfere . . . Frank makes all the decisions, and there are times when I do mind when Frank and the family sort of gang up against me. There seems to have been quite a lot of that going off in our household lately. You see they want me to do what they want. They keep making changes in the house. They annoy me when when they want to take over in the house. Frank and the family make all the decisions – what we do; what's to be done in the house sort of thing. I think I should be given the preference of deciding what's to be done. They think I'm not capable. But I disagree. I think while I can organise the house I should be allowed to. But I keep quiet because I think, well, it's better to keep the peace. (Ford and Sinclair, 1987, pp. 69–70)

The ageism of our society affects women differently to men. We see, for example, that an older man may be considered 'distinguished' whilst an older women loses her charms. This is very clearly reflected in the media's exhortations that women 'keep young and beautiful' (Itzin, 1986). Daughters are taught that they will replace mothers, that their power comes through joining with father, and so Freda's experience is probably not unusual. As Barbara Macdonald says

> It becomes clear that the present attitude of women in their twenties and thirties has been shaped since childhood by patriarchy to view the older woman as powerless, less important than the fathers and the children, and there to serve them both; and like all who serve, the older woman soon becomes invisible. (Macdonald and Rich, 1984, p. 40)

When mothers become less able to care for their husbands and children, then the daughter is expected to move in and replace her. Ageism and sexism combine to perpetuate the oppression of women, it sets up barriers between younger and older women, between daughter and mother as they compete to be 'best carer'.

Burden of Care

In the social policy literature the picture we are presented with is the very real, albeit one-sided, one of the burden of care many daughters take on and tackle in relative isolation. For the daughter it can mean having no life of her own and suffering the psychological and physical stresses that caring alone for a very dependent person brings. In physical terms caring can mean anything from providing meals and housework support, through help with personal care like washing, dressing and toileting, to being 'on duty' constantly throughout the day and often being woken at night. It can involve the daily grind of doing almost everything for another person – lifting an incontinent elderly person onto the toilet every half-hour (Hicks, 1988, p. 39) or, where for example, they have Alzheimer's disease, having to be their brain 'here's your knife, here's your fork, eat your dinner . . .' (Lewis and Meredith, 1988, p. 43); and if the elderly person is suffering from dementia, becoming resigned to the fact that throughout all this they may not even recognise you.

Suzanne Steinmetz interviewed 104 adult children who were caring for dependent elderly relatives. Many had been caring, without support, for long periods and the burden of that caregiving was obvious to the interviewer. A typical response to the question 'Do you find this caregiving a burden?' came from a sixty-year-old daughter who had been caring for her eighty-four-year old mother for three years; she says 'It's distressing. I would not describe it as a burden, I don't consider my mother to be a burden . . . ' (Steinmetz, 1989, p. 221). It is difficult for the daughter to see the 'burden of caregiving' as something different from saying her mother is a burden. Women's caring *for* and caring *about* are not easily separated. To be a 'caring' daughter is to take on the burden of the caring work, to do otherwise is to be 'selfish'.

The work involved in the caring relationship cannot in reality be divorced from the quality of the relationship between the two people involved. The stresses on the daughter of caring for her elderly mother and the stress on the mother of being in such a dependent position must have an effect on the mother-daughter relationship. For example, Cherrill Hicks tells us of a sixty-three year old widow, Delia Holland, caring alone for her eighty-two year old mother who has Parkinson's disease and is partially paralysed after five strokes. Delia says 'She's taken over my life; I live her life more than mine'. Not unnaturally Delia finds herself resenting her mother of this, especially since the illness has changed her mother from a quiet, non-dominant person to a demanding and verbally aggressive one (Hicks, 1988).

A mother's domineering and aggressive attitude in such a situation may not be wholly due to a medical condition but could be a reflection of the distress a mother feels at having to depend so heavily on her daughter coupled with the embarrassment and frustration of her position. Accepting full care from a daughter may be a particular issue for a mother who has always prided herself on her independence and ability to care for others.

Caring for an elderly relative in Western culture, like motherhood, is an unrewarded and isolating activity. Other relatives tend to maintain some distant relationship when the 'chosen' main carer takes up their role, support from 'caring' agencies is sadly lacking. The lack of support for the carers of elderly people is a reflection of the lack of respect for elderly people in a society which values productivity above all else. Caring for an elderly person is devalued, the only societal reward consists of the knowledge of having fulfilled obligations based on duty and love.

This is not to say that in other cultures the burden of care does not fall on the females of the family. In India, for example, a daughter-in-law, or a number of daughters-in-law may be responsible for the physical care of elderly parents. Again, as in motherhood, the carer may not be working in isolation but may have the support of other women within the extended family. For Asian women living in Britain this may not be the case, and support may be even less easy to find because of the structural racism of social services, and the racist assumption that 'other cultures' will 'care for their own'.

Easier access to social service provision and/or the ability to pay for nursing care may ease the burden of physical care for some middle-class carers. However, the societal and moral imperative for women to take care of their own, and particularly for daughters to look after aged parents is not easily ignored, and even where it is financially possible to pay for help, the daughter may not be able to give herself 'permission' to do so, and she will in any case continue to assume responsibility for the quality of that care.

Caring Relationships

Underlying the acts of care by daughters for mothers are a range of emotional involvements and a variety of relationships which must be related to the previous mother/daughter relationship.

Joan Barefoot (1986) illustrates this well in her novel *Duet for Three*. The conflictual relationship between a daughter in her sixties and her eighty-year-old and increasingly physically dependent mother is shown in relation to their separate recollections of their shared history. One feels that it is not just through her professed duty to God that the daughter June continues to look after a mother who she feels has never shown her any real love and affection, but also perhaps in order to try and finally receive that love (although she is unable at this stage to open up to it when it is offered).

The mother, Aggie, has never identified with her daughter who from being born is seen as so unlike her and so like her unloved husband. At a time when she needs her daughter's care she finds herself with little respect for this daughter who seems never to have been able to live her own life to the full, but has always found her duty to God prevailing. June sees her mother's increasing dependency paradoxically as her means of escape as she initially pursues the idea of her mother going into a nursing home, but of course this also is not without its burden of guilt. For June her relationship with her mother was already difficult and had been since she was a child, but for some daughters who have shared happier times with their mothers the blow of caring for someone who does not recognise them or who is unrecognisable as mother, as often happens with dementia, may be more difficult to bear. One of Claire Ungerson's respondents, Mrs Hall, who has shared a long and close relationship with her mother, finds herself trying to care for her seventy-six year old mother who is suffering from senile dementia. Her mother is incontinent and very confused, she 'flies at' her daughter and will not allow her to do any of the personal caring tasks for her. Mrs Hall says

> Oh, it upsets me. I've turned off, really. I don't think she's my mum, really. We were always so close. If I wasn't well she'd come and look after the family; she used to do everything. (Ungerson, 1987, p. 118)

Ungerson found that a number of the daughters and daughters-in-law caring for mothers and mothers-in-law found themselves using an emotional cut-off mechanism in order to cope with caring tasks. It is easier to carry out these tasks as though one were a stranger than allow the emotions of the long history shared together to surface.

For the daughter who does not feel the bonds of mutual affection with her mother it can be extremely difficult to ignore the strictures of a society which believes daughters should care for their elderly parents. This, combined with some unfinished business in the mother-daughter relationship, for example if the daughter feels she never has had the affection she needs from her mother, can lead to a forced and distressful relationship of care, as for one of Cherrill Hicks's respondents:

> We never got on very well. She was never a good mother to me when I was a child. I was a bright kid, won prizes, I'd be in school plays – she'd never come and see them. I wouldn't say I like her or dislike her. I don't think I've ever loved her because she's never loved me. If she wasn't my mother I wouldn't have anything to do with her. (Hicks, 1988, p. 32)

The term 'role-reversal' is often used in situations where adult children becomes carers to their elderly parents (although Steinmetz makes the case for changing the terminology to 'generational inversion': 1989, pp. 47–9). For some daughters caring for their elderly mothers 'role-reversal', as the accepted terminology, may be the only way they can express their experience of the relationship, although what they are actually experiencing may be much more complex than that of daughter as mother and mother as child, as the term implies. For some daughters this 'role-reversal' may even seem to have taken place much earlier in life, perhaps in childhood, where the daughter felt herself to be more the carer than the cared-for in the relationship with her mother.

Fischer has highlighted the potential changes in power within the mother-daughter relationship that 'role-reversal' may convey. She points out that role-reversal is not a straightforward handing over of power from mother to daughter but may reflect a variety of scenarios. A daughter physically caring for her mother may feel she holds little power either over her mother's life or her own, particularly where her mother continues to treat her as a child.

> She tells me what to do all the time as if I were a five-year-old. She always tells me not to forget this and that. She tries to dominate me. [a sixty-two year old daughter caring for her ninety-three year old mother] (Steinmetz, 1989, p. 54)

A mother and daughter who have competed to be 'best carer' may struggle for the power base when one of them (that is the mother) is now clearly in more need of care than the other. Or a mother who has cared for others all her life may with some relief accept that caring from her daughter and slip easily into the role of being mothered herself, whilst the daughter may also get some pleasure out of being able to fulfil this socially approved role.

As with mothering itself, 'power' for the daughter here actually means responsibility, but for an elderly mother it may be felt as a loss of person power to determine her own life. For a mother used to being independent this loss of personal power coupled with a loss of dignity may be more than she can tolerate, resulting in anger and aggressive behaviour. A daughter may feel her life has been taken over and controlled by her mother to the extent that her anger and frustration is translated into verbal and/or physical abuse of her mother.

It is unlikely that power is simply reversed but involves a protracted process of negotiation between mother and daughter which will have its own effect on their relationship (Lewis and Meredith, 1988). Both mother and daughter may feel the loss of their previous relationship as a new way of relating is in process.

Research by Bromberg (1983a; 1983b) lends credence to the notion of supportive relationships between mothers and adult daughters and negates the concept of 'role-reversal'. Mother and daughter do not 'swop roles' in the sense of daughter becoming the adult and mother becoming the child – a myth perpetuated by ageist theory where elderly people are regarded as children – but rather take on different tasks in response to changing needs.

A mother and daughter who have been previously close and mutually supportive are likely to retain that supportiveness even though the ways in which they offer each other support may change. Jane Lewis and Barbara Meredith point out that among their respondents a mutually supportive relationship was more easily sustained as mothers became increasingly dependent on physical care, where the daughter did not also have a husband and children to care for, where the mother was not suffering from mental illness and where mother and daughter 'seemed to have maintained their own identities and regarded each other with an affection beyond that induced by the filial bond'

(Lewis and Meredith, 1989, p. 51). All the completely mutually supporting relationships they found in their small study were between single women carers and their mothers, usually based on friendship, independence and shared interests. For example one daughter says

> My mother and I lived together because we chose to, we liked each other . . . we shared a common home – we could laugh together . . . I was an independent person, so was my mother, we were living together, I wasn't just looking after her. (Lewis and Meredith, 1989, p. 54)

For some women this sharing had meant their mothers doing the work in the home and looking after them whilst they worked outside the home. When the mother's deteriorating health meant that the daughter took on more of the tasks of care the mutually supportive relationships were sustained by companionship

> It was good having someone else to share life with. I could still enjoy talking to her and she continued to take a vast interest in what I did. I used to enjoy giving her pleasure – making a fuss of parties and celebrations, bringing things home from holidays. (Lewis and Meredith, 1989, p. 56)

The care of the daughters was appreciated by the mothers and the daughters felt they also got something from this relationship. There is also a feeling of mutual interest and mutual concern that suggests an interdependent adult-adult relationship in which power is not such an issue. This then is not 'role-reversal' but a mutuality of care provided by both mother and daughter for each other and changing 'as needs, abilities, and opportunities make necessary or appropriate' (Kraus, 1990).

Where the element of real choice as to whether or not to care for one's elderly mother (or be cared for by one's daughter) is missing, as it is for so many daughters and mothers, and where having taken on that task, whether willing or not, one is left to cope alone with it, the actual quality of the mother-daughter relationship is distorted. The changes which may take place in the relationship at this time may also reflect on how the daughter faces and deals with her mother's death.

DEATH OF MOTHER

Where mother and daughter are close companions the daughter faces the loss of that companionship when her mother dies, if in looking after her mother she has also lost an independent social life she may find it an even more daunting prospect. Stella is a single woman caring for her mother. She says

> We're very alike, we talk a lot, that's one of the problems – it's very much like a marriage. The sort of relationship I was living before was a normal, independent adult life, even though we were in the same house. The emotional relationship was not so intense. I'm worried about whether I'll be able to cope when she dies. (Hicks, 1988, p. 57)

Similarly in Katherine Allen's study of single women one women 'who had lived with her mother, supported her financially and served as her confidant', was deeply affected by her mother's death:

> She was 82. She had lived her life, and I was grateful I had been able to keep her home because so many people get to the point where they can't be taken care of at home. Oh, it took me months to get over coming home to an empty house. It's an awful feeling. I'd expect her to be sitting in that chair . . . I missed her terrible and it took months. (Allen, 1989; p. 89)

Guilt and Grief

> Her death brought immense relief, but the guilt of feeling that relief added an intolerable dimension to my inconsolable grief. (Pitfield, 1985, p. 166)

When the mother dies there may be, as well as a profound sense of loss, a feeling of relief at a burden of care lifted, a feeling of regret at not enough done or said, a feeling of guilt at not being a 'perfect' daughter or a 'perfect' carer.

Excessive guilt in bereavement has been seen by psychoanalysts as proof of an ambivalent relationship. Melanie Klein (1937) saw guilt as the bereaved person's anger turned inwards as a defence against the 'triumph' over the dead. Since the daughter's relationship with her mother is almost by definition seen as ambivalent, the daughter's feelings of guilt and self-reproach on the death of her mother fit well into this theory. What this ignores, of course, is the fact that these theories, which fit so well together, are based on Western patriarchal notions of both the mother-daughter relationship and the process of bereavement.

Guilt can equally be viewed as a straightforward accompaniment to responsibility. If women see themselves and are seen as wholly responsible for the care of their dependents, then any 'failure' in that care (including death) will carry with it some degree of guilt feelings. Perhaps a few women who have totally devoted themselves to the care of their mother in her dying days, weeks, and even years may escape intense guilt feelings – but for most daughters there will be something they can reproach themselves for in what they did or did not do or say.

The grief that accompanies the loss of one's mother may be profound. It may be felt that what has been lost in the mother's death is not only the person but some part of oneself. The connection between mother and daughter at some deep level whether or not they had a a 'good' or 'bad' relationship cannot be explained away via the theory of a 'lack of separation' between them.

On the evening of her mother's death Simone de Beauvior was in touch with this depth of despair

> Suddenly, at eleven, an outburst of tears that almost denigrated into hysteria.
> Amazement. When my father died I did not cry at all. I had said to my sister, 'It will be the same for Maman'. I had understood all my sorrows until that night: even when they flowed over my head I recognised myself in them. This time my despair escaped from my control: someone other than myself was weeping in me. (Beauvoir, 1969, p. 28)

With the mother's death the possibility of the daughter's re-conciliation with the mother – an underlying theme in the mother-daughter literature – is gone. That reconciliation may take place at the death-bed of the mother, as in novels (for example see Smedley, 1973; Yezierska, 1925). But it is more likely that the daughter will reach some stage of understanding of herself and her relationship with her mother some time after her mother's death, when there will be no opportunity to go back to her mother and share her new insights with her. This can be a cause of great sadness to the daughter. Two friends of Judith Arcana told her

> How lucky you are; your mother is here; she is alive. When we came to know ourselves, to understand some, at least, of what we had wanted from our mothers, of what they had done with us; when we came to a space in which we could have taken this on, our mothers were dead. (Arcana, 1979, p. 166)

The mother's death itself may lead to a better understanding of one's mother – having foreclosed the possibility of ever getting whatever perfect love was expected from mother she can be considered in a more realistic light as the woman she was.

Separation Revisited

Of course there are those who will say that perhaps it is not possible to come to an understanding of oneself and one's mother while the mother is alive. If we believe that mother-daughter separation is necessary for the daughter's psychological growth into adulthood, then for some daughters the death of their mother is their release into adulthood and an identity of their own.

There is some suggestion in the literature that whatever the daughter's age, if she has continued to have a close and connected relationship with her mother then she will find herself with some emptiness within herself which is not only about loss but is about her ability or rather inability, to stand on her own two feet, to be independent. It is as if the daughter should be capable of fully functioning without the support of her mother (or anyone else's support) from an early age, and that failure to do so is the reason for the depths of her grief when her mother dies. Whereas a widow's need to learn to 'cope alone' is not only accepted but required (it should be seen that she was dependent on her husband) a daughter should, if she is developmentally mature enough, continue to function as usual apart from some brief interlude of 'normal' bereavement after her mother's death.

Where mother and daughter have lived together and been so close as to function in a similar way to a married couple then one would expect a larger degree of adaptation to be allowed for the daughter. The daughter may have until this time been viewed as in a childlike role in relation to her mother in spite of the adult functions she has performed (providing financially and sharing mutual care with the mother). Katherine Allen (1989) points out that 'The loss of a parent . . . gave women who lived with their parents all their lives their first sense of independence.' At age sixty-two one of Allen's respondents 'felt like an adult for the first time in her life': she had never been alone until her parents died and then her life changed because she 'had to go out and do things and make friends'.

The opportunity to be independent may however be more the issue here than the degree of separation and maturity achieved. As we have already seen in relation to daughters as carers the time leading up to the mother's death is likely to be one where the daughter is carrying out fully the job of provider and carer, and is certainly not in a 'dependent' position. For independence we should perhaps substitute 'freedom', from the responsibility of care and the opportunity to please oneself.

David Gutmann (1979) has suggested a link between the onset of mental illness in older women 'with failure to separate from the mother, whether or not the mother is still alive' (Abramson, 1987, p. 9). In David Gutmann's terms how well a daughter adapts to the death of her mother will depend on the extent to which the daughter has already separated from her mother since those who are 'less separated' may 'refuse to let their mother die'. Again we see that women are expected to find the internal strength to cope with loss and to carry on as fully functioning adults (that is taking care of others). Not being able to do this, looking to others for support, is seen as narcissistic and immature. Women do not appear to have the right to be mature and have their needs met in the way men are. That women may indeed have lost their central source of support when their mother dies is seen as evidence of their lack of psychological separation and growth, as proof that they are not yet grown, rather than as evidence that women are mutually supportive and that mothers and daughters can offer each other a great deal in terms of emotional and practical support. One of Arcana's respondents sounds almost apologetic when she says

> In relation to my mother, I was never an adult until she died, ad when she died I was left like a child without a mother. I feel a very strong tie to my mother even now. At 62 I would like to have a mother. I could cry. (Arcana, 1979, p. 167)

Surely she is entitled to feel this without her maturity being questioned. Only in a society where we pretend that being 'grown up' means not needing the care and support of others is it seen as ludicrous for a sixty-two year old to still need a mother. Because women are more able to express this need than men, and because they are seen to have a greater need (bearing in mind men's emotional needs are usually met by women without men having to ask or even admit need), then this need becomes woman's 'failure', her inability to be an adult.

With a clear belief that a daughter's maturity hinges on the degree to which she has separated from her mother, Jane Abramson (1987) set about conducting a study to see how far separation affects later adaptation to loss and in particular to the mother's death. When she found no correlation between adaptation to maternal loss and degree of separation, Abramson concluded that her study had been too small or that she had made the assessments 'too early'.

The competency and able functioning of some of the women she interviewed who were, under Abramson's criteria, not separated enough she puts down to 'narcissism' (using others as a 'prop'), 'superficial functioning' and the development of a 'false-self': she believes that had she interviewed them later they 'might have performed less impressively'. This demonstrates yet again that we reach research conclusions via our own biases, all the while upholding those theories we started out with.

Reconciliation

The death of the mother is only in the physical sense a final separation. The relationship lives on in the daughter's mind and there is still a lot of work to be done on it. When the sharpness of the grief lessens, when the daughter takes control of the crying which seems to come from some very deep place within her, and when she begins to forgive herself and her mother for all the things they should have done and said but didn't, then she may start to feel the 'ordinary' sadness of her loss.

Whether or not we consider it to be with the 'internalised mother' the conversations go on in the daughter's head. The relationship has the potential for change in this way after the mother's death. The sadness of not being able to 'check it out' is difficult but perhaps is part of the process of integrating the dead mother into the self.

> Slowly I find myself being weaned from her material presence. Yet, filled with her as never before. It is I now who represent us both. I am our mutual past. I am my mother and my self. She gave me love, to love myself, and to love the world. I must remember how to love. . . .
> I knew a beautiful woman once. And she was my mother. I knew a tenderness once. And it was my mother's. Oh, how happy I was to be loved.
> And now I mourn her. I mourn that cornerstone. I mourn her caring. I mourn the one who always hoped for me. I mourn her lost image of me. The lost infant in myself. My lost happiness. I mourn my own eventual death. My life now is only mine. . . .
> Every blade, every leaf, every seed in my portion of the world had shifted. Your presence hovers everywhere, over house, over garden, over dreams, over silence. You are within me. I'll not lose you. (Toby Talbot, 1980)

Towards the end of *Duet for Three* June and Aggie have been sorting out a lifetime's accumulation of belongings stored in the attic. Some of it comes out of their shared history but mainly it tells something of Aggie's life before June was born. June looks at the carefully-kept items and photographs from Aggie's past for some answers as to who this woman, her mother, is and who she has been. She realises that she knows very little

> June wonders what came over Aggie, admitting fear, so unlike her. Although she is no longer so sure of precisely what is like Aggie, and what is unlike. There are all those faces,

without much resemblance to one another; the girl sitting in a farmhouse kitchen, stitching pillowcases; the young woman in that family photograph, who made that dress; the mother who apparently danced and sang with her child, although the child cannot remember; the widow who sat staring out of the windows after her husband dies; the woman who punched holes in walls, and rose before dawn, and sat with her feet up on the kitchen counter in the mornings, laughing with the dairy man; the one kneading dough and hitting cash register keys; the one with her nose buried in a book; the one sipping her first drink, laughing about how it tickled; the one who stitched a nightgown for her daughter, and took that daughter back, along with a grandchild, even though she didn't want to; the one whose eyes were rimmed with redness on a few occasions, although she would not weep in front of June; when her granddaughter finally left home, when her friend finally moved away; the one defying June and God with irritating, blasphemous questions.

The one who sometimes in the mornings looks up despairingly from wet sheets. And also the dead one with the secret, from the dream last night. (Barefoot, 1986, p. 248)

The daughter has to stop looking at the mother with a childlike gaze, just as the mother has to recognise the adult her daughter has become.

A daughter's recognition of her mother as a woman may not come until it is too late to converse with her, or it may just seem impossible to have that conversation while she is here. The reconciliation with the mother, the daughter's understanding of their connections and the acceptance of their differences, may be something she needs to come to terms with within herself.

Some mothers, in contemplating their own death, may feel the need to tell their daughters how they feel before it is too late to do so, as did Ann Scott's mother probably 'in a whirlwind of emotion' after reading Simone de Beauvoir's *A Very Easy Death*. She writes to her daughter

> . . . when one is in one's terminal illness it is too late to talk about one's feelings, past and actual. . . . So I want to tell you

now, for you to remember then (in case I don't get another moment like this in the next twenty years) that I love you devotedly, no matter how bitchy you are sometimes; that I think you are getting to be a bigger and better person as you grow older; that I admire you for your struggles to mature and liberate yourself; that I respect your intellect; that I am proud to have had a hand in your upbringing; and that I hope we shall be friends as long as I live. It's strange that I have this attachment to you, since we are such different characters. (quoted in Payne, 1983, p. 373)

Some are aware, because they have been there themselves, that their daughters may need some form of communication with them after their death. Anne Sexton, finding herself at forty, on a plane thinking about her dead mother and wishing she could speak with her thought of her daughter in this same position, wrote her a letter for those moments when she wouldn't be there, the central message of which was

1. I love you.
2. You *never* let me down.
3. I know. I was there once. I *too*, was 40 and with a dead mother who I still needed. . . . (quoted in Payne, 1983, p. 18)

Both these communications took the form of letters which is perhaps an easier way than direct conversation to say what one is feeling, especially for middle-class mothers and daughters.

It is noticeable that such communications from mothers to daughters are usually a complete expression of love, while those from daughters to mothers are more a process of working out the complexities of the daughter's feelings towards the mother, and often can be hurtful. When these letters are actually sent (some are not but are kept as part of the daughter's own working-out process) it may be very difficult for the mother to respond. For what should she do? Take on board the blame for the daughter's feelings and blame herself for being a mother? Tell the daughter how she herself has been hurt at times and try to share out the guilt? Having worked through her feelings of humiliation and anger at having received such a letter one mother finally writes to her daughter

I know that I love and care for you, perhaps as Johann says at the end of *Scenes from a Marriage*, – 'in my inadequate way', and I think you love and care for me, too. So what more is there to say? (quoted in Payne, 1983, p. 365)

9 "But We're Not One"

But we're not one, we're worlds apart.
You and I.
Child of my body, bone of my bone,
Apple of my eye.

(Rosalie Sorrels, 1974)

The story of a mother and daughter relationship is two stories. It is the story of two different lives, of two different people separated by generation and by the changing role of women, yet connected by blood, by body and by womanhood. The literature on mother-daughter relationships has to date been biased towards the daughter's perception of the relationship. The mother-daughter relationship has been viewed from the perspective of the daughter attempting to grow up and find her own identity. In this it has also been the story of individual development rather than the development of a relationship between two people. The development of the mother as an individual has hardly been viewed at all. But in order to attempt to understand the relationship we need also to have some understanding of the mother within it and some understanding of the process of negotiation between mother and daughter as their relationship proceeds and changes.

MOTHER'S STORY

Our attempt to understand the mother's story is complicated by the fact that we are considering the mother as a *mother* rather than as a woman. Motherhood carries with it massive cultural expectations to which both the mother and the daughter relate. We have seen how this affects the daughter's view of her mother, how being a powerless child in the face of an 'omnipotent' mother affects the child's view of her mother; how the mother as socialiser and carrier of cultural norms appears as restrictive and controlling to the daughter as well as her carer; how the daughter whilst experiencing the mother's power over her also sees the mother's powerlessness within wider society; how mother as solely responsible for the development of the daughter carries the blame for any failure in this area; and in failing to be the 'perfect mother' is bound to be a disappointment to the daughter.

No wonder the daughter feels ambivalent – should she support the mother in her powerless position within patriarchy, or reject the mother and align with the more powerful father? Does supporting the mother mean offering oneself as victim of patriarchy or joining forces to overcome its power?

Mothers have written about their experiences of motherhood (Lazarre, 1987; Rich, 1977; Gieve, 1989) but this has tended to be about the early stages where the woman is experiencing changes in her identity and in how she is responded to because she is now a mother. This work has not been related in any depth to becoming and continuing as the mother of a daughter, so, for example, although we get some flavour of this from Marianne Grabrucker's account (1988) of the first three years of her daughter's life, her analysis is very much about her daughter's socialisation than about her own experience.

What we do have available about the experience of early motherhood speaks to the ambivalence in that early relationship with the infant – whether male or female

> the murderous alternation between bitter resentment and raw-edged nerves, and blissful gratification and tenderness . . . caught up in the waves of love and hate, jealousy even of the child's childhood; hope and fear for its maturity; longing to be free of responsibility, tied by every fibre of one's being. (Rich, 1977, p. 21)

It also speaks to the costs to women in Western society of exclusive, isolated, devalued motherhood (Lazarre, 1976). These accounts remind us of the cycle of life as the daughter become mother thinks back to her own mother and perhaps begins to see her in a different light.

In Lazarre's account we see not only the longing for her dead mother (the specifics of which affect the way she wishes to mother) but some glimpse of different motherhoods in the contrast between her white, middle-class mother who went off to work each morning leaving her in the care of a maid, and her Black working-class mother-in-law who had been home with her four children 'from the day of their birth until they marched victoriously off to college'. Lazarre is well aware that the glorification of such motherhood comes from the view of a child who desperately wanted her mother and not from the viewpoint of that mother struggling to raise her children in poverty and surrounded by racism.

Mother as Woman

> Don't call me Mama
> Don't call me Mother
> See me for what I am
> A Woman.
> [. . .]
> My Motherhood is not my Womanhood
> Just another dimension
> of me
> A Woman . . .
>
> (Carole Stewart, 1987, p. 34)

Of course all mothers are women. Some are white women, some are Black women, some Jewish, some Catholic, some rich, some poor, some heterosexual, some lesbian, some ablebodied, some differently abled. Once a woman has become a mother, 'mother' becomes a part of her identity and will to a greater or lesser extent change that identity. It is all too easy for the daughter to see it as the whole of her identity, either because she looks no further than her own needs in relation to her mother, or because her mother presents little else of her self. As Dorothy West says of her mother:

> But I still cannot put my finger on the why of her. What had she wanted, this beautiful woman? Did she get it? I would look at her face when it was shut away, and I would long to offer her a penny for her thoughts. But I knew she would laugh and say. 'I was thinking it's time to start dinner,' or something equally far from her yearning heart.
> I don't think she ever realised how often she made the remark, 'Speech was given man to hide his thoughts.' At such times I would say to myself, she will die with her secrets. I had guessed a few, but they had been only surface deep, easy to

flush out. I know that the rest went with her on her flight to heaven. (West, 1982)

Why might it be so difficult for a mother to share her 'secrets' with her daughter? Perhaps Ying-Ying St Clair, the fictional mother in Amy Tan's *The Joy Luck Club*, gives us a clue

> For all those years I kept my mouth closed so selfish desires would not fall out. And because I remained quiet for so long now my daughter does not hear me. . . . All these years I kept my true nature hidden, running along like a small shadow so nobody could catch me. And because I moved so secretly now my daughter does not see me. . . .
> And I want to tell her this: We are lost, she and I, unseen and not seeing, unheard and not hearing, unknown by others. (Tan, 1989, p. 67)

Mothers are expected to be unselfish – indeed not to have a 'self' at all but to be there to meet the needs of her children. When the children are grown it may not be so easy to break that habit of keeping one's own needs to oneself. A daughter then may accuse her mother of not stating her needs, of 'playing the martyr'.

But what of the mother who does disclose her own needs? Does the daughter then feel offended, as in Margaret Atwood's short story 'Significant Moments in the Life of my Mother' when in response to the mother's admission that she would have liked to have been an archaeologist the daughter says

> I must have been thirty-five at the time, but it was still shocking and slightly offensive to me to learn that my mother might not have been totally contented fulfilling the role in which fate had cast her: that of being my mother. What thumbsuckers we all are, I thought, when it comes to mothers. (Atwood, 1987, p. 19)

Or when the daughter sees the mother develop and change, and even take on some of the daughter's values and way of life, she may feel she has 'lost' her mother, as in Michelene Wandor's story 'Meet My Mother':

> And I think, once upon a time I had a mother who was just what she should be. Manipulative, bigoted, a pain in the

neck, didn't understand me, didn't want to understand me, wanted me to be all the things she thought I should be. Once upon a time I could dread going round to visit her on Sunday, I could be on guard against her attacks, and secretly I could enjoy eating her home-made biscuits, made with butter, delicious and crumbly, and I could take material round for her to make clothes for me, and borrow a knitting pattern from her, and this was our exchange. Once upon a time I had a mother. Now she's gone, and I don't know what I'm going to do. (Wandor, 1987, p. 36)

The mother will have to be freed from 'the domination of the daughter' so that she can be represented 'more honestly as a separate, individuated being whose daughters cannot even begin to imagine the mysteries of her life' (Washington, 1989, p. 352). For this we need to take more heed of what the mother is actually saying and less about the daughter's or societal inter-pretations of mother's experiences.

ADULT RELATIONSHIP

It may indeed be painful for the adult daughter to begin to see her mother as also a woman. The daughter's view of her mother is likely always to be constrained by her experience of being mothered. We don't all have the benefit of seeing our mother's story written before us, and perhaps the story is easier to give and less difficult to take if someone else's daughter has asked. Yet it is in this ability to see each other as 'separate' adults that much of the mother-daughter literature lodges its hopes for a supportive and non-conflictual relationship between mothers and daughters.

The feminist mother-daughter literature asks in effect that daughters try to see their mothers as the 'imperfect' women they are, carrying out their mothering in particular, often constraining social circumstances; and asks mothers to see their daughters as independent adult women rather than as the 'products' of their endeavours. Mothers are excused their faults because daughters begin to have some understanding of the constraints under which they operate. But because it is essentially about the daughter this work stops short of really exploring the mother's experiences as her daughter becomes an adult.

It is difficult indeed to find anything written about the mother's feelings towards her daughter once that daughter is no longer a small child. Although many studies have been done which give us some insight into the daughter's feelings and attitudes towards her mother from the daughter's adolescence to middle-age, we do not have the benefit of a similar insight into the mother's feelings. One can only guess at how mothers feel.

Mary Stott in *Ageing for Beginners* tells us that she has met 'quite a few women who have made no bones about 'hating' their mother' and she has met 'even more elderly women who are hurt and bewildered because their daughters seem to dislike and despise them'. She goes on

> A letter in the feminist magazine *Spare Rib* a year or two ago asked, 'Why do our daughters seem to hate us so? Why even if they are "fond" of us do they think so poorly of us?' 'Recently', the writer continued, 'a woman told me that she had invited her parents to a gathering. When she told her friend this they opted not to come. 'If you've invited your parents you can't expect us to come too'. On another occasion this woman had attended a women's conference and gone into a workshop on 'motherhood'. As she sat down two younger women walked to the door, one saying, 'I'm not going to stay here if a woman of that age is going to listen to everything I say.' She summed up: 'Something has happened to make the daughters of some of the most active and independent women the world has ever known feel that their mothers are shameful and foolish . . . and the mothers acquiesce in this.' What else can we do, I wonder, but acquiesce? (Stott, 1981, p. 55)

Here we see the results of theoretical distortions on the lived experience of the mother-daughter relationship, White, middle-age class daughters (for that is the group I believe is being referred to here) have been encouraged, even forced, to see their mothers in a hostile light through the literature, the workshops, the therapy.

Where the experiences of other groups of women don't seem to fit this model, this is explained away. For example, Dennis Marsden and Sheila Abrams (1987) in exploring the relationship of care between mothers and daughters through the life-cycle, found 'a marked social class difference in the emotional tone of these caring relationships, with middle-class daughters more prone to reject their mothers, despite the mothers' lower level of incapacity'. Middle-class daughters were more prone than working-class daughters to express feelings of rejection or hatred. Marsden and Abrams suggest that what we 'may be seeing here [is] greater middle-class articulacy, curbed by fewer inhibitions about revealing family discord to the middle-class interviewer' (p. 200). Well maybe, or maybe white, working-class women do have different relationships with their mothers than white, middle-class women who may be closer to and more influenced by dominant interpretations of that relationship.

Just as daughters may be unable to see beyond the mother role to the woman, so the mother may only see the culmination of her responsibilities and care in the daughter. The mother may have certain expectations of her daughter which may relate to her own life and her own belief in what is best. The societal message to mothers is clear – the way their children 'turn-out' is down to them and no one else. It may be difficult, then, to relinquish some feeling of control over the actions of the daughter. Yet even where the mother is able to see her daughter as a person in her own right she may be accused of no longer acting like a mother, of denying her daughter a mother to whom she can turn, even of expecting the daughter to mother her. No wonder separation is an 'elusive concept' (Payne, 1983, p. 334) for really it isn't possible to split off mother and woman, to view one without viewing the effects of the other, the daughter cannot be expected to relate to her mother only as a woman, or the mother to relate to her daughter only as a woman, for they are connected in their relationship as mother and daughter as well as in their womanness.

The difficulty seems to lie in retaining and valuing this connection whilst respecting the fact that one's mother or one's daughter has a different life, different ambitions, different hopes, fears, needs. A mother may be confused by the very different life her daughter chooses, particularly where this involves a move across class barriers, holding different political viewpoints, or expressing sexuality in a different way. The daughter may then move into a world the mother herself has no understanding of. The daughter may not understand why her mother cannot see that her life is 'better'. The changing expectations of women may be enough to set up this confusion.

We start with a problem (not being psychologically separate and the daughter therefore hating the mother who would seem to hold her back): we resolve it by both mother and daughter seeing the other person as a separate adult. But does this problem (lack of separation) exist in the first place and is this resolution as simple as it looks? Perhaps what we start with is connection and an ideology of motherhood and mother-daughter relationships which seeks to disconnect. New theories of development which allow for connection in relationships and the growth of the individual through attachments start us on the path to rethinking the mother-daughter relationship in theory and a chance to experience it differently in practice.

The myth that women somehow lack a 'sense of self' because of a lack of separation from their mothers is questioned by the knowledge we have that children are born with a sense of self (Stern, 1985), that mothers are positive influences in the daughter's ego development (Grotevant and Cooper, 1983), and that it is socialisation processes, which are more than the mother's responsibility, which can be held to account for girls being taught that their identity comes solely through caring for others.

It should be clear by now that the separation myth is perpetuated to keep mothers and daughters separated, not, as it is claimed, to aid the psychological development of the daughter. We need to replace such distorting concepts as 'separation' with 'differentiation through attachment' (Berzoff, 1989), and 'dependency' with interdependency and mutual dependency, whilst getting rid altogether of such denigrating and misleading terms as 'role-reversal' in relation to older people and their adult children, rather than replacing it with the equally misguided 'generational inversion' (Steinmetz, 1989).

The development of theories based on connection, the celebration of the daughter's heritage through the literature of matrilineage, and a better understanding of the social context of mothering and mother-daughter relationships, have already led us to an understanding of the distortions of that relationship. There is much further to go in challenging and changing dominant prescriptions of motherhood and daughterhood.

The mother's voice needs to be heard more, we need to have a better understanding for her continuing development, especially as it relates to her attachment to her daughter. We need to think about the complexity of mother-daughter relationships, and that there are indeed a variety of relationships and not one way of relating which then becomes the 'norm' against which other relationships are judged and found wanting. For this we need to have a better understanding of women's history and experiences, for, as Adrienne Rich points out 'The more we learn of actual female history (to take but one example, of the history of black women) the less we can generalise about the failure of mothers to cherish and inspirit daughters in a strong, female tradition' (Rich, 1973, p. 91). We may also learn more about the pride and connection daughters feel towards their mothers, and mothers towards their daughters.

All of this requires the sharing of women's own experiences and the continual challenging of imposed reality. It also requires a breaking-out from the dichotomies and hierarchies of patriarchal thought and from the oppressive interpretations of racism and classism.

At the level of individual relationships, Susan Kraus gives some ideas for developmental tasks for both mother and adult daughter which validate and maintain their connection rather than seeing it as a problem. She suggests that mothers and daughters 'broaden the lens' (Lerner, 1985), that is learn more about each other's lives, histories, interpretation of experiences by asking rather than by anticipating. That they 'separate wishful thinking from facts', that is, that they come to terms with their real relationship rather than hold onto fantasies of 'perfect' mother, 'perfect' daughter. That mother and daughter 'learn about the larger contexts', about the social constraints and socialisation they have both experienced and the differences between them in this experience. In order to nurture and develop their relationship all of this can be done within a context of a commitment to their relationship, and to enhance this Kraus suggests developing mother-daughter 'rituals' which means determining to spend some special time with each other. The response that other family members may have to this is revealing. Kraus facilitated a group in which several women started to do some of this work of developing their relationships with their mothers, Kraus tells us

> the following family responses were encountered: 'You couldn't stand her guts last month and now you want to spend the weekend alone?' 'You two are so different that you'll never have anything in common.' 'You don't spend enough time with your own kids and now you're spending a whole Saturday with your Mom?' 'When are you going to grow up and stop depending on your mother?' (Kraus, 1990, p. 41)

We should be asking, why is the mother-daughter relationship so threatening to others?

For those daughters and mothers who experience their relationship as tense and conflictual, the above may seem impossible to even start, let alone positively develop. Whilst the myths of problematic mother-daughter relationships remain strong in our culture, it may prove difficult for individual mothers and daughters to overcome problems in their experience of the relationship. Questioning the myths, the patriarchal language and theories can lead to changing perceptions and to a different understanding of experiences, and finally to some changes in those experiences.

But challenging will not be easy, for it requires not only individual but global responses in the replacing of a patriarchal imperative to separate mother from daughter, with a matriarchal ethic of reciprocity and transformative power (Kuykendall, 1982).

An increasing number of feminist writers are looking towards a matriarchal future, not in the sense imposed by patriarchy, of mothers dominating children and men, but one where mothers will 'define motherhood, determine the conditions of motherhood and determine the environment in which the next generation is reared' (Love and Shanklin, 1978). The mother-daughter connection is essential in this, not in order to exclude the father, but for women to claim mothering back and for men and women to learn to value what Ruddick has termed 'maternal thinking' (Ruddick, 1990).

In such a society mothers and daughters would be free to relate in much more positive ways, while the positive relations of mothers and daughters now may take us some way towards that future. As the French psychoanalyst Luce Irigaray says:

> The mother/daughter, daughter/mother relation constitutes an extremely explosive core in our societies. To think it, to change it, leads to shaking up the patriarchal order.
>
> (Luce Irigaray, 1981 translation.)

Bibliography

Abramson, J. B. (1987) *Mothermania: A Psychological Study of Mother-Daughter Conflict*, (New York: D. C. Heath and Co.).

Alibhai, Y. (1989) 'Burning in the Cold' in Gieve (ed.) op. cit.

Allatt, P., Keil T., Bryman A., Bytheway B. (eds) (1987) *Women and the Life Cycle* (London: Macmillan).

Allen, K. R. (1989) *Single Women and Family Ties: Life Histories of Older Women* (London: Sage).

Alta, (1974) 'Placenta Praevia' in *Momma: a start on all the untold stories* (New York: Times Change Press).

Anderson, B. and Zinsser, J. P. (1989/90) *A History of Their Own* Volume One (1989); Volume Two (1990) (Harmondsworth: Penguin).

Angelou, M. (1984) *I Know Why The Caged Bird Sings*, (London: Virago; (1970) New York, Random House).

Angelou, M. (1974) *Gather Together In My Name* (New York: Random House; London: Virago).

Apter, T. (1985) *Why Women Don't Have Wives: Professional Success and Motherhood* (London: Macmillan).

Apter, T. (1990) *Altered Loves: Mothers and Daughters During Adolescence* (Hemel Hempstead: Harvester Wheatsheaf).

Arcana, J. (1979) *Our Mothers Daughters* (London: Shameless Hussy Press; page numbers taken from 1981 edition, London: The Women's Press).

Astra, (1986) *Back You Come Mother Dear* (London: Virago).

Atwood, M. (1982) *Lady Oracle* (London: Virago).

Atwood, M. (1987) 'Significant Moments in the Life of My Mother' in Park and Heaton (eds) op. cit.

Badinter, B. (1980) *The Myth of Motherhood* (London: Souvenir Press).

Bakan, D. (1966) *The Duality of Human Existence* (Chicago: Rand McNally).

Ballou, J. W. (1978) *The Psychology of Pregnancy* (Toronto: Lexington Books).

Ballou, M. and Gabalac, N. W. (1985)) *A Feminist Position on Mental Health* (Springfield, IL: Charles C. Thomas).

Bandura, A. (1977) *Social Learning Theory* (Englewood Cliffs, NJ: Prentice-Hall).

Bardwick, J. M. and Douvan, E. (1971) 'Ambivalence: The Socialisation of Women' in V. Gornick and B. K. Moran (eds) *Women in Sexist Society: Studies in Power and Powerlessness* (New York: Basic Books).

Barefoot, J. (1986) *Duet For Three* (London: The Women's Press).

Bart, P. (1977) 'The Mermaid and the Minotaur, a Fishy Story that's Part Bull' in *Contemporary Psychology*, 22, (11).

Bart, P. (1981) 'Review of Choderow's Reproduction of Mothering' pp. 147–152, in Trebilcot (ed.) op. cit.

Baruch, G. and Barnett, R. C. (1983) 'Adult Daughters Relationships with their Mothers' in *Journal of Marriage and the Family*, 45, 601–6.

Bass, E. (1984) 'There are Times in Life When One Does The Right Thing' in *Our Stunning Harvest* (Philadelphia: New Society).

Bateson, G. (1972) *Steps to an Ecology of Mind* (New York: Jason Aronson).

Bell, C. and Newby, H. (1976) 'Husbands and Wives: the dynamic of the differential dialectic' in D. Barker and S. Allen (eds) *Dependency in Work and Marriage*, (New Jersey: Longman).

Beauvoir, S. de (1963) *Memoirs of a Dutiful Daughter* (Harmondsworth: Penguin).

Beauvoir, S. de (1969) *A Very Easy Death* (Harmondsworth: Penguin).

Beauvoir, S. de (1972) *The Second Sex* (Harmondsworth: Penguin).

Beauvoir, S. le Bon de (1989) in P. Forster and I. Sutton (eds) *Daughters of de Beauvoir* (London: The Women's Press).

Bernard, J. (1974) *The Future of Motherhood* (Harmondsworth: Penguin).

Bernay, T. and Cantor, D. W. (eds) (1986) *The Psychology of Today's Woman: New Psycholoanalytic Views.* (Hillside, NJ: The Analytic Press).

Berzoff, J. (1985) 'Valued Female Friendships: Their Function in Promoting Women's Psychological Development', unpublished doctoral dissertation, Boston University.

Berzoff, J. (1989a) 'From Separation to Connection: Shifts in Understanding Women's Development', *Affilia: Journal of Women and Social Work,* Spring (1).

Berzoff, J. (1989b) 'Fusion and Heterosexual Women's Friendships: Implications for Expanding Our Adult Developmental Theories' in *Women and Therapy,* 8(4).

Bettleheim, B. (1985) 'The Problem of Generations' in E. Erikson (ed) *The Challenge of Youth* (New York: Anchor Press).

Bibring, G. L., Dwyer, T., Huntingdon, D., Valenstein, A. (1961) 'A study of the psychological processes in pregnancy and of the earliest mother-child relationship', *Psychoanalytic Study of the Child,* 16, 9–72.

Bickerton, T. (1988) 'Mothers and Daughters' in S. Krzowski and P. Land (eds) *In Our Experience* (London: The Women's Press).

Biller, H. B. (1976) 'The Father and Personality Development: Paternal Deprivation and Sex Role Development' in Lamb (ed) op. cit.

Biller, H. B. (1981) 'The Father and Sex Role Development' in Lamb (ed) op. cit.

Blos, P. (1967) 'The Second Individuation Process of Adolescence' in A. Freud (ed) *Psychoanalytic Study of the Child* (New York: International University Press)

Bourne, G. (1972) *Pregnancy* (London: Cassell and Co.).

Bowlby, J. (1969) *Attachment and Loss* (London: Hogarth).

Bowlby, J. (1988) *A Secure Base* (London: Routledge).

Breen, D. (1975) *The Birth of the First Child* (London: Tavistock).

Breen, D. (1989) *Talking with Mothers* (London: Free Association Press).

Bristol Child Health and Development Study (1986) 'West Indians: No link between disadvantage and attainment', *Education,* 25 April 383.

Bromberg, E. M. (1983a) 'Mother-daughter relationships in later life: the effect of quality of relationship upon mutual aid', *Journal of Gerontological Social Work,* 6, 75–92.

Bromberg, E. M. (1983b) 'Mother-daughter relationships in later life: Negating the Myths' in *Aging,* 340, 15–20.

Brown, P., Macintyre, M., Mopeth, R. and Prendergast, S. (1981) 'A Daughter: a thing to be given away' in Cambridge Women's Study Group, *Women in Society* (London: Virago).

Brown, G. W. and Harris, T. (1978) *Social Origins of Depression: A Study of Psychiatric Disorder in Women* (London: Tavistock).

Bruch, H. (1978) *The Golden Cage: The Enigma of Anorexia Nervosa* (Shepton Mallet: Open Books).

Bryan, B., Dadzie, S., and Scafe, S. (1985) *The Heart of the Race: Black Women's Lives in Britain* (London: Virago).

Cambridge Women's Study Group (1981) *Women in Society* (London: Virago).

Caplan, P. J. (1981) *Barriers Between Women*, (Lancaster: MTP Press).

Caplan, P. J. and Hall-McCorquodale, I. (1985) 'Mother Blaming in Major Clinical Journals' in *American Journal of Orthopsychiatry*, 55(3) July, 345–53.

Caplan, P. J. (1989) *Don't Blame Mother: Mending the Mother-Daughter Relationship* (New York: Harper & Row).

Carlson, R. (1970) 'On the structure of self esteem: Comments on Ziller's formulation', *Journal of Consulting and Clinical Psychology*, 34, 264–8.

Carlson, R. (1971) 'Sex Differences in Ego Functioning: exploratory studies of agency and communion', *Journal of Consulting and Clinical Psychology*, 37, 267–77.

Chaplin, J. (1988) *Feminist Counselling in Action* (London: Sage).

Charnas, S. McKee (1989) *Walk to the End of the World and Motherlines*, (London: The Women's Press).

Chasseguet-Smirgel, J. (1964) *Female Sexuality* (Paris: Editons Payot; 1981, London: Virago).

Chernin, K. (1985) *In My Mother's House: A Daughter's Story* (London: Virago).

Chernin, K. (1986) *The Hungry Self*, (London: Virago).

Chesler, P. (1972) *Women and Madness* (Garden City, NY: Doubleday).

Chesler, P. (1987) *Mothers on Trial* (New York: McGraw Hill).

Chesler, P. (1990) *Sacred Bond: Motherhood under Siege* (London: Virago).

Choderow, N. (1978) *The Reproduction of Mothering: Psychoanalysis and the sociology of gender* (Berkeley: University of California Press).

Choderow, N. and Contratto, S. (1982) 'The Fantasy of the Perfect Mother' in B. Thorne and M. Yalom (eds) *Rethinking the Family* (New York: Longman).

CIBA Foundation (1984) *Child Sexual Abuse within the Family* Independent Publication.

Cline, S. and Spender, D. (1987) *Reflecting Men at twice their Natural Size* (London: André Deutch).

Cobbe, Frances Power (1894) *Life of Frances Power Cobbe by Herself* (London: R. Bentley)

Cobham, R. and Collins, M. (eds) (1987) *Watchers and Seekers: Creative Writing by Black Women in Britain* (London: The Women's Press).

Cochran, M. (1985) 'The mother-daughter dyad throughout the life cycle' in *Women and Therapy*, 4(2) 3–8.

Cohen, G. (1978) 'Women's Solidarity and the Preservation of Privilege' in P. Caplan and J. Bujra (eds) *Women United and Women Divided: Cross Cultural perspectives on Female Solidarity*, (London: Tavistock).

Cohler, B. J. and Grunebaum, H. U. (1981) *Mothers, Grandmothers and Daughters* (London: Wiley).

Colette, S. G. (1966) *My Mother's House & Sido* (Harmondsworth: Penguin).

Collins, P. H. (1990) *Black Feminist Thought: Knowledge, Consciousness and the Politics of Empowerment*, (London: Unwin Hyman).

Collins, P. H. (1987) 'The Meaning of Motherhood in Black Culture and Black Mother/Daughter Relationships' *Sage: A Scholarly Journal on Black Women*, 4(2) 4–11.

Common Thread Collective (Cotterill, J., Kennerley, A., Nathan, P. and Wilding, J.), (eds) (1989) *The Common Thread: Writings by Working-Class Women* (London: Mandarin).

Cornwell, J. (1984) *Hard Earned Lives: Accounts of Health and Illness from East London* (London: Tavistock).

Crisp, A. H. (1967) 'Anorexia Nervosa' in *Hospital Medicine*, 713.

Dalley, G. (1988) *Ideologies of Caring: Rethinking Community and Collectivism* (London: Macmillan).

Daly, A. (1982) *Inventing Motherhood: The Consequences of an Ideal* (London: Hutchinson).

Daly, M. (1979) *Gyn/Ecology* (London: The Women's Press).

Davidson, C. N. and Broner, E. M. (1980) *The Lost Tradition; Mothers and Daughters in Literature* (New York: Unger).

Deutch, H. (1947) *The Psychology of Women*, Volume One: Girlhood; Volume Two: Motherhood (London: Research Books).

De Salvo, L. (1989) *Virginia Woolf: the Impact of Childhood Sexual Abuse on her Life and Work* (London: The Women's Press).

Dill, B. T. (1979) '"The Means to Put My Children Through". Child Rearing Goals and Strategies among Black Female Domestic Servants' in Rodgers-Rose op. cit.

Dinnerstein, D. (1976) *The Rocking of the Cradle and the Ruling of the World*, (New York: Harper and Row; 1978, London: Souvenir Press, 1987, London: The Women's Press).

Dix, C. (1986) *The New Mother Syndrome: coping with post-natal depression* (London: Allen and Unwin).

Dodd, C. (1990) *Conversations with Mothers and Daughters* (London: Optima).

Driver, E. and Droisen, A. (1989) *Child Sexual Abuse: Feminist Perspectives* (London: Macmillan).

Du Bois, B. (1983) 'Passionate Scholarship: Notes on Values, Knowledge and Method in Feminist Social Science' in G. Bowles and R. Duelli Klein (eds) *Theories of Women's Studies*, (London: Routledge and Kegan Paul).

Dyhouse, C. (1981) *Girls Growing Up in Late Victorian England* (London: Routledge and Kegan Paul).

Dyhouse, C. (1986) 'Mothers and Daughters in the Middle-Class Home, 1870–1914' in J. Lewis (ed.) *Labour and Love: Women's Experience of Home and Family, 1850–1940* (Oxford: Basil Blackwell).

Edwards, Susan S. M. (1987) 'Provoking her own demise: from common assault to homicide' in J. Hanmer and M. Maynard (eds) *Women, Violence and Social Control* (London: Macmillan).

Ehrenreich, B. and English, D. (1979) *For Her Own Good: 150 years of expert's advice to women* (London: Pluto Press).

Ehrensing, R. H. and Weitzman, E. L. (1970)) 'The mother-daughter relationship in anorexia nervosa', *Psychosomatic Medicine* 32, 201–8.

Eichenbaum, L, and Orbach, S. (1984) *What Do Women Want?* (London: Fontana).

Eichenbaum, L., and Orbach, S. (1985) *Understanding Women* (Harmondsworth: Penguin).

Eichenbaum, L., and Orbach, S. (1987a) 'Separation and Intimacy: Crucial practice issues in working with women in therapy' in Ernest and Maguire, (eds) op. cit.

Eichenbaum, L., and Orbach, S. (1987b) *Bittersweet: Love, Envy and Competition in Women's Friendships* (London: Century Hutchinson).

Eisler, R. (1990) *The Chalice and the Blade: Our History, Our Future* (London: Unwin).

Elias-Button, K. (1980) 'The Muse as Medusa' in Davidson and Broner (eds) op. cit.

Emecheta, B. (1977) *Second Class Citizen* (London: Fontana).

Enders-Dragaesser, U. (1988) 'Women's Identity and Development within a Paradoxical Reality' *Women's Studies International Forum*, 11(6) 583–90.

Erikson, E. H. (1956) 'The Concept of Ego Identity' *Journal of the American Psychoanalytic Association* 4, 56–121.

Erikson, E. H. (1965) *Childhood and Society* (Harmondsworth: Penguin).

Erikson, E. H. (1971) 'Womanhood and the Inner Space' in *Identity, Youth and Crisis* (London: Faber and Faber).

Ernst, S. and Maguire, M. (eds) (1987) *Living with the Sphinx: Papers from The Women's Therapy Centre* (London: The Women's Press).

Ernst, S. (1987) 'Can a Daughter be a Woman? Women's identity and psychological separation' in Ernst and Maguire (eds) op. cit.

Evans, M. (ed.) (1985) *Black Women Writers: Arguments and Interviews* (London: Pluto Press).

Evers, H. (1983) 'Elderly Women and Disadvantage: perceptions of daily life and support relationships' in D. Jerrome (ed.) *Ageing in Modern Society* (London: Croom Helm).

Evers, H. (1984) 'Old women's self-perception of dependency and some implications for service provision', *Journal of Epidemiology and Community Health*, 38, 306–9.

Evers, H. (1985) 'The Frail Elderly Woman: emergent questions in aging and women's health' in E. Lowin and V. Olesen (eds) *Women, Health and Healing: Towards a New Perspective* (London: Tavistock).

Evert, K. (1987) *When You Are Ready: a woman's healing from childhood physical and sexual abuse by her mother* (Walnut Creek, Calif.: Launch Press).

Fagot, B. I. (1978) 'The Influence of Sex on Child or Parental Reactions to Toddler Children' *Child Development*, 49, 459–65.

Fairbairn, W. R. D. (1952) *Psychoanalytic Studies of the Personality*, (London: Tavistock).

Fischer, L. R. (1979) 'When Daughters Become Mothers', unpublished doctoral dissertation, University of Massachusetts.

Fischer, L. R. (1981) 'Transitions in the Mother-Daughter Relationship', *Journal of Marriage and the Family*, August.

Fischer, L. R. (1986) *Linked Lives: Adult daughters and their Mothers* (New York: Harper and Row).

Fishburn, K. (1980) 'The Nightmare Repetition: the mother-daughter conflict in Doris Lessing's *Children of Violence*'in Davidson and Broner (eds) op. cit.

Fishman, P. M. N. (1978) 'Interaction: The Work Women Do', *Social Problems* 25(4) 397–406.

Flax, J. (1978) 'The Conflict Between Nurturance And Autonomy in The Mother Daughter Relationship and within Feminism' *Feminist Studies* 4(2).

Fodor, I. G. (1974)) 'The Phobic Syndrome in Women: Implications for treatment' in V. Frank and V. Burtle (eds) *Women in Therapy: New psychotherapies for a changing society* (New York: Brunner/Mazel).

Ford, J. and Sinclair, R. (1987) *Sixty Years On: women talk about old age* (London: The Women's Press).

Formanek, R. and Gurian, A. (eds) (1987) *Women and Depression: a life-span perspective* (New York: Springer).

Forster, P. and Sutton, I. (eds) (1989) *Daughters of de Beauvoir* (London: The Women's Press).

Forward, S. and Buck, C. (1981) *Betrayal of Innocence* (Harmondsworth: Penguin).

Franz, C. E . and White, K. M. (1985) 'Individuation and Attachment in personality Development: extending Erikson's theory' *Journal of Personality* 53(2), June.

French, M. (1987) *Her Mother's Daughter* (London: Heinemann).

Freud, S. (1905) *Three Essays on Sexuality*, The Standard Edition of the Complete Works of Sigmund Freud, Vol VII (London: Hogarth Press). (1953)

Freud, S. (1977) *On Sexuality*, edited by A. Richards, Pelican Freud Library, Vol 7 (Harmondsworth: Penguin).

Friday, N. (1979) *My Mother, My Self* (London: Fontana).

Friedrich, M. (1988) 'The Dependent Solution: Anorexia and Bulimia as defenses against anger', *Women and Therapy* 7(4), 53–71.

Fromm, E. (1956) *The Art of Loving* (New York: Harper and Row).

Gabriel, A. (1985) 'Recovering from Religion' in Hemmings (ed.) op. cit.

Gavey, N., Florence, J., Pezaro, S., Tan, J. (1990) 'Mother Blaming, the Perfect Alibi: Family Therapy and the Mothers of Incest Survivors' *Journal of Feminist Family Therapy*, 2(1) 1–25.

Gavron, H. (1966) *The Captive Wife* (London: Routledge and Kegan Paul).

Giaretto, H. (1981) 'A comprehensive child sexual abuse treatment program' in P. B. Mrazek and C. H. Kempe (eds) *Sexually Abused Children and their Families*, (Oxford: Pergamon).

Gieve, K. (ed.) (1989) *Balancing Acts: On Being a Mother* (London: Virago).

Gilbert, L. and Webster, P. (1982) *Bound by Love: the sweet trap of daughterhood* (Boston: Beacon Press).

Gilbert, L. A., Hanson, G. R., and Davis, B. (1982) 'Perceptions of parental role responsibilities between mothers and fathers', *Family Relations*, 1(2) 261–9.

Gilligan, C. (1982) *In a Different Voice: psychological theory and women's development* (London: Harvard Press).

Glendinning, C. and Millar, J. (eds) (1987) *Women and Poverty in Britain*, (Brighton: Wheatsheaf).

Glenn, N. D. (1975) 'Psychological well-being in the post-parental stage: some evidence from national surveys', *Journal of Marriage and the Family*, 37, 105–10.

Gordon, M. (1982) *The Company of Women* (London: Corgi; published New York: Random House, 1980).

Gornick, V. (1988) *Fierce Attachment: a memoir* (London: Virago).

Grabrucker, M. (1988) *There's A Good Girl: Gender stereotyping in the first three years of life: a diary*, trans. W. Philipson (London: The Women's Press).

Graham, H. (1980) 'Women's accounts of anger and aggression against their babies' in N. Frude (ed.) *Psychological approaches to child abuse* (London: Batsford).

Graham, H. (1982) 'Coping: Or how mothers are seen and not heard' in S. Friedman and E. Sarah (eds) *On the Problem of Men* (London: The Women's Press).

Graham, H. (1983) 'Caring: A Labour of Love' in J. Finch and D. Groves (eds) *A Labour of Love: Women, Work and Caring* (London: Routledge and Kegan Paul).

Graham, H. (1987) 'Women, Poverty and Caring' in Glendinning and Millar (eds) op. cit.

Greene, A. L. and Boxer, A. M. (1986) 'Daughters and sons as young adults: restructuring the ties that bind' in N. Datan, A. Greene, H. Reese (eds) *Life Span Developmental Psychology* (Hillside, NJ: Lawrence Erlbaum).

Grenwal, S., Kay, J. and Parmar, P. (eds) (1988) *Charting the Journey: Writings by Black and Third World Women*, (London: Sheba Feminist Press).

Griffin, S. (1977) 'Forum: On wanting to be the mother I wanted', *MS*, V(7), January, 98–105.

Griffin, C. (1985) *Typical Girls? Young Women from School to the Job Market*, (London: Routledge and Kegan Paul).

Griffiths, V. (1987) 'Adolescent girls: transitions from girlfriends to boyfriends?' in Allatt et al. (eds) op. cit.

Grimshaw, J. (1986) *Feminist Philosophers: Women's perspectives on philosophical traditions* (Brighton: Wheatsheaf).

Grotevant, H. and Cooper, C. (eds) (1983) *Adolescent development in the Family* (San Francisco: Jossey Bass).

Gump, J. (1972) 'Sex role attitudes and psychological well being' *Journal of Social Issues*, 28, 79–92.

Gupta, R. (1988) 'Women and Communalism; a tentative enquiry' in Grenwal et al. (eds) op. cit.

Gutmann, D. (1979) 'The Clinical Psychology of Late Life: Developmental Paradigms', paper presented at the West Virginia Gerontology Conference 'Transitions of Aging' May 23–6, 1979, Morgantown, MV; quoted Abrahamson (1987) op. cit., p. 9.

Hale, J. (1980) 'The Black Woman and Child Rearing' in Rodgers-Rose (ed.) op. cit.

Hall, K. (1989) 'My Mother' in Common Thread Collective (eds) op. cit.

Hall, N. (1980) *The Moon and the Virgin: reflections on the archetypal feminine* (London: The Women's Press).

Hammer, S. (1976) *Mothers and Daughters: Daughters and Mothers* (London: Hutchinson).

Hargreaves, O. J. and McColley, M. (1986) (eds) *The Psychology of Sex Roles* (London: Harper and Row).

Hartley, R. E. (1966) 'A Developmental View of Female Sex-Role Identification' in B. J. Biddle and E. J. Thomas (eds) *Role Theory* (New York: Wiley).

Hartsock, N. (1981) *Money, Sex and Power: an essay on domination and community* (New York: Longman).

Haywood, J. (1989) 'I Was Three Once' in Common Thread Collective (eds) op. cit.

Hemmings, S. (ed.) (1985) *A Wealth of Experience: the lives of older women* (London: Pandora Press).

Herman, J. and Hirschman, L. (1977) 'Father-Daughter Incest', *Signs* 2(4), 735–56.

Herman, J. L. and Lewis, H. B. (1986) 'Anger in the Mother-Daughter Relationship' in Bernay and Cantor (eds) op. cit.

Herman, N. (1989) *Too Long a Child: the mother-daughter dyad.* (London: Free Association Press).

Hicks, C. (1988) *Who Cares: looking after people at home* (London: Virago).

Hoffman, L. W. (1977) 'Changes in family roles, socialisation and sex differences' in *American Psychologist* 32, 644–57.

Hooks, B. (1982) *Ain't I a Woman: Black Women and Feminism* (London: Pluto Press).

Hooper, C. A. (1987) 'Getting Him off the Hook', *Trouble and Strife* 12, Winter.

Hopkinson, L. P. (1988) *Nothing to Forgive: a daughter's life of Antonia White,* (London: Chatto and Windus).

Horner, M. S. (1972) 'Towards an understanding of achievement-related conflict in women', *Journal of Social Issues,* 28, 157–75.

Horney, K. (1950) *Neurosis and Human Growth,* (New York: W. W. Norton).

Hoschschild, A. (1989) *The Second Shift: Working Parents and the Revolution* (London: Viking).

Humm, M. (1990) *The Dictionary of Feminist Thought* (Hemel Hempstead: Harvester/Wheatsheaf).

Hunt, A. (1978) *The Elderly at Home* (London: Her Majesty's Stationery Office).

Irigaray, L. (1981) 'And the one doesn't stir without the other', trans. H. V. Wenzel, *Signs,* Autumn, 1981, 60–7.

Itzin, C. (1986) 'Media Images of Women: the social construction of ageism and sexism' in S. Wilkinson (ed.) *Feminist Social Psychology: developing theory and Practice* (Milton Keynes: Open University Press).

Jackson, J. (1972) 'Black Women in a Racist Society' in C. Willie, B. Kramer and B. Brown (eds) *Racism and Mental Health* (Pittsburgh: University of Pittsburgh Press).

Jacobson, E. (1965) *The Self and the Object World,* (London: Hogarth Press).

Jamieson, L. (1986) 'Limited Resources and Limited Conventions: working-class mothers and daughters in urban Scotland c.1890–1925' in J. Lewis (ed.) *Labour and Love* (London: Blackwell).

Jeffries, S. (1985) *The Spinster and her Enemies: feminism and sexuality* 1880–1930, (London: Pandora Press).

Jewish Women in London Group (1989) *Generations of Memories: Voices of Jewish Women* (London: The Women's Press).

Johnson, E. S. (1978) 'Good relationships between older mothers and their daughters: a causal model' *Gerontologist*, 18, 301–6.

Johnson, M. M. (1982) 'Fathers and "Femininity" in Daughters: a review of the research' in *Sociology and Social Research*, 67 (1).

Johnson, T. H. (ed.) (1958) *The Letters of Emily Dickinson* (Cambridge, Mass: The Belknap Press).

Jolly, H. (1981) *Book of Child Care: the complete guide for today's parents* (London: Sphere).

Jones, G. (1977) 'An Interview' *Massachusetts review*, 18 (Winter) 692.

Jones, J. (1982) 'My mother was much of a woman: black women, work and the family under slavery' *Feminist Studies*, 8(2) 235–69.

Jordon, J. V. and Surrey, J. L. (1986) 'The Self-in-Relation: empathy and the mother-daughter relationship' in Bernay and Cantor, op. cit.

Jordon, J. (1972) 'White English/Black English: The Politics of Translation' in June Jordon, *Moving Towards Home: Political essays* (1989) (London: Virago).

Joseph, G. (1981) 'Black Mothers and Daughters: Their Roles and Functions in American Society' in Joseph and Lewis (eds) op. cit.

Joseph, G. and Lewis, J. (eds) (1981) *Common Differences: Conflicts in Black and White Perspectives* (Garden City, NY: Anchor).

Joseph, G. I. (1983) 'Review of Women, Race and Class' *Signs*, 9(1) 134–6.

Joshi, H. (1987) 'The Cost of Caring' in Glendinning and Millar (eds) op. cit.

Jung, C. G. (1971) 'Psychological aspects of the Kore' in C. G. Jung and C. Kerényi, *Essays on a Science of Mythology, the Myth of the Divine Child and the Mysteries of Eleusis* (trans. R. F. C. Hull) (Princeton, NJ: Princeton University Press). Bollingen Series 22, 1971.

Jung, C. G. (1972) 'Psychological Aspects of the Mother Archetype' in *Four Archetypes* (London: Routledge and Kegan Paul).

Justice, B. and Justice, R. (1979) *The Broken Taboo: sex in the family*, (London: Peter Owen).

Kaplan, J. L. (1978) *Oneness and Separateness: From Infant to Individual* (New York: Simon and Schuster).

Kea, K. (1987) 'An open letter to battering mother explainers' *Women's Studies International forum*, 10(2) 213–14.

Keith, L. (1990) 'Caring Partnerships' *Community Care*, Inside Supplement, 22 February 1900, v/vi.

Kempe, R. S. and Kempe, C. H. (1978) *Child Abuse*, (London: Fontana).

Kennedy, H. (1989) 'Wanting it All' in Gieve (ed.) op. cit.

Kestenberg, J. S. (1976) 'Regression and reintegration in pregnancy' *Journal of American Psychoanalytic Association* 24, 213–50.

Kitzinger, C. (1987) *The Social Construction of Lesbianism* (London: Sage).

Kitzinger, S. (1978) *Women as Mothers*, (London: Fontana).

Kitzinger, S. (ed.) (1988) *The Midwife Challenge* (London: Bandora Press).

Klein, G. (1976) *Psychoanalytic Theory: An Exploration of Essentials* (New York: International University Press).

Klein, M. (1937) 'Love, Guilt and Reparation' in *Love, Guilt and Reparation and other works 1921–1945* (New York: Dell, 1975).

Klein, M. (1946) 'Notes on some schizoid mechanisms', *The Writings of Melanie Klein* Vol. 3 (London: Hogarth Press).

Klein, M. (1959) 'Our Adult World and its Roots in Infancy', *Envy and Gratitude and other works 1946–1963* (New York: Dell, 1975).

Kohlberg, L. (1966) 'A cognitive developmental analysis of children's sex role concepts and attitudes' in E. E. Maccoby (ed.) *The Development of Sex Differences* (Stanford, Calif.: Stanford University Press).

Kohut, H. (1971) *The Analysis of the Self* (New York: International University Press).

Koppelman, S. (ed.) (1985) *Between Mothers and Daughters: Stories across a generation* (New York: The Feminist Press).

Kraus, S. J. (1990) 'On adult daughters and their mothers: a peripatetic consideration of developmental tasks', *Journal of Feminist Family Therapy*, 2(1) 27–42.

Krzowski, S. and Land, P. (eds) (1988) *In Our Experience: Workshops at the Women's Therapy Centre* (London: The Women's Press).

Kuykendall, E. H. (1982) 'Towards an Ethic of Nurturance: Luce Ingaray on Mothering and Power' in Trebilcot (ed.) (1983) op. cit.

Ladner, J. (1972) *Tomorrow's Tomorrow: The Black Woman* (New York: Anchor Books).

Laing, R. D. and Esterson, A. (1964) *Sanity, Madness and the Family* (London: Tavistock).

Lamb, M., Owen, M., Chase-Lonsdale, L. (1979) 'The father-daughter relationship: past, present and future' in C. B. Kopp and M. Kirkpatrick (eds) *Becoming Female* (New York: Plenum).

Lamb, M. E. (ed.) (1976) *The Role of the Father in Child Development,* 1st edition (London: Wiley).

Lamb, M. E. (ed.) (1981) *The Role of the Father in Child Development,* 2nd edition (London: Wiley).

Lawrence, M. (1984) *The Anorexic Experience* (London: The Women's Press).

Lazarre, J. (1987) *The Mother Knot* (London: Virago; 1976, New York: McGraw-Hill).

Leach, P. (1977) *Baby and Child* (London: Michael Joseph).

Lebsock, S. (1982) 'Free Black Women and the Question of Matriarchy: Petersburg, Virginia 1784–1820', *Feminist Studies*, 8(2)) 271–92.

Lee, C. M. (ed.) (1978) *Child Abuse: A Reader and a Sourcebook* (Milton Keynes: University Press).

Lees, S. (1986) *Losing Out: Sexuality and Adolescent Girls* (London: Hutchinson).

Lerner, H. Goldhor (1985) *The Dance of Anger: a woman's guide to changing the patterns of intimate relationships* (New York: Harper and Row).

Lessing, D. (1952) *Martha Quest* (London: MacGibbon and Kee).

Leuptow, L. B. (1980) 'Social change and sex role change in adolescent orientations towards life, work and achievement, 1961–1975', *Social Psychology* 13(1) 18–59.

Levine, P. (1990) 'Love, Friendship and Feminism in Later 19th century England', *Women's Studies International Forum*, 13(1–2) 63–78.

Lewis, J. (1986) *Labour and Love: women's experience of home and family, 1850–1940* (Oxford: Blackwell).

Lewis, J. and Meredith, B. (1988) *Daughters Who Care: daughters caring for mothers at home* (London: Routledge).

Lewis, M. (1972) 'Parents and Children: sex role development' *School Review*, 80, 228–40.

Lewis, C. and O'Brien, M. (eds) (1987) *Reassessing Fatherhood: new observations on fathers and the modern family* (London: Sage).

Lewis, M. and Weintraub, M. (1972)) 'The father's role in the child's social network's in Lamb (ed.) op. cit.

Lilienfield, J. (1980) 'Reentering Paradise: Cather, Colette and Woolf and their Mothers' in Davidson and Broner (eds) op. cit.

London Borough of Lambeth (1987) *Whose Child? The report of the public inquiry into the death of Tyra Henry)* (London: London Borough of Lambeth).

Lorde, A. (1981) 'An open letter to Mary Daly' in C. Moraga (ed.) *This Bridge Called My Back* (Watertown, Mass.: Persephone Press).

Lorde, A. (1984) *Sister Outsider: Essays and Speeches* (Freedom, Calif.: The Crossing Press).

Love, B. and Shanklin, E., (1978) 'The Answer is Matriarchy' in G. Vida (ed.) *Our Right to Love* (Englewood Cliffs, NJ: Prentice-Hall) reprinted in Trebilcot (ed.) (1983) op. cit.

Lynn, D. (1974) *The Father: His Role in Child Development* (Monteray, Calif.: Brooks/Cole).

Macdonald, B. and Rich, C. (1984) *Look Me In The Eye: old women, aging and ageism* (London: The Women's Press).

MacDonald, S. Peck (1980) 'Jane Austen and the Tradition of the Absent Mother' in Davidson and Broner (eds) op. cit.

MacLeod, M. and Saraga, E. (1988) 'Challenging the Orthodoxy: Towards a Feminist Theory and Practice', *Feminist Review* 28 January, 16–55.

MacLeod, S. (1981) *The Art of Starvation* (London: Virago).

Maglin, N. Bauer (1980) 'Don't never forget the bridge that you crossed over on: The Literature of Matrilineage' in Davidson and Broner (eds.) op. cit.

Maguire, M. (1987) 'Casting the evil eye: women and envy' in Ernst and Maguire (eds.) op. cit.

Mahler, M. S. (1968) *On Human Symbiosis and the Visissitudes of Individuation* (New York: International University Press).

Mahler, M. S., Pine, F., and Bergman, A. (1975) *The Psychological Birth of the Human Infant* (London: Hutchinson).

Mairs, N. (1986) 'On Being Raised by a Daughter' in *Plain Text* (Tuscan, Arizona: University of Arizona Press). Quoted in Kraus, op. cit.

Malan, D. H. (1979) *Individual Psychotherapy and the Science of Psychodynamics* (London: Butterworth).

Marcus, J. (ed.) (1981) *New Feminist Essays on Virginia Woolf* (London: Macmillan).

Margolin, G. and Patterson, G. R. (1975) 'Differential consequences provided by mothers and fathers to their sons and daughters' *Developmental Psychology* 11, 537–8.

Marsden, D. and Abrams, S. (1987) '"Companions", "Liberators", "Intruders" and "Cuckoos in the Nest" a sociology of informal caring relationships over the life cycle' in Allatt et al. (eds) op. cit.

Marshall, P. (1959) *Brown Girl, Brownstones* (London: Virago (1982)).

Martin, H. Reimensnyder (1923) 'Mrs Gladfelter's Revolt' in Koppleman (ed.) op. cit.

Martin, J. and Roberts, C. (1984) *Women and Employment: A lifetime perspective*, Department of Employment/Office of Population Census and Surveys. (London: HMSO).

Martineau, H. (1877) *Autobiography in three volumes* ed. by M. Weston Chapman (London: Smith, Elder and Co.)

Masson, J. (1985) *The Assault on Truth: Freud's Suppression of the Seduction Theory* (Harmondsworth: Penguin).

Masson, J. (1989) *Against Therapy* (London: Collins).

Matsui, Y. (1989) *Women's Asia* (London: Zed Books).

McAdoo, H. P. (1985) 'Strategies Used By Black Single Mothers Against Stress', *Review of Black Political Economy* 14 (2–3), 153–66.

McConville, B. (1987) *Mad to be a Mother* (London: Century).

McDougall, J. (1979) 'The Homosexual Dilemma: a clinical and theoretical study of female homosexuality' in I. Rosen (ed) *Sexual Deviation* (Oxford: Oxford University Press).

McNaron, T. A. H. (1985) *The Sister Bond: a feminist view of a timeless connection* (Oxford: Pergamon).

McRobbie, A. (1978) 'Working class girls and the culture of femininity' in Women's Studies Group, *Women take Issue: Aspects of Women's Subordination* (Birmingham: Centre for Contemporary Cultural Studies).

Mead, M. (1970) *Culture and Commitment: a study of the generation gap* (New York: Doubleday).

Meltzer, H. (1943) 'Sex differences in children's attitudes to parents', *Journal of Genetic Psychology* 62, 311–26.

Menninger, K. (1942) *Love Against Hate* (New York: Harcourt, Brace and Co.)

Miller, J. Baker (ed.) (1973) *Psychoanalysis and Women* (Harmondsworth: Penguin).

Miller, J. Baker (1978) *Towards A New Psychology of Women* (Harmondsworth: Penguin).

Mischel, W. (1966) 'A Social Learning View of Sex Role Differences' in Mitchell, J. (1974) *Psychoanalysis and Women* (London: Allen Lane).

Morrison, T. (1974) *Sula* (New York: Bantam).

Moss, H. A. (1973) 'Sex, age and state as determinants of mother-infant interactions' in L. J. Stone, H. T. Smith and L. B. Murphy (eds) *The Competent Infant* (London: Tavistock).

Mossberg, B. A. Clarke (1980) 'Reconstruction in the House of Art: Emily Dickinson's "I Never Had a Mother"' in Davidson and Broner (eds) op. cit.

Mrazek, P. B. and Bentovim, A. (1981) 'Incest and the Dysfunctional Family System' in P. B. Mrazek and C. H. Kempe (eds) *Sexually Abused Children and their Families* (Oxford: Pergamon).

Murcott, A. (1983) '"It's a pleasure to cook for him": Food, Mealtimes and Gender in Some South Wales Households' in E. Gamarnikov, D. Morgan, and J. Purvis (eds) *The Public and The Private* (London: Heinemann).

Myers, M. (1980) 'Unmothered Daughters and Radical Reformers: Harriet Martineau's career' in Davidson and Broner (eds) op. cit.

Myers, L. (1975) *Black Women and Self Esteem* in M. Millman and R. M. Kanter (eds) *Another Voice: Feminist Perspectives on Social Life and Social Science* (Garden City, NY: Anchor).

Neisser, E. G. (1967) *Mothers and Daughters* (London and New York: Harper and Row).

New, C. and David, M. (1985) *For the Children's Sake: making childcare more than women's business* (Harmondsworth: Penguin).

Newson, J. and Newson, E. (1976) *Seven Years Old in the Home Environment* (London: Allen and Unwin).

Nissel, M. and Bonnerjah, L. (1982) *Family Care of the Handicapped Elderly: Who Pays?* (London: Policy Studies Institute).

Oakley, A. (1972) *Sex, Gender and Society* (Aldershot: Temple Smith).

Oakley, A. (1979) *Becoming a Mother* (Oxford: Martin Robertson).

Oakley, A. (1980) *Women Confined* (Oxford: Martin Robertson).

Oakley, A. (1981a) *Subject Women* (Oxford: Martin Robertson).

Oakley, A. (1981b) 'Normal Motherhood: an exercise in self control?' in B. Hutter and G. Williams (eds) *Controlling Women: The Normal and the Deviant* (Beckenham: Croom Helm).

Olsen, T. (1956) 'I Stand Here Ironing' from *Tell Me A Riddle* (London: Virago, 1980).

Olsen, T. (1980) *Silences* (London: Virago).

Olsen, T. (1985) *Mother to Daughter: Daughter to Mother* (London: Virago).

Ong, Bie Nio (1985) 'Understanding Child Abuse: Ideologies of Motherhood' *Women's Studies International Forum*, 8(5), 411–19.

Ong, Bie Nio (1986) 'Child Abuse: Are Abusing Women Abused Women?' in C. Webb (ed.) *Feminist practice in Women's Health Care* (London: Wiley).

Orbach, S. and Eichenbaum, L. (1987) *Bittersweet: Love, Envy and Competition in Women's Friendships* (London: Hutchinson).

Palozzoli, M. S. (1974) *Self Starvation* (London: Chaucer)

Parikh, I. J. and Garg, P. K. (1989) *Indian Women: An Inner Dialogue* (London: Sage).

Park, C. and Heaton, C. (eds) (1987) *Close Company: Stories of Mothers and Daughters* (London: Virago).

Parker-Smith, B. J. (1985) 'Running Wild in their Soul: The Poetry of Carolyn Rodgers' in M. Evans, *Black Women Writers: Arguments and Interviews* (London: Pluto Press).

Parmar, P., Kay, J., and Lorde, A. (1988) 'Frontiers' in Grenwal et al. (eds) op. cit.

Parton, N. (1985) *The Politics of Child Abuse*, (London: Macmillan).

Parton, C. and Parton, N. (1989) 'Women, the Family and Child Protection' *Critical Social Policy*, 24, Winter 1988–9, 38–49.

Payne, K. (1983) *Between Ourselves: Letters between Mothers and Daughters* (London: Michael Joseph).

Pederson, F. A. (ed) (1980) *The Father-Infant Relationship* (New York: Praeger).

Phoenix, A. (1988) 'Narrow definitions of culture: the case of early motherhood' in S. Westwood and P. Bhachu (eds) *Enterprising Women: Ethnicity, Economy and Gender Relations* (London: Routledge).

Pitfield, N. (1985) 'Making Gardens in the Wilderness' in Hemmings (ed.) op. cit.

Plath, A. S. (ed.) 1976) *Letters Home* (London: Faber and Faber).

Price, J. (1988) *Motherhood: what it does to your mind* (London: Pandora Press).

Pulling, J. (1987) *The Caring Trap* (London: Fontana).

Qureshi, H. and Walker, A. (1989) *The Caring Relationship: Elderly People and their Families* (London: Macmillan).

Radford, J. (1989) 'My Pride and Joy' in Gieve (ed.) op. cit.

Radicalesbians (1970) 'The Woman Identified Woman', reprinted in S. L. Hoagland and J. Penelope (eds) *For Lesbians Only: A Separatist Anthology* (London: Onlywomen Press, 1988).

Rafkin, L. (ed.) (1987) *Different Daughters: a book by mothers of lesbians* (Pittsburgh, Penn./San Francisco: Cleis Press).

Raphael-Leff, J. (1983)) 'Facilitators and Regulators: Approaches to Mothering' *British Journal of Medical Psychology*, 56, 374–90.

Raymond, J. (1986) *A Passion for Friends* (London: The Women's Press).

Rich, A. (1973)) 'Jane Eyre: The Temptations of a Motherless Woman' in Rich (1980) op. cit.

Rich, A. (1977) *Of Women Born: Motherhood as Experience and Institution* (London: Virago).

Rich, A. (1978a) 'Splitting' in Rich, A. (1978) *The Dream of a Common Language* (New York: W. W. Norton).

Rich, A. (1978b) 'Disloyal to Civilisation: Feminism, Racism and Gynephobia' in Rich (1980) op. cit.

Rich, A. (1980) *On Lies, Secrets and Silence: Selected Prose 1966–1978* (London: Virago).

Robbins, J. Hamerman (1985) 'A Legacy of Weakness: Unresolved Issues in the Mother-Daughter Arrangement in a Patriarchal Culture' in Robbins et al. (eds) op. cit.

Robbins, J. Hamerman, and Siegal, R. J. (eds) (1985) *Women Changing Therapy* (New York: Harrington Park Press).

Roberts, N. (1989) 'Little Moments in a Lancashire Childhood' in Common Thread Collective (eds) op. cit.

Rodgers, C. (1969) *Songs of a Blackbird* (Chicago: Third World Press).

Rodgers-Rose, L. F. (1979) (ed.) *The Black Woman* (Beverley Hills, Calif.: Sage).

Robinson, C. R. (1985) 'Black Women: A tradition of self-reliant strength' in Robbins et al. (eds) op. cit.

Rohrbaugh, J. (1981) *Women: Psychology's Puzzle* (London: Abacus).

Rosenkrantz, P., Vogel, S., Bee, H., Broverman, L., and Broverman, D. (1968) 'Sex Role Stereotypes and Self Concepts in College Students' *Journal of Consulting and Clinical Psychology*, 32, 287–95.

Ross, M. (1988) 'Pushing the boundaries: Mo Ross talks to Jackie Kay and Pratibha Parmar' in Grenwal et al. (eds) op. cit.

Rothman, B. Katz (1989) *Recreating Motherhood: Ideology and Technology in a Patriarchal Society* (New York: Norton).

Rothman, S. (1978) *Women's Proper Place: a history of changing ideals and practices, 1870– present* (New York: Basic Books).

Rubin, J., Provenzano, F., and Luna, Z. (1974) 'The Eye of the Beholder: parent's views on sex of newborns' *American Journal of Orthopsychiatry*, 44(4) 512–19.

Ruddick, S. (1990) *Maternal Thinking: Towards a Politics of Peace* (London: The Women's Press).

Russ, J. (1975) 'Autobiography of My Mother' in Koppelman (ed.) op. cit.

Sa'adawi, N. el (1980) *The Hidden Face of Eve: Women in the Arab World* (London: Zed Books).

Sage: A Scholarly Journal on Black Women (1984) 1(2) 'Mothers and Daughters I' Special Issue.

Sage: A Scholarly Journal on Black Women (1987) 4(2) 'Mothers and Daughters II' Special Issue.

Sanguiliano, I. (1978) *In Her Time* (New York: William Morrow).

Sarton, M. (1974) *Collected Poems (1930–1973)* (New York: Norton).

Savage, W. (1986) *A Savage Enquiry: Who Controls Childbirth?* (London: Virago).

Sayers, J. (1986) *Sexual Contradictions: Psychology, Psychoanalysis and Feminism* (London: Tavistock).

Sears, R. (1970) 'Relation of early socialisation experiences to self concept and gender role in middle childhood' *Child Development* 41, 267–89.

Segal, L. (1987) *Is The Future Female?* (London: Virago).

Sexton, A. (1961) 'Housewife' in *All My Pretty Ones* (Cambridge Mass.: Riverside Press).

Shaaban, B. (1988) *Both Right and Left Handed: Arab Women Talk about their Lives* (London: The Women's Press).

Shainess, N. (1986) 'Antigone: Symbol of Autonomy and Women's Moral Dilemmas' in Bernay and Cantor (eds) op. cit.

Sharpe, S. (1976) *Just Like a Girl: How girls learn to be women* (Harmondsworth: Penguin).

Sharpe, S. (1987) *Falling in Love: Teenage Mothers talk* (London: Virago).

Shengold, L. (1978) 'Assault on a Child's Individuality: a kind of soul murder' *Psychoanalytic Quarterly* 47, 419–24.

Skinner, C. (1986) *Elusive Mister Right: the social and personal context of a young woman's contraception* (London: Carolina).

Slesinger, T. (1935) 'Mother to Dinner' in Koppelman (ed.) op. cit.

Smedley, A. (1973) *Daughter of Earth* (New York: The Feminist Press).

Smith-Rosenberg, C. (1975) 'The female world of love and ritual: relations between women in nineteenth century America', *Signs* 1, 1–29.

Sorrels, R. (1974) excerpts from lyrics of 'Apple Of My Eye' in R. Sorrels (ed.) *What, Women and Who, Myself, I am* (Pleasantville, NY: Wooden Shoe).

Spelman, E. V. (1990) *Inessential Woman: Problems of exclusion in feminist thought* (London: The Women's Press).

Spender, D. (1980) *Man Made Language* (London: Routledge and Kegan Paul).

Spender, D. and Sarah, E. (1980) *Learning to Lose: sexism and education* (London: The Women's Press).

Spender, D. (1982) *Invisible Women: The schooling scandal* (London: Writers and Readers; reprinted 1989, London: The Women's Press).

Spring, J. (1987) *Cry Hard and Swim: the story of an incest survivor* (London: Virago).

St. John, R. Anyiam (1987) 'Mama' in Cobham and Collins (eds) op. cit.

Stack, C. (1974) *All Our Kin* (New York: Harper and Row).

Statham, J. (1986) *Daughters and Sons: experiences of non-sexist child raising* (London: Basil Blackwell).

Steedman, C. (1986) *Landscape for a Good Woman* (London: Virago).

Steedman, C., Urwin, C., and Walkerdine, V. (1985) *Language, Gender and Childhood* (London: Routledge and Kegan Paul).

Steele, B. F., and Pollack, C. B. (1978) 'General Characteristics of Abusing Parents' in Lee (ed.) op. cit.

Steinmetz, S. K. (1989) *Duty Bound: Elder Abuse and Family Care* (London: Sage).

Stern, D. (1985) *The Interpersonal World of the Infant: A view from psychoanalysis and developmental psychology* (New York: Basic Books).

Stevenson, A. (1982) 'Poem to my Daughter' in *Minute By Glass Minute*, (Oxford: Oxford University Press).

Stewart, C. (1987) 'Don't Call Me Mama' in Cobham and Collins (eds) op. cit.

Stivens, M. (1978) 'Women and their Kin: Kin, class and solidarity in a middle-class suburb of Sydney, Australia' in P. Caplan and J. M. Bujra (eds) *Women United, Women Divided* (London: Tavistock).

Stott, M. (1981) *Ageing For Beginners* (London: Blackwell).

Sturdivant, S. (1980) *Therapy with Women: A Feminist Philosophy of Treatment* (New York: Springer).

Symonds, A. (1971) 'Phobias after Marriage: Women's declaration of dependence' *American Journal of Psychoanalysis*, 31(2) 144–52. Reprinted in J.B. Miller (ed) (1972) *Psychoanalysis and Women* (Harmondsworth: Penguin).

Talbot, T. (1980) *A Book About My Mother* (New York: Farrar, Straus and Giroux).

Tan, A. (1989) *The Joy Luck Club* (London: Heinemann).

Tanner, N. (1974) 'Matrifocality in Indonesia and Africa and among Black Americans' in M. Rosaldo and L. Lamphere (eds) *Women, Culture and Society* (Stanford, Ca: Stanford University Press).

Tivers, J. (1987) *Women Attached: the daily lives of women with young children* (London: Croom Helm).

Tizard, B. and Hughes, M. (1984) *Young Children Learning* (London: Fontana).

Treblicot, J. (1983) *Mothering: Essays in Feminist Theory* (Savage, Maryland: Rowman and Littlefield).

Ullman, L. (1977) *Changing* (London: Weidenfield and Nicolson).

Ungerson, C. (1987) *Policy is Personal: Sex, Gender and Informal Care* (London: Tavistock).

Urwin, C. (1984) 'Power Relations and Emergence of Language' in J. Henriques et al. (eds) *Changing the Subject: psychology, Social regulation and Subjectivity* (London: Methuen).

Urwin, C. (1985) 'Constructing Motherhood: the persuasion of normal development' in Steedman et al. (eds) op. cit.

Valentine, D. (1989) review of Kathy Evert's *When You Are Ready* op. cit. *Affilia*, 4(2), 101–3.

Walker, A. (1984) *In Search of Our Mother's Gardens* (London: The Women's Press).

Walker, M. (1966) *Jubilee* (Bantam, NY: Houghton Mittlin).

Walkerdine, V., and Lucey, H. (1989) *Democracy in the Kitchen: Regulating Mothers and Socialising Daughters* (London: Virago).

Walters, M., Carter, B., Papp, P., and Silverstein, O. (1988) *The Invisible Web: gender patterns in family relationships* (New York: The Guildford Press).

Walters, M. (1988) 'Mothers and Daughters' in Walters et al. op. cit.

Wandor, M. (1987) 'Meet My Mother' in Park and Heaton (eds) op. cit.

Washington, M. H. (1975) *Black Eyed Susans* (Garden City, NY: Doubleday).

Washington, M. H. (ed.) (1989) *Invented Lives: narratives of Black Women 1860–1960* (London: Virago).

Welburn, V. (1980) *Postnatal Depression* (London: Fontana).

West, D. (1982) 'My Mother Rachel West' in Washington (ed.) (1989) op. cit.

Westkott, M. (1986) *The Feminist Legacy of Karen Horney* (New Haven, Cann.: Yale University Press).

Weston Chapman, M. (ed.) *Harriet Martineau's Autobiography* (London: Smith, Elder and Co.).

Williams, C. (1988) 'Gal . . . You came From Foreign' in Grenwal et al. (eds) op. cit.

Willmott, P. and Young, M. (1960) *Family and Class in a London Suburb*, (London: Routledge and Kegan Paul).

Wilson, A. (1978) *Finding a Voice: Asian Women In Britain* (London: Virago).

Wilson, E. (1989) 'In a Different Key' in Gieve (ed.), op. cit.

Winnicott, D. W. (1954) 'The Depressive Position in Normal Emotional Development' in *Collected Papers: through Paediatrics to Psychoanalysis* (London: Tavistock).

Winnicott, D. W. (1956) 'Primary Maternal Deprivation' in *Collected papers*, op. cit.

Winnicott, D. W. (1958) 'The First Year of Life' in Winnicott (1965) op. cit.

Winnicott, D. W. (1960) 'The relationship of a mother to her baby at the beginning' in Winnicott (1965) op. cit.

Winnicott, D. W. (1965) *The Family and Individual Development* (London: Tavistock).

Winnicott, D. W. (1971) *Playing and Reality* (London: Tavistock).

Wodak, R. and Shultz, M. (1986) *The Language of Love and Guilt: Mother-daughter relationships from a cross-cultural perspective* (Amsterdam and Philadelphia: John Benjamin).

Wolff, C. (1977) *Love Between Women* (London: Duckworth).

Woodward, J. (1988) *Understanding Ourselves: the uses of therapy* (London: Macmillan).

Woolf, V. (1931) 'Professions for Women' in M. Barrett (ed.) (1979) *Virginia Woolf: Women and Writing* (London: The Women's Press).

Woolf, V. (1927) *To the Lighthouse* (1977 ed., London: Grafton).

Woolf, V. (1976) 'A Sketch of the Past' in J. Sculkind (ed.) *Moments of Being, unpublished autobiographical writings* (Brighton: Sussex University Press).

Young, M., and Willmott, P. (1958) *Family and Kinship in East London* (London: Routledge and Kegan Paul).

Young, M., and Willmott, P. (1973) *The Symmetrical Family* (London: Routledge and Kegan Paul).

Yezierska, A. (1925) *Bread Givers* (New York: George Braziller).

Zimmerman, B. (1980) '"The Mother's History" in George Eliot's Life, Literature and Political Ideology' in Davidson and Broner, op. cit.

Zuckerberg, J. Offerman (1980) 'Psychological and Physical Warning Signals regarding Pregnancy, Adaptation and early Psychotherapeutic Intervention' in B. Blum (ed.) *Psychological Aspects of Pregnancy, Birth and Bonding* (New York: Human Science Press).

Index

254